Palgrave Macmillan Series in International Political Communication

Series Editor: Philip Seib, University of Southern California (USA)

From democratization to terrorism, economic development to conflict resolution, global political dynamics are affected by the increasing pervasiveness and influence of communication media. This series examines the participants and their tools, their strategies and their impact. It offers a mix of comparative and tightly focused analyses that bridge the various elements of communication and political science included in the field of international studies. Particular emphasis is placed on topics related to the rapidly changing communication environment that is being shaped by new technologies and new political realities. This is the evolving world of international political communication.

Books Appearing in this Series

Media and the Politics of Failure: Great Powers, Communication Strategies, and Military Defeats
By Laura Roselle

The CNN Effect in Action: How the News Media Pushed the West toward War in Kosovo
By Babak Bahador

Media Pressure on Foreign Policy: The Evolving Theoretical Framework
By Derek B. Miller

New Media and the New Middle East
Edited by Philip Seib

The African Press, Civic Cynicism, and Democracy
By Minabere Ibelema

Global Communication and Transnational Public Spheres
By Angela M. Crack

Latin America, Media, and Revolution: Communication in Modern Mesoamerica
By Juanita Darling

Japanese Public Opinion and the War on Terrorism
Edited by Robert D. Eldridge and Paul Midford

African Media and the Digital Public Sphere
Edited by Okoth Fred Mudhai, Wisdom J. Tettey, and Fackson Banda

Islam Dot Com: Contemporary Islamic Discourses in Cyberspace
By Mohammed el-Nawawy and Sahar Khamis

Explaining News: National Politics and Journalistic Cultures in Global Context
By Cristina Archetti

News Media and EU-China Relations
By Li Zhang

Kurdish Identity, Discourse, and New Media
By Jaffer Sheyholislami

Al-Jazeera English: Global News in a Changing World
Edited by Philip Seib

Civic Engagement, Digital Networks, and Political Reform in Africa
By Okoth Fred Mudhai

Egyptian Revolution 2.0: Political Blogging, Civic Engagement, and Citizen Journalism
By Mohammed el-Nawawy and Sahar Khamis

Egyptian Revolution 2.0

Political Blogging, Civic Engagement, and Citizen Journalism

Mohammed el-Nawawy and Sahar Khamis

palgrave
macmillan

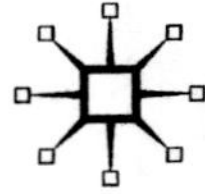

EGYPTIAN REVOLUTION 2.0

First published in 2013 by
PALGRAVE MACMILLAN®
in the United States—a division of St. Martin's Press LLC,
175 Fifth Avenue, New York, NY 10010.

Where this book is distributed in the UK, Europe and the rest of the world, this is by Palgrave Macmillan, a division of Macmillan Publishers Limited, registered in England, company number 785998, of Houndmills, Basingstoke, Hampshire RG21 6XS.

Palgrave Macmillan is the global academic imprint of the above companies and has companies and representatives throughout the world.

Palgrave® and Macmillan® are registered trademarks in the United States, the United Kingdom, Europe and other countries.

ISBN: 978–1–137–02091–8

Library of Congress Cataloging-in-Publication Data is available from the Library of Congress.

A catalogue record of the book is available from the British Library.

Design by Newgen Imaging Systems (P) Ltd., Chennai, India.

First edition: May 2013

10 9 8 7 6 5 4 3 2 1

Contents

Preface

During the past 20 years, the Arab media environment has evolved dramatically. As recently as the early 1990s, Arab publics were forced to depend on state-provided information and had no substantive way to respond. Any efforts to stimulate participatory public discourse were frustrated by an absence of venues and were likely to be met by repressive reaction from the government.

This began to change in 1996 with the birth of Al-Jazeera. A pan-Arab voice could be heard throughout the region, and it spoke of topics that had long been forbidden in public discussion. Government corruption, the role of women, and other such matters were reported on Al-Jazeera's newscasts and debated—often heatedly—on the channel's talk shows. As people watched this on their television screens, they began talking more openly about the same issues and looked for forums where they could express themselves.

Roughly a decade later, access to the Internet was spreading slowly within the Arab world, and people began to take advantage of new sources of information and new ways in which they, as individuals, could participate in civic discourse. The oligarchic (and geriatric) rulers of the region were slow to recognize how the political terrain was shifting as new technologies became more widely used.

A clear path can be found from Al-Jazeera's founding in 1996 to the events of the "Arab spring" of 2011. As communication technology became more sophisticated and more accessible, more people joined in conversations about their future. After years of simmering frustration about economic and political oppression, public sentiment finally boiled over and swift, dramatic change swept across much of the region.

In *Egyptian Revolution 2.0,* two of the world's top scholars of Arab media, Mohammed el-Nawawy and Sahar Khamis, provide a valuable detailed analysis of how new media—and particularly the use of blogs—contributed to this sweeping change. Their focus on the blogosphere is particularly welcome because blogs can constitute the conversation of democratic yearnings and, eventually, the discourse of democracy itself. The authors note the value of blogs providing homes for "individual expression and diversity of opinions," and these are crucial to sustaining political reform.

Blogging is empowering because the medium fosters activism and encourages citizen journalism. People are able to tell others about their own lives and what is going on around them. This opportunity invites people to participate in the public sphere. Egypt's prospects for democracy in the years ahead are largely dependent on how thoroughly populated that public sphere remains. No one is certain how the relatively new phenomenon of "cyberactivism" will affect political progress and societal stability, but at the heart of the Arab uprisings that began in 2011 was a longing on the part of individuals to take more control of their own lives and to have more say in their communities, large and small. Through blogging and the use of social media, this goal—unattainable for so long—comes within reach.

The events that began in the Arab world in 2011 will have global repercussions for years to come. *Egyptian Revolution 2.0* will be a useful guide as the future is explored.

PHILIP SEIB

Acknowledgments

The authors are grateful to the following people for their precious contributions through the different stages of writing and producing this book: Philip Seib, editor of the Palgrave Macmillan Series in International Political Communication; director of the Center on Public Diplomacy; and professor of Journalism, Public Diplomacy and International Relations at the University of Southern California, for his unsurpassed encouragement and support and for his belief in the idea of this book; Mike Wirth, assistant professor in the Art Department at Queens University of Charlotte for designing the book cover; Kathryn Vaughn, a dual masters in Public Policy/MBA candidate at the School of Public Policy and the School of Business at the University of Maryland, College Park, for providing thorough edits and thoughtful remarks on the final draft of this book; Emily Kellner, an undergraduate student in the Department of International Studies at Queens University of Charlotte, for her help with compiling the academic literature for this book; and Donna Nasserghodsi, an undergraduate student in the Department of Communication at the University of Maryland, College Park, for compiling the book's index.

The authors are also thankful to the current and former editorial staff at Palgrave Macmillan, especially Farideh Koohi-Kamali, the editorial director for the Academic Program; Isabella Yeager, editorial assistant; and her predecessor, Sarah Nathan, for their continuous assistance, support, and valuable editorial advice throughout the process of producing this book.

Last but not least, both authors would like to express their gratitude and appreciation to their families for their unconditional love and support, without which this book would not have been completed.

CHAPTER 1

Blogging as Cyberactivism: Introductory Themes

Who would have expected that a group of young digital activists, blogging, tweeting, chatting, and texting, could have sparked the massive wave of political change that swept the Arab world, and came to be known as the "The Arab Spring" or "The Arab Awakening"? The answer could very well be "no one"! That's mainly because for a number of years the Arab world has been witnessing a perplexing paradox, namely, the gap between the vibrant and active media landscape, where many resistant and oppositional voices could be heard, on the one hand, and the dormant and stagnant political landscape, which did not exhibit any serious signs of active change, popular participation, or true democratization, on the other hand. One explanation that some Arab media scholars (Seib, 2007; Khamis, 2007, 2008) used to account for this puzzling gap was the notion of "safety valves," that is, that Arab media, especially the opposition press, were being exploited by the autocratic ruling regimes as a platform for people to vent their angry feelings and resentment toward their authoritarian governments, instead of taking decisive steps in the direction of radical reform and transformation, thus substituting words for action (Seib, 2007).

It was not until the latest wave of political upheaval swept the Arab region that Arab media, or more precisely new media in the Arab world, started to become effective tools for "public will mobilization," which usually "crystallizes around a social condition that is recognized as problematic; it coalesces into a collective consensus about how the problem can and should be ameliorated; and it can erupt, through coordination of resources and collective resolve, into social action" (Salmon et al., 2010, p. 159).

This book contributes to understanding how new media in the Arab world, especially political blogs, changed from being just safety valves to becoming effective "mobilization tools," through analyzing the role played by the Egyptian political blogosphere in paving the road for the Egyptian popular revolution of 2011, as well as its multiple roles during and after the revolution.

The Egyptian revolution was characterized by the instrumental use of social media, especially Facebook, Twitter, YouTube, and text messaging by protesters, to achieve a number of pragmatic goals, such as group networking, on-the-ground organizing, and offering practical advice on how to confront police brutality or how to avoid arrest. Each type of social media played a different role that is closely related to its own nature and functions. For example, the social network best suited for the task of organizing the protesters was Facebook, "where information could be spread to thousands of people in an instant and then shared between friends," and this "dissemination was far faster than leaflets, with the added benefit that those receiving the messages were already interested and trusted the source" (Idle & Nunns, 2011, p. 20). This highlights the value of social media in terms of creating networks that enable peer-to-peer communication between users, especially since networks are multifaceted communication systems comprising relations that allow for "dynamic, emergent, adaptive, and flexible associations" (Howard, 2011).

Different social media tools lend themselves to different types of networks. Facebook, for example, is built on linkages between "friends," whereas Google Moderator and Twitter allow anyone to comment on a subject. Google Moderator allows for commentary and voting on subjects by all users. Twitter allows users to create a subject for discussion and post a comment, or "tweet," about that subject (which could include a link to other content), which can then be picked up by other users and "retweeted" multiple times, until it becomes widespread. Thus, tools like Twitter lead to an environment where the best ideas and content, regardless of who posted it, can spread and gain great influence in a type of "meritocracy" of ideas and information (Maher, 2011). By combining these multiple functions of different types of online media together in one effective communication network during the 2011 revolution, it is easy to understand how Egyptian political activists won their battle against the regime both online and, most importantly, offline.

However, we argue that while these types of social media were crucial for the actual execution of instrumental, organizational roles during the revolution, political blogs have played a different, but equally valuable, role through providing important venues for the exchange of ideas and the formulation of collective public opinion. Over the past seven years, blogs paved the way for the eruption of the revolution by widely sharing an antigovernmental discourse that revealed the former Egyptian regime's dysfunctions and malpractices, such as corruption, violations of human rights, and limitations on freedom and democratic practice.

Through analyzing the discourses in five of the most popular Egyptian political blogs, we highlight the role played by political blogs in encouraging civic engagement and public participation through (1) acting as effective tools for supporting the capabilities of the democratic activists by allowing forums for free speech and political networking opportunities and (2) providing a virtual space for assembly, which allows for the exchange of civic discourse, deliberation, and articulation that goes beyond simply supporting the capability of the protestors to plan, organize, and execute peaceful protests on the ground.

Additionally, the book explores how political blogs, as new media avenues, can provide forums for citizen journalism through enabling ordinary citizens to document not only the protests, but, most importantly, the underlying causes that led to the eruption of these protests in the first place, such as governmental brutality, limitations on freedom of expression, flaws in the political system, official corruption, and violations of human rights, as well as allowing them to disseminate these words and images to each other, and, most importantly, to the outside world.

Moreover, we argue that the discourses and deliberations in the Egyptian political blogosphere also highlighted and optimized the communication struggle that erupted between the people, on the one hand, and their repressive government, on the other hand, which was as fierce as the political struggle on the ground. Through analyzing the postings on these political blogs, the book reveals how the Egyptian people engaged in a political struggle to impose their own agenda and ensure the fulfillment of their demands, while at the same time engaging in a communication struggle to make their authentic voices heard and tell their side of the story. While the dictatorial Egyptian regime took many measures to block the flow of information and inhibit mobilization efforts, thus combining the repression of protestors on the streets with the suppression of the truth in the media arena, the Egyptian people resisted these persistent efforts to both silence the peoples' voices and present the state's fabricated versions of the story, through asserting their own will and protecting their political rights. We argue that political blogs provided a venue through which such acts of resistance and empowerment were exercised and exemplified.

To better understand these points, however, it is essential to provide a brief overview of the changing communication landscape in the Arab world, especially before and after 1990, in order to assess the implications of new media venues, such as blogs, on transforming the political and communication landscapes in the Arab world. This provides the necessary context for analyzing the role played by political blogs before, during, and after the Egyptian revolution.

The Shifting Communication Landscape in the Arab World: The Impact of New Media

Prior to 1990, most media ownership in the Arab world lay largely with governments, and most media functioned under strict governmental supervision and control. A number of authors (Rugh, 2004; Boyd, 1999; Mellor, 2007; Abdel-Rahman, 1985, 2002) argued that in this era, Arab media were mostly controlled by governments mainly to keep laypeople largely uninformed and thus incapable of effectively participating in ongoing political controversies and rational debates.

A new media revolution erupted in the Arab world after 1990, inspired by the introduction of both satellite television channels and the Internet (Khamis & Sisler, 2010). In the 1990s, Internet penetration started to spread throughout the Arab world. Although the region has generally suffered from being on the low end of the digital divide (Abdulla, 2007, p. 35), facing many challenges, including the lack of human and economic information technology (IT) resources, illiteracy and computer illiteracy, the lack of funds for IT research and development, and the lack of solid telecommunication infrastructures (Abdulla, 2007, p. 35), this situation is rapidly changing, since many Arab countries are currently striving hard to increase Internet penetration rates.

Ironically, although many Internet websites and blogs are used to defy and resist autocratic governments and dictatorial regimes in the Arab world, a number of these governments took steps to encourage Internet proliferation and accessibility, mainly in order to boost economic development, as in the case of the Egyptian government (Abdulla, 2006, p. 94). This provides more evidence of the highly ambivalent and complex relationship between media and governments in the Arab world (Khamis & Sisler, 2010).

Overall, it could be said that the introduction of satellite television channels and the Internet represented an important shift from the monolithic, state-controlled, and government-owned media pattern to a much more pluralistic and diverse media scene, where many varied and competing voices representing different political positions and orientations could be heard at the same time, adding to the richness of ongoing political debates and the formation of a wide array of public opinion trends (Khamis, 2007, 2008; Atia, 2006).

The rise in social media usage in the Arab world followed a rise in overall Internet and mobile phone penetration in the region. A study by Philip Howard (2011, pp. 19–20), encompassing predominantly Muslim countries throughout the world, shows that mobile phones and Internet penetration has increased dramatically over the last ten years, with technology adoption rates in these countries among the highest of all developing nations. The same study indicated that since 2001, the increase in Internet users has outstripped the increase in computers per household, likely reflecting the use of Internet cafés (which can be found in both urban and rural areas) and libraries, as well as the collective use of computers among family members and circles of friends.

The Internet allows for the dissemination of cultural content in the Arab world (Howard, 2011, p. 163). Much of the user-generated content is transmitted using social media, such as Facebook, blogs, the video-sharing portal YouTube, Twitter, and short message service (SMS) or text messaging. These media enable peer-to-peer communication between users and can be linked to each other, allowing users to transmit their ideas and images to large numbers of people. Therefore, it is safe to say that the Internet is one of the most important avenues through which public opinion trends and public spheres are both shaped, as well as reflected, in modern Arab societies (Zelaky et al., 2006, p. 5). The significance of the introduction of the Internet stems from the fact that it defies boundaries, challenges governmental media censorship, and provides an alternative voice to traditional media outlets that echo official, governmental policies and views. In other words, it enables the inflow and outflow of information simultaneously through a "virtually defined . . . emerging cyberworld that knows no physical boundaries" (Salmon et al., p. 159). Thus, it provides invaluable opportunities for public will mobilization across borders.

The Internet is also a rapidly growing and expanding medium, especially among youth. Recent research studies indicate that Internet use is increasingly more prevalent among younger age groups within the Arab world, especially the 20- to 30-year-old age group, which uses the net more avidly compared to the rest of the population, and those younger than 20 years old are the group growing most rapidly in the Arab world (Abdulla, 2007, p. 50). This can very well explain why and how new media were effectively deployed by young people in the Arab world to trigger political reform and pave the way for democratization.

Howard (2011, p. 182) notes that through social media, citizen journalists who are dissatisfied with traditional media's version of events are telling their own stories, and that "these patterns of political expression and learning are key to developing democratic discourses." He observed that social media not only help start democracies but also help entrench existing ones, and that the "networked design" of social media is the key factor threatening authoritarian regimes since "these are the communication tools for the wealthy, urban, educated elites whose loyalties or defection will make or break authoritarian rule" (Howard, 2011, p. 11).

Social media can also serve as channels for expressing collective consciousness and national solidarity. Freeland (2011) argues that opponents of a dictator need to feel that their views are widely shared and that enough of their fellow citizens are willing to join them. He indicates that "what really stops people who are oppressed by a regime from protesting is the fear that they will be part of an unsuccessful protest. When you are living in these regimes, you have to be extremely afraid of what happens if you participate and the regime doesn't change." Therefore, he contends that satellite television and social networking have made it easier to let each individual know that his/her views are shared by enough people to make protesting worthwhile and safe (Freeland, 2011). This was, indeed, applicable in the case of the Egyptian revolution.

After providing this overview of the dynamically shifting Arab communication landscape, which provided the needed environment for an equally transformative Arab political scene, we can now focus our attention on how blogs, in particular, can play an effective part in this vibrant and transitory moment of contemporary Arab history, through their multiple roles.

Blogging: Definitions, Types, and Functions

A blog can be defined as "a Web page that is updated frequently, with the most recent entry displayed at the top of the page" (Rheingold, 2008, p. 103). It can also be defined as virtual spaces "with minimal to no external editing, providing on-line commentary, periodically updated and presented in reverse chronological order, with hyperlinks to other online sources" (Drezner & Farrell, 2004, p. 5). By definition, "a blog...[or] 'weblog' is a form of online diary where anyone with access to the Internet can create a platform from which they may reveal to the world whatever is on their minds" (Seymour, 2008, p. 62). One of the main distinguishing features of blogs has been their autonomy and independence from authoritarian and governmental control and domination, and blogs have been described as "a new form of communication that shifts mainstream control of information to the audience. Emergent technology allows bloggers to express views and blog readers to engage in meaningful conversation, thus empowering news audiences to become information providers" (Chung et al., 2007, p. 305). Additionally, besides providing the opportunity for the author to express himself or herself, blogs allow other Internet users to comment on the online stories referred to as blog posts (Drezner & Farrell, 2004), thus widening the scope of public participation in online discussions and opinion exchange.

This activity has been made possible through some of the characteristics of blogging, such as the fact that it is free of charge and easily accessible. In just a couple of minutes, a person can create an account with Blogger, or WordPress, or some other blog hosting service, and start blogging. If we compare this to the process of television, newspaper, or magazine production, we can easily tell that blogging requires no special resources, whether economic, in terms of budget, or human, in term of training or skills. Therefore, it has fewer barriers, compared to mainstream media, in terms of who can participate and who can become a "sender" and/or a "receiver." It is this openness and accessibility of blogging that provides it with the potential to be such a powerful tool for participatory democracy, and to possibly bring about change in the public sphere. These possibilities will be questioned and debated in the rest of this chapter. However, the fact remains that today any Internet user can maintain a blog without additional training (Ward & Cahill, 2007), and blogs are easily available to anyone, provided they have Internet access. Blogging also allows building relationships online, since the structure of blogs allows readers to reach posts, read others' comments, and post multiple comments, thus providing for a meaningful conversation (Kline & Burstein, 2005). Additionally, the Internet provides a certain degree of anonymity; therefore, bloggers can express their views without identifying their names, localities, or any other personal information. This could, in turn, make them feel less threatened when they expose their views and ideas to an online community. Some scholars, such as McCullagh (2008), found that the anonymous nature of blogging encouraged Internet users to post personal information that may have been threatening and/or private. Along the same lines, Muhtaseb and Frey (2008) suggested that anonymity might encourage Internet users to freely express their opinions online, thus allowing bloggers to post their views with less restrictions and constraints.

Another feature of the growing blogging process has been "linking conversations and other existing blogs, increasing the ebb and flow of information. This forms hubs or nodes within networks, where bloggers aggregate information, and give orientation and relevance—and also become effective filters of information. They act like fishers, who pick the most relevant pieces of information out of the net" (Kreutz, 2009, p. 30). This interconnected and closely networked web of blogs leads to the creation of a "blogosphere." This is another distinguishing characteristic between blogs and mainstream media. Newspapers and other forms of traditional news media have a vertical structure, with a flow of information going from the news agency to the audience (Barlow, 2007, pp. 90–93). The viewing or reading audience is not passive, but the expectation is that the journalists are the truly active party. Blogs, on the other hand, are more like Facebook or Twitter accounts, existing as pieces of a larger social network on the horizontal platform that is the Internet (Barlow, 2007, pp. 93–94). In this horizontal world, blogs are interconnected with one another in the mass that we call the blogosphere (Tremayne, 2007, p. xi). They are not truly independent entities, but are connected literally by links to one another (Tremayne, 2007, p. xi). Blogs are more subject to the conversation within the social network of blogging as a whole, and they are expected to stay in dialogue. The multiple links between different online journals form this blogosphere, which is a collective enterprise with multiple reporters (Posner, 2005). Through this blogosphere, different individual blogs can be electronically linked to each other. These links allow bloggers to stay updated on others' blogs and allow blog readers to have easy access to similar pages.

The first blogs appeared in 1999 in the United States, when two software products, Blogger and Pitas, were created and made available to the public (Herring et al., 2007). The industry immediately witnessed growth in both the number of bloggers and the number of websites that offered online space for personal journals. Already in 2004, five years after the first blogs appeared in cyberspace, research identified millions of individual blogs (Rainie, 2005) on multiple websites, including Livejournal, DiaryLand, and Xanga (Tremayne, 2007). Therefore, it is obvious that the blogosphere has witnessed a tremendous growth since its birth in 1999. The number of blogs jumped from a few hundred in the late 1990s to millions in the early years of the new millennium. The ease of starting a new blog and the relatively low cost associated with maintaining it are among the primary reasons for this rapid growth (Drezner & Farrell, 2004). According to a 2005 report issued by Technorati (http://technorati.com), which is the most popular search engine for blogs, there was close to 70 million blogs worldwide (Tsekeris, 2009, p. 51).

Today, blogs take on various forms, styles, and formats. "The spectrum of interactivity in the medium ranges from tightly controlled formats with little [or no] audience participation to versions that are mostly built from the bottom up through the participation of their audience" (Rutigliano, 2007, p. 225). The world of blogging includes two opposing principles: "monologues and dialogues. The blogger can conduct a one-way conversation, or can invite reaction through threaded archives whose only constraint is the uni-directionality of time" (Hall, 2006, p. 22).

Other distinctions are between "traditional" and "news" blogs (Kent, 2008). Traditional blogs allow individuals to express their personal opinions on different subjects, and they tend to be narcissistic. In other words, traditional blogs focus on the blogger's opinions, thoughts, and experiences, while news blogs focus on analyzing news, and tend to have links to actual news stories. Often, news blogs focus on a particular subject area, such as politics, science, or international news. According to Kent (2008), news blogs tend to be more popular because they relate to a wider audience. Other classifications of blogs are based on topic (Ward & Cahill, 2007) and popularity (Cammaerts, 2008). Blogs differ in terms of the popularity level: A-list blogs are the most influential sites, which have a considerable amount of hyperlinks, whereas B-list blogs are read by a smaller community of Internet users (Herring et al., 2007). There are no typical blogs, as the very purpose of blogs is to allow individual expression and diversity of opinions.

Overall, we can contend that blogging, which is one of the most distinguishing phenomena of the Web 2.0 era, "has become more and more widespread and influential, potentially de-stabilizing the traditional linear model and the socio-political status quo... [and leading] to an unperceived and unimaginable conversational complexity of overlapping virtual communities" (Tsekeris, 2009, p. 51). "Not only does [blogging] provide many viewpoints on shared experiences, but it often also serves as a collective databank used to jog the faulty memories of those who write or report for major media" (Gill, 2004, p. 2). In this context, Sullivan (2002), as cited in Papacharissi (2007), noted that "blogging is arguably the most significant media revolution since the arrival of television, providing the ability to make arguments, fact-check them and rebut them in a seamless and endless conversation" (p. 21).

Also, it would be useful to distinguish between two other types of blogs, namely, activist blogs and public-sphere blogs. Activist blogs, which have been most closely related to the literature concerning blogs as a catalyst for political change, have been defined by Marc Lynch (2007) as being "directly involved in political movements, [with activists] using blogs to coordinate political action, spread information, and magnify the impact of contentious politics." He mentions the weblogs of the Muslim Brotherhood and the blogs associated with the *Kefaya* opposition movement in Egypt as good examples of activist blogs, since both of them used their blogs' postings to rally their supporters around their causes and to urge them to organize public actions, such as demonstrations, strikes, and protests (Lynch, 2007).

Public-sphere blogs, by contrast, are defined by Lynch (2007) as being "deeply engaged in arguments about domestic politics, but not in organized activism. In other words, they provide a platform for the expression of varying opinions around current issues and public affairs, but without offering channels or venues for actual public action on the ground." In examining the potential for blogs to act as a catalyst for political change, we can argue that these blogs may not directly give birth to the same degree of offline activism and on-the-ground organization as in the case of activist blogs. However, their role in providing important platforms for discussion and debate, especially in the absence of a truly vibrant and active civil society, as in the case of Egypt, for example, is invaluable in terms of setting the stage for transitioning to democratization and reform.

Since blogs serve as a platform for the views of the individual blogger on a multitude of diverse subjects, one of the criticisms of blogs has been that the factionalized platforms and limited audience-reach negatively affect their ability to touch the general public and to incite change, suggesting their limited role as catalysts for transformation. However, blogs should not be totally discredited as an impractical tool for inspiring real change, given their ability to contribute to creating the healthy environment for debate and discussion that is needed for change, but the expectation should be for slow and gradual, rather than fast and sudden, change. Also, the other types of social media, such as Facebook and Twitter, which have been credited with instigating change, could be considered a variation of blogging, or, more accurately, a form of "microblogging." "Microblogging is a new form of communication in which users can describe their current status in short posts distributed by instant messages, mobile phones, email or the Web.... Compared to regular blogging, microblogging fulfills a need for an even faster mode of communication. By encouraging shorter posts, it lowers users' requirement of time and thought investment for content generation" (Java et al., 2009). Blogging could be seen as the wider umbrella under which various forms of cyberactivism can be incorporated.

This compels us to provide a definition of the term "cyberactivism," along with other concepts that constitute the theoretical framework of this study, such as civic engagement and citizen journalism, in order to better understand their utilization and applicability in this book.

Conceptual Framework: Cyberactivism, Civic Engagement, and Citizen Journalism

The role of social media before, during, and after the Egyptian revolution was especially important in three intertwined ways, namely, enabling cyberactivism, which was a major trigger for street activism; encouraging civic engagement, through aiding the mobilization and organization of protests and other forms of political expression; and promoting a new form of citizen journalism, which provides a platform for ordinary citizens to express themselves and document their own versions of reality. Therefore, it is crucial to provide definitions for these terms in order to better understand their relevance and applicability in the context of the Egyptian revolution.

Howard (2011, p. 145) defines cyberactivism as "the act of using the internet to advance a political cause that is difficult to advance offline," adding that "the goal of such activism is often to create intellectually and emotionally compelling digital artifacts that tell stories of injustice, interpret history, and advocate for particular political outcomes." Cyberactivism differs from mobilization because of the latter's focus on planning, execution, and facilitation of actions. However, they are both closely interrelated, since cyberactivism can help to foster and promote civic engagement, which, in turn, gives rise to various forms of mobilization.

The term "civic engagement" refers to the process through which civil society is invited to participate in ongoing political, economic, and social efforts that are meant to bring about positive change. The Coalition for Civic Engagement and Leadership at the University of Maryland indicated that

> civic engagement is acting upon a heightened sense of responsibility to one's communities. This includes a wide range of activities,

> including developing civic sensitivity, participation in building civil society, and benefiting the common good. Civic engagement encompasses the notions of global citizenship and interdependence. Through civic engagement, individuals—as citizens of their communities, their nations, and the world—are empowered as agents of positive social change for a more democratic world.

Along the same lines, Edwards (2004) defined civic engagement as

> a composite of associational life and voluntary interaction...that provides societies with sturdy norms of generalized reciprocity (by creating expectations that favors will be returned), channels of communication through which trust is developed (by being tested and verified by groups and individuals), templates for collaboration (that can be used in wider settings), and a clear sense of the risks of acting opportunistically (that is, outside networks of civic engagement, thereby reinforcing cooperative behavior, or at least conformity with "civic values")....These positive social norms will produce a "society that is civil." (p. 76)

There are two forms of civic engagement: cooperative and expressive. The cooperative, or collaborative, type of civic engagement includes "broader public interests, whereas expressive forms are more individualistic and correspond to more narrowly defined interests" (Putnam, 2000, p. 45). The cooperative form of civic engagement has been on the decline, and this has led to the weakening of the "civility of contemporary political discourse" (Putnam, 2000, p. 46).

A better understanding of the term civic engagement requires a deeper comprehension of a closely intertwined term, namely, civil society. Edwards (2004) defined civil society as "a reservoir of caring, cultural life and intellectual innovation, teaching people...the skills of citizenship and nurturing a collection of positive social norms that foster stability, loosely connected under the rubric of 'social capital'" (p. 14). According to Diamond (1999),

> Civil society is the realm of organized social life that is open, voluntary, self-generating, at least partially self-supporting, autonomous from the state, and bound by a legal order or set of shared rules. It is distinct from "society" in general in that it involves citizens acting collectively in a public sphere to express their interests, passions, preferences, and ideas...to hold state officials accountable. (p. 221)

Most importantly, "According to much contemporary democratic theory, civil society forms the bedrock of good democratic governance—and this sentiment is echoed in more popular political discourse" (Browers, 2006, p. 5). Therefore, "The most noticeable change has been a distinct shift of focus in discussions of democratization from the state to society—that is, from theories that view the state as the locus of political change to theories that see the impetus for change as arising in a non-governmental realm" (Browers, 2006, p. 19).

In analyzing the discourses in the five blogs under study to determine their relevance to the notion of civic engagement, we will utilize the functions of civil society, which were outlined by Larry Diamond (1999) as follows: "checking and limiting" the state influence (p. 241); "supplement[ing] the role of political parties in stimulating political participation" (p. 242); enhancing "education for democracy"; "structuring multiple channels, beyond the political party, for articulating, aggregating, and representing interests" (p. 243); helping with a "transition from clientelism to citizenship at the local level" (p. 244); "generat[ing] a wide range of interests that may . . . mitigate the principal polarities of political conflict"; "recruiting and training new political leaders" (p. 245); developing "explicit democracy-building purposes, beyond leadership training" (p. 246); "widely disseminat[ing] information and so empower[ing] citizens in the collective pursuit and defense of their interests and values"; "mobiliz[ing] . . . new information and understanding" (p. 247); "developing techniques for conflict mediating and resolution and offering these services" (p. 248); "strengthen[ing] the social foundations of democracy"; and developing "freedom of association" (p. 249).

While we do not anticipate finding evidence of the existence of all of these functions in the postings in the five analyzed blogs, we will attempt to use them as a general framework to better understand the role of political blogs in contributing to creating an active civil society and promoting civic engagement, through explaining which of these functions were better exemplified in the studied blogs, and why, how, and to what extent. We will also point to the absence of other functions and provide explanations for it, whenever applicable.

An equally significant concept worth defining is citizen journalism, which provides ordinary citizens with the opportunity to document their own version of reality and to tell their own side of the story. It is distinguished from professional journalism in that ordinary citizens use digital media tools to report on events on the ground, upload text and videos directly to the Internet, and feed the information and videos to media outlets. Therefore, we can contend that citizen journalism "is a promising new breed of news-making that has been championed by various scholars...[for] granting ordinary citizens a novel, hands-on role" (Reich, 2008, p. 739). It "gives people a voice and therefore power. The people's participation itself and what they produce are regarded with the hope to contribute to an informed citizenry and democracy" (Nip, 2006, p. 212). It also assumes that "average citizens are capable of intelligent judgment, mature understanding, and rational choice if offered the opportunity; in other words, that democracy as 'self-government' is not a dream but a practical premise" (Rosen, 1994, p. 18).

Citizen journalism can be utilized as a "problem-solving" tool when it comes to the complex issues that need to be addressed by the press. In this context, Lemert (1981), as cited in Haas (2007), called on journalists to provide citizens with "mobilizing information, or information about how to join up with relevant civic organizations that work on given problems" (p. 41). According to Haas (2007), journalists can enhance the effectiveness of the "problem-solving model" within the context of citizen journalism by addressing two basic questions: "First, journalists need to consider whether given problems could be adequately addressed by citizens themselves or whether those problems would require more deep-seated, systemic intervention by government officials. Second, journalists need to consider whether given problems could be adequately addressed through local intervention, whether citizen-based or governmental, or whether those problems would require intervention of a broader regional, state, national, or even international scope" (p. 43).

Addressing the two questions mentioned above in the context of the problem-solving model requires three conditions, according to Haas (2007), First, journalists need to join forces with experts, citizens, and even government officials, particularly when it comes to tackling complicated issues that cannot be solved by the citizens themselves; second, "journalists should be involved with the 'processes,' but not with the 'outcomes,' of citizens' efforts to solve problems" (p. 44); and third, journalists should not be neutral, but they should have a stand or a position with regard to political issues. Haas (2007) indicates that

> the claim that journalists can remain politically neutral is both illusionary and counterproductive. It is illusionary because news reporting will by necessity always be based on the perspectives of certain sources of information, and counterproductive because pretending otherwise merely serves to deflect attention away from the particular political interests embedded within those perspectives. (pp. 76–77)

We will apply Haas's problem-solving model that is mentioned above in our analysis of whether the discourses in the five blogs under study reflect a form of citizen journalism. Here again, our aim is not to necessarily apply all of the points mentioned in this model. Rather, we will highlight which ones were most applicable and which were not, and why this was the case.

After providing an overview of the definitions, multiple roles, and diverse types of blogs, as well as the definitions of the key terms and concepts that constitute the theoretical framework of this study, we now turn our attention to providing a brief overview of the five blogs under study, and the similarities and differences between them.

Five Political Blogs: Background, Similarities, and Differences

This book focuses on analyzing five of the most popular Egyptian blogs, which were founded by five pioneering and prominent bloggers and political activists, namely, Wael Abbas, Abdel Monem Mahmoud, Nawara Negm, Maikel Nabil (who was the only blogger arrested after the revolution), and Mahmoud Salem (who uses the pseudonym "Sandmonkey" on his blog).

The purpose of this analysis, as previously mentioned, is to see how the discourses and deliberations on these blogs provided the necessary environment for active civic engagement and vibrant citizen journalism, both of which contributed significantly to the eruption of the Egyptian revolution and aided its ultimate success.

The focus on the Egyptian blogosphere in particular in this book stems from the fact that the Egyptian bloggers represent "the largest structural cluster in the Arabic blogosphere, undoubtedly in part because Egypt has a large online population, and the largest population of any Arab country" (Etling et al., 2009, p. 15). Moreover, Egypt has been considered a pioneering political player and a strategic heavyweight in the whole region of the Arab world throughout the twentieth century and the beginning of the twenty-first century. "For these, and for many other reasons, what happens in Egypt matters throughout the region. Egypt may not dictate or shape what happens, as a conscious strategy of regional hegemony (much as it might, sometimes, wish it could), but despite the emergence of other centers of regional power and influence... Egypt and Egyptians continue to offer the observer of the region a way of getting to grips with what is going on [politically] by concentrating on one country" (Jones, 2007, pp. 11–12).

Addressing the important questions related to the multiple roles of political blogging before, during, and after the Egyptian revolution in the rest of this book necessitates providing a brief overview of each of the blogs under study and their similarities and differences, as well as understanding the process through which they were selected.

Here it is worth mentioning that our main goal is not comparing and contrasting these five blogs, but rather providing the reader with a snapshot of how and why they may or may not have reflected the concepts of civic engagement and citizen journalism and to what extent. However, we believe that highlighting some of the similarities and differences between them, whether in terms of the nature of the target audience, the language used, or the political and ideological orientation, is of utmost importance in terms of analyzing their roles and functions.

Wael Abbas founded his blog *Egyptian Awareness* "http://misrdigital.blogspirit.com" in 2004. Wael started his career as a journalist in *Al-Dostour* newspaper and the German news agency dpa, and did some freelancing for various foreign newspapers, such as *The Washington Post* and *Slate* magazine. His blog started as a journalistic endeavor, but then turned into an activism venue. Through his blog, he tries to report on stories (such as the calls for political change) that are not covered by traditional mainstream media, which, according to him, are subject to government restrictions. This helped in building credibility for his blog, and he started receiving videos of torture inside prisons, violence on the streets, and other types of human rights violations, which he exclusively posted on his blog. His blog was characterized by its bold and aggressive attacks on the Mubarak regime. The blogger and the posters on his blog oftentimes use profanities to express the extent of their dissatisfaction with the government's policies and to vent their anger. Abbas frequently posts videos to document certain incidents of police brutality and aggression against innocent civilians. He also includes links to other interesting or relevant media articles. This could be directly related to his journalistic background. He earned his wide fame and popularity as a blogger from the controversial and sensitive nature of some of the items posted on his blog, such as the video of two police officers sodomizing a bus driver inside a police station.

Nawara Negm started her blog *Popular Front of Sarcasm* "http://tahyyes.blogspot.com" in 2006. She is an editor and translator at the Egyptian Radio and Television Union. Negm's father is a famous poet and her mother a renowned writer. Both her parents are well known for their political activism and opposition to successive governments in Egypt, which led to their multiple imprisonments. Therefore, she is a political activist and an opponent of the ruling regime, almost by default. Her blog is equally fierce and outspoken as that of Wael Abbas when it comes to criticizing the government and exposing its malpractices. However, her blog has fewer profanities and milder language than Abbas's blog, and she exhibits relatively more self-censorship and self-regulation. She sometimes relies on posting videos and including links to other relevant articles, although to a lesser degree than Abbas. Negm should be credited with being one of the most active bloggers before, during, and after the revolution.

Abdel Monem Mahmoud started his blog *Ana Ikhwan* (which is translated to 'I am a Brotherhood' in English) "http://www.ana-ikhwan.blogspot.com" in 2006. The name of his blog in Arabic *Ana Ikhwan* translates as "I am of the Muslim Brotherhood," which makes a brave statement about his ideological position, in a rather rare and unusual fashion, taking into account the fact that the Muslim Brotherhood had been an outlawed group in Egypt until very recently. The ban on this group was only lifted after the revolution. Mahmoud officially canceled his membership in the Brotherhood to avoid what he referred to as "a possible conflict of interest with being a journalist." However, he still believes in the Brotherhood's ideologies and embraces its values. Although he was naturally critical of the ruling regime in Egypt and its practices, the tone of his attacks and criticisms is less harsh, compared to the two previously mentioned bloggers, since he refrains from including or posting profanities or offensive comments on his blog. Also, although he worked as a journalist in the *Al-Dostour* online newspaper in Egypt and the *Al-Jazeera Mubasher* channel in Egypt, he engaged in fewer journalistic activities on his blog, such as posting videos or including links to other media articles, in comparison to Abbas and Negm. He decided to stop blogging after the revolution in order to devote more time to his journalistic career. This decision could have been linked to the lifting the ban on the Muslim Brotherhood group, which meant that its supporters did not have to restrict themselves to dissident activities anymore, whether online or offline, since they could now participate openly, whether in political life or through mainstream media outlets.

Maikel Nabil started his blog "www.maikelnabil.com" in 2006. He was a political activist and a member of the Democratic Front Party, which is an independent political party. His blog is also harshly critical of the Egyptian regime and its policies, which sometimes translates into the use of profanities and offensive language, as in the case of Abbas's blog. He also includes a fair amount of video posts and links to other relevant articles to support his posts. Nabil's blog deals with a wide range of topics, including politics, religion, and Egyptology. It could be considered the most controversial of all the analyzed blogs, due to the unconventional nature of his postings, which include his objection to mandatory military service, his outspoken support for Israel, his declared agnostic position, not to mention his harsh criticism of the Supreme Council of the Armed Forces (SCAF). In fact, after the revolution, specifically in April 2011, a military court sentenced Nabil to three years in prison on charges of "insulting the military and publishing false information," due to his blog posts, which criticized the army's role during the revolution and clearly stated that "the army and the people have never been one hand." Commenting on Maikel's sentence, a writer in *The Guardian* claimed that "by…imprisoning Maikel Nabil, the Egyptian army megaphoned his simplistic rantings and elevated him from a small-time provocateur to a prisoner of conscience" (Talat, 2011). In a personal interview with Nabil before his arrest, he commented on his "anti-military" stand by saying, "I am a member of a movement called 'No for Compulsory Military Service', which is a youth movement…I am the founder of this movement, which is the first Egyptian movement ever to be opposed to the military establishment."

Mahmoud Salem started his blog *Rantings of a Sandmonkey* "www.sandmonkey.org" in 2004, so he was one of the pioneer bloggers in Egypt. His blog is characterized by its bold and somewhat sarcastic tone in criticizing the political status quo. It is the only blog among the five that is in the English language, although some of the posts in this blog get translated to Arabic. In a personal interview with Salem, he told the authors that his blog "presents a very secularized, anti-Islamist perspective." He added that he is trying to advocate the point of view that "not everybody who lives in an Islamic country such as Egypt is for terrorism." As for his target audience, he indicated that he aims for "an international audience." He added, "I also target highly educated people inside Egypt. This is because I believe that if there is ever going to be change in Egypt, it is going to come from the more educated social class who can read and write [in] English." Most interestingly, this blogger constantly uses the pseudonym "Sandmonkey" on his blog since he started it back in 2004. It was not until he was arrested and beaten by the police while delivering medical supplies to Tahrir Square during the Egyptian revolution in early February 2011 that he decided to reveal his real name and identity and to declare his role in posting dozens of graphic videos showing police officers beating and torturing their victims. He won the best English-language blog—a people's choice award—in the Deutsche Welle's International Blog Awards. In its citation, Deutsche Welle said, "The activist blogger's witty and courageous writing has called for freedom and democracy in Egypt long before this year's uprising" (Davies, 2011).

It is worth noting that all five bloggers were personally interviewed for the purpose of obtaining a detailed account of the history of their blogs, their philosophy of blogging, their target audiences, as well as their goals and objectives.

There are several similarities among the five blogs under study. One main similarity among them is that they were all highly critical of the now-ousted Egyptian government and, therefore, they could be said to represent the opposition. In this context, it would be worth noting that these bloggers exemplify a new form of political activism that has been launched by relatively young people utilizing new media technologies, such as the Internet, to reach their growing followers. They focus on the government's failure to address people's political concerns and its attempts to suppress freedom of opinion and expression and all forms of political activism on the Egyptian street. They also shed light on the government's violations of human rights, with special emphasis on the incidents of the government's harassment of political bloggers.

Another major similarity among the five blogs is that they cover salient political themes, such as fighting against violations of human rights and limitations on freedom and democratic practice, and exposing the government's corruption. Moreover, all five blogs called for drastic reforms in the political system in Egypt, and they proposed ideas for restructuring and revitalizing the Egyptian civil society and contributing to the creation of a new form of political life in Egypt. These calls for change that started out on these blogs, as far back as 2004, were important triggers for political activism in Egypt and, in turn, for the Egyptian revolution.

As for the differences between the five blogs, they exemplified diversity in terms of gender (four males and one female blogger), ideology (one of the five bloggers adopts the Muslim Brotherhood ideology; one is a declared agnostic; one is a secular; and the remaining two represent liberal, undeclared ideological orientations), language (four of the blogs are in Arabic and one is in English), and self-identification (four bloggers always identified themselves by using their real names and posting a short biography and some photos of themselves, while the fifth has always been anonymous until recently).

The selection process of these blogs started out by contacting Amira Al-Hussaini, the Middle East/North Africa editor of Global Voices (www.globalvoicesonline.org)—a transnational virtual forum that "attempts to cover the global blogosphere by surveying, selecting and translating blogs from around the world, [including the Middle East] in English and seven other major languages" (Dahlgren, 2009, p. 166). The Global Voices website "clearly tilts toward the idea of global public spheres" (Dahlgren, 2009, p. 166). We asked the Global Voices' editor to provide us with a list of what she perceived were the most popular political blogs in Egypt, or the blogs that she thought had an impact on the Egyptian political public sphere. The editor sent us a list of 25 popular political blogs in Egypt.

Then, we used Alexa.com to rank these 25 blogs. Alexa.com is a website traffic ranking service that provides the ranking of any site based on the total number of visits over a three-month period. Based on the Alexa.com ranking of the blogs from the most to the least visited, we reduced the number of blogs on the list from 25 to 12 blogs. The blogs' rankings in the new, reduced list ranged between 120,000 and 1.5 million over the three-month period (May through July 2009) that preceded our work on this study. These rankings are very high by political blogs' standards, or by any website's standards for that matter. These high rankings indicate that the dozen blogs included in the modified list are considered among the most significant platforms in terms of framing the ongoing discussions and deliberations in the virtual political public sphere in Egypt and, hence, are most appropriate for the purpose of this book.

We used other criteria for filtering and selecting blogs from the modified list. We ruled out the blogs that did not have public participation or postings from readers, as such blogs could not provide an indication of the extent to which they may impact or reflect the dynamics of the Egyptian political blogosphere. This filtering step reduced our list of blogs to 10. From this list, we chose the five abovementioned blogs, as they represent some of the most popular, pioneering, and influential blogs in Egypt.

Here it is worth mentioning that the visibility and popularity of bloggers can be a double-edged sword. On the one hand, their increased fame and visibility in the domestic and international journalism and human rights domains might have helped to put pressure on the now-ousted Egyptian government, not to harass them out of fear that it would be viewed as opposed to the freedom of expression. On the other hand, the bloggers' visibility might have increased the likelihood that they would be arrested or harassed if they posted something that did not appeal to the former government. It is worth mentioning in this context that two of these bloggers—Abbas and Mahmoud—were repeatedly harassed by the former Egyptian government because of the daring topics covered in their blogs. In the case of Abbas, he was detained a few times by security officials, while Mahmoud was arrested and imprisoned several times, mainly due to his Muslim Brotherhood links. The case of Nabil, who was sentenced to three years in prison after a military trial, shows that these practices were still very much in place even after the revolution.

Research Methodology

This study utilized two qualitative research techniques, namely, textual analysis and in-depth personal interviews, which are believed to supplement and strengthen one another.

Textual analysis, which can also be referred to as "interdiscursive analysis," entails "seeing texts in terms of the different discourses, genres and styles they draw upon and articulate together" (Fairclough, 2003, p. 3). Conducting textual analysis requires studying the actual text and interpreting the meaning(s) constructed through that text. Meanings in a text can either be explicit (i.e., overtly stated) or implicit (i.e., assumed or implied) (Fairclough, 2003, pp. 10–11).

According to Norman Fairclough (2003), interpretation of meanings in a text is "partly a matter of understanding . . . what words or sentences or longer stretches of text mean, understanding what speakers or writers mean (the latter involving problematic attributions of intentions)." But it is also "partly a matter of judgment and evaluation: for instance, judging whether someone is saying something sincerely or not, or seriously or not; judging whether the claims that are explicitly or implicitly made are true; judging whether people are speaking or writing in ways which accord with the social, institutional etc. relations within which the event takes place, or perhaps in ways which mystify those relations" (Fairclough, 2003, p. 11).

Context plays a critical role in textual analysis in the sense that the meanings in a text have to be interpreted with the cultural context in mind (McKee, 2006). Since various cultures have different interpretive approaches, a particular text does not necessarily have to produce one correct interpretation. In other words, there can be multiple interpretations of the same text, and these interpretations may not be the same as the one intended by the creator of that text (McKee, 2006). This post-structuralism or cultural relativism, which is the basic characteristic of textual analysis, means that "different ways of thinking about the world might be equally valid" (McKee, 2006, p. 52).

Furthermore, as Acosta-Alzuru and Kreshel (2002) rightly point out, "Textual analysis recognizes that meaning is a social production. The method is different from content analysis. Whereas the latter is interested in the recurrence of patterns in the manifest content, the goal of textual analysis is the study of the latent content of texts through a study of their signification. The object of a textual analysis is not the meanings of the texts, but rather the construction of those meanings through the text" (pp. 46–47).

This complex process requires, according to Stuart Hall (1975), three distinctive stages, namely, "a long preliminary soak in the text, which allows the analyst to focus on particular issues while preserving the 'big picture'; a close reading of the chosen text and preliminary identification of discursive strategies and themes; and an interpretation of the findings within the larger framework of the study" (p. 15).

We selected two main themes that seemed to be overarching and overlapping among the five blogs and that, most importantly, could be considered among the main triggers of the Egyptian revolution, namely, (1) violations of human rights and limitations on freedom, which includes issues such as arrests, torture, murder, forging election results, ban on the formation of political parties, and other restrictions on political participation, as well as malpractices and abuse of power by the SCAF and (2) governmental corruption, which includes financial crimes, such as theft, fraud, and money laundering, committed by high-ranking officials.

While there is certainly an overlap between these two highly interlinked themes, we will deal with each one of them in a separate chapter, because there is also enough distinction between them, especially in terms of how they were handled and discussed in the Egyptian political blogosphere, to justify devoting a separate analytical chapter to each of them.

To analyze each of these themes with sufficient depth and details, we selected threads from the five blogs under study that seemed to best capture the gist of the abovementioned themes. We were keen to mention the date when each thread was posted and, whenever possible or relevant, the underlying context for posting it, to help the reader gain a deeper understanding of each of the analyzed threads and the circumstances under which it was posted.

We particularly focused on the threads that exhibited sufficient deliberation, vibrant discussion, and high level of interactivity, as demonstrated not only by the number of posters or the volume of comments, but, most importantly, by the quality of the exchanged discourses. This was necessary to enable us to conduct a thorough textual analysis of these threads and to draw meaningful conclusions and come up with informative patterns.

This last point explains our decision to focus on blogs that exemplified a "dialogue," rather than a "monologue" (Hall, 2006); those that were "news" blogs, rather than "traditional" blogs (Kent, 2008); "A-list" blogs, rather than "B-list" blogs (Herring et al., 2007); and "public sphere" blogs, rather than "activist" blogs (Lynch, 2007), since they are the ones that provide the best examples of platforms of free expression and exchange of ideas, where the connection to the notions of civic engagement and citizen journalism could be best tested.

It is also worth mentioning that it was for the same reason that this study focused on blogs, in the first place, as a form of social media, rather than on Facebook or Twitter, for example, since Facebook posts or tweets do not provide sufficient content or enough context to understand the notions at hand or to analyze them using textual analysis, which could have posed the risk of "reading too much into too little." The analyzed threads in chapters 4 and 5 will be classified according to three main functions, namely, whether they urge public mobilization, offer documentation, or provide a platform for deliberation.

Besides relying on a textual analysis of the five blogs under study, this book also relies on extensive, in-depth personal interviews with political bloggers, human rights activists, professional journalists, political activists, and other leading figures in order to deepen the understanding of the issues under study and to provide a fuller and more comprehensive context through which they could be better analyzed. In that sense, it can be argued that both of these qualitative research methodologies, namely, textual analysis and in-depth personal interviews, complement each other.

Chapters' Outline

This book consists of six chapters. This first chapter sets the stage for the rest of the book through providing the reader with an overview of the book's main themes, objectives, and structure, and explaining the basic terms and concepts used in the book, such as cyberactivism, civic engagement, and citizen journalism.

Chapter 2, "Political Blogging: (Re)Envisioning Civic Engagement and Citizen Journalism," explores the process of political blogging and its potential implications on reviving the phenomena of civic engagement and citizen journalism. The chapter will explain how virtual public sphere(s), alongside intertwined civil spheres, can serve as platforms for self-expression and citizen journalism and as spaces where political and democratic practices are played out. The chapter will lay the theoretical foundations of this book through exploring the concepts of civic engagement and citizen journalism and their relevance to the transformations that new media, especially political blogs, have triggered in the overall political culture in the Arab world, in general, and Egypt, in particular. In doing so, the chapter explores how online public sphere(s), as exemplified in political blogs, could carry the implications of freedom and renewal found in online discourses, alongside the freedom to pull into separate, fragmented political discussion communities, and the degree to which they can contribute to boosting civic engagement and providing platforms for citizen journalism.

Chapter 3, "The Arab Political Blogosphere: The Case of Egypt," will shed light on the transformative Arab media landscape before and after the latest revolutions in the Arab world. In doing so, it will explain how and why Arab media changed from safety valves to effective mobilization tools, with a special focus on the role of new media, especially political blogs in the Arab world, in general, and Egypt, in particular, in inducing political change and paving the way for democratization. The chapter will also discuss the barriers and challenges that Arab bloggers, especially Egyptian bloggers, have been facing in their day-to-day online activism. The chapter will rely on an extensive literature review of the transformative political and media landscapes in the Arab world, as well as in-depth personal interviews with political bloggers, human rights activists, media professionals, and leading political figures. This chapter will also provide a general overview of the Egyptian political environment and the relationship between the Egyptian government and civil society, on the one hand, and the Egyptian government and the media, on the other hand, before, during and after the Egyptian revolution. In doing so, it will pay special attention to the critical role played by new media outlets, especially political blogs, in paving the way for this historical revolution.

Chapter 4, "Blogging on Violations of Human Rights and Limitations on Freedom," addresses how these important themes, which were major triggers for the Egyptian revolution, were tackled in the discourses on the five blogs under study. The Egyptian government under Mubarak suffered from a very poor human rights record due to massive arrests of opponents, political activists, and media figures, in addition to the widespread torture and maltreatment of lay citizens at the hands of police officers. This chapter presents the findings of the textual analysis of selected threads from the five blogs under study that revolve around the violations of human rights in Egypt and their multiple implications. The chapter also deals with another main trigger of the Egyptian revolution, which was the lack of a healthy democratic environment in the country, as evidenced in the flawed constitution and fraudulent parliamentary elections, in addition to the absence of genuine freedom of expression, as evidenced by the arrests and harassment of political activists, journalists, and bloggers. The textual analysis of selected threads in this chapter will revolve around mobilization, documentation, and deliberation among the participants in these threads.

Chapter 5, "Blogging on Governmental Corruption," will present the findings of the textual analysis of selected threads from the five blogs under study that deal with another major problem that existed under the Mubarak regime, namely, massive corruption, which was widespread among high-ranking political officials and leading figures in the country and characterized several government branches and institutions. The chapter will shed light on how the five blogs tackled this theme and identify the similarities and differences between them when it comes to mobilization, documentation, and deliberation.

Chapter 6, "The Future of Political Blogging in Egypt: Looking Ahead," will sum up the most significant findings of this book, based on the indications from the textual analysis of the five blogs under study, in addition to the authors' critical analysis of the relevant literatures and the findings from in-depth interviews with political bloggers, political activists, human rights activists, journalists, and leading political figures. The chapter will also provide an overview of how the Egyptian revolution has been triggered by new media, in general, and political blogs, in particular. It will also discuss the potential implications of the role of new media in shaping the political future of the Arab world, in general, and Egypt, in particular, as well as recommend further research in this important area of study.

CHAPTER 2

Political Blogging: (Re)Envisioning Civic Engagement and Citizen Journalism

Introduction

This chapter lays out the theoretical framework for this book through exploring the process of political blogging, as a form of online democracy, and its potential implications on (re)envisioning the phenomena of civic engagement and citizen journalism. It starts by introducing the notion of political blogging and its many implications, especially in terms of contributing to the creation of a new form of online democracy, which can lead to the rise of a virtual public sphere(s). It also investigates how political blogging can actually energize and revitalize civil society through boosting and encouraging the growth of active civic engagement and actual political participation, and it discusses how and why this may, or may not, be the case. Finally, it sheds light on the closely interlinked process of citizen journalism and how it may impact the phenomenon of political blogging, as well as how it may be impacted by it. In doing so, it explores the multifaceted characteristics of both political blogging and citizen journalism and how and why they may overlap with, or diverge from, each other.

Political Blogging and Revitalizing Online Democracy

There is increasing agreement among scholars that blogs form an online public sphere where issues are raised, debated, and sometimes lead to action (Ward & Cahill, 2007). Despite the fact that blogging is a relatively new phenomenon, "it shows some signs of potentially evolving into a miniature public sphere of its own, one of shared interests rather than shared geography" (Froomkin, 2004, p. 10). In particular, political blogs "may be considered to be a manifestation of Habermas'...notion of a public sphere involving convergence of people...from various walks of life who share in discourse" (Trammell et al., 2006, p. 23). In other words, blogs could be said to contribute to the creation of new "virtual public spheres" (el-Nawawy & Khamis, 2009).

The term "public sphere" was coined by the contemporary German philosopher Jürgen Habermas, and it refers to the space "between civil society and the state, in which critical public discussion of matters of general interest was institutionally guaranteed" (Habermas, 1989, p. xi). The public sphere was exemplified in the intellectual discussions and deliberations that took place among members of the aristocracy or the "bourgeois" at the salons and coffee houses during seventeenth- and eighteenth-century Europe. This was mostly a "sphere of private people [coming together] as a public" to discuss matters of shared interest and to engage in stimulating debates (Habermas, 1989, p. 27).

Universality (i.e., "access is guaranteed to all citizens") and equality (i.e., citizens convene and participate in discussions with no restrictions) characterize the ideal public sphere (Sparks, 1998, p. 112). The Habermasian public sphere seeks synthesis and resolution and seeks to regulate forces of fragmentation. However, it is important to bear in mind that the ideal public sphere, as envisioned by Habermas, is not necessarily a physical sphere. "It is a metaphorical term that is used to describe the virtual space...where people's conversations, ideas and minds meet" (McKee, 2005, p. 4). In other words, what matters for Habermas is not the physical space where the deliberations are taking place, but rather the presence of "shared social spaces" (Haas, 2004, p. 180). Therefore, his notion of the public sphere "can be applied to assess the democratic potential of face-to-face dialogue, mediated deliberation, and more complex, hybrid forms like those found in Internet discussion forums" (Haas, 2004, p. 180) and blogs.

The rational-critical debates and dialogical interactions that form the gist of Habermas' public sphere have acquired a new meaning in the Internet world. In his discussion of deliberative communication, Habermas "addressed the Internet only in a footnote, pointing out that interaction on the Internet...has democratic significance in so far as it undermines censorship of authoritarian regimes" (Rasmussen, 2007, p. 2). Unlike the traditional public sphere, which was characterized by face-to-face interactions and then by the mass media, the

Internet "propels a more differentiated public sphere... [that is] more niche-oriented, both because of a more diverse media-scape, and because of a more ethnically and culturally pluralistic society in general" (Rasmussen, 2007, p. 8).

It is for these reasons that some scholars hailed the new communicative and deliberative possibilities enabled by this new "virtual public sphere(s)" online (el-Nawawy & Khamis, 2009). For example, Goode (2005) argued that the Internet can contribute to "the renaissance of dialogue, the advent of the 'electronic coffee house'... in which citizens would (re) discover the art of speaking, debating, and discursively testing the claims of the powerful and of each other" (p. 107). Likewise, Dahlberg (2007) argued that "the Internet is of great interest to deliberative democrats because it offers two-way, relatively low cost, semi-decentralized, and trans-national communication through which government and corporate power may (in principle) be bypassed and rational-critical deliberation fostered" (p. 50). Along the same lines, Janack (2006) argued that

> the Internet's capacity for near-instantaneous, two-way, decentralized communication has made cyberspace a potentially attractive site for extended informal political deliberation. Furthermore, because markers of gender, race, and class are less obvious in an online environment, some have considered the Internet as a more democratic and egalitarian venue in which individuals could exchange ideas with less interference from personal prejudices. (pp. 283–284)

The alternative, anti-hegemonic nature of the Internet, and its related applications, such as blogging, has allowed politically marginalized groups to "use [it] as a means for the formation of counter-publics, the articulation of identities and oppositional discourses, and the contestation of the discursive boundaries of the mainstream public sphere" (Dahlberg, 2007, p. 60). Along the same lines, Simone (2006) argued that

> the web provides an outlet for developing and disseminating counter-discourse. Subaltern voices can find their way into popular consciousness with or without the support of the mainstream press. So, while use of the web may not result in a revolution, it is becoming as indispensable for critical debate as the newspaper was in the bourgeois public sphere. (p. 361)

Some of the optimists, who support the role of blogging in energizing online democracy and creating virtual public spheres, such as

Coleman (2005), referred to blogs as "sophisticated listening posts of modern democracy" (p. 274). He contended that

> [to] blog, is to declare your presence; to disclose to the world that you exist and what it's like to be you; to affirm that your thoughts are at least as worth hearing as anyone else's; to emerge from the spectating audience as a player and maker of meanings. . . . [B]logging is a source of nourishment for a kind of democracy in which everyone's account counts. (Coleman, 2005, p. 274)

Blogs also are believed to provide a venue through which individual participants can express their political views away from the constraints set by political systems and the restrictions set by traditional media. "That is why blogs have become a key source of information and analysis for people who prefer to trust their own judgment rather than depend upon the spin, censorship and narrow agenda of the usual sources" (Coleman, 2005, p. 276). The "bottom-up" nature of the blogs allows for expanding the public sphere through providing the opportunity to "enter into an 'authentic two-way conversation', enabling people to provide feedback in an open manner—and more easily than before" (Kreutz, 2009, p. 31).

In fact, one of the biggest differences between blogging and traditional news media lies in the creation of "virtual space" for audience interaction. As previously mentioned, the Internet as a medium facilitates the opening of multiple spaces and enables the creative, inventive use of virtual space by the audience. It carries with it "the ability to enable immediate, person to person and person-to-masses (and sometimes both at once) communication" (Warnick, 2007, p. 8). Blogging is just one way of shaping and utilizing this space to engage in political discourse.

A function of blogging as a platform is the ability to comment on a post and reply to other posters' comments, thus enabling back-and-forth conversation and two-way interaction online. This is very different from how audiences engage with each other, or with news senders, through traditional media. It is therefore important to see blog posting as moving beyond a single written work and into a conversation, which allows for a circular, rather than a linear process of communication. The ability to have conversations within blogs allows us partially to move back to what Habermas desired in his ideal type of public sphere: "a public space for debate, opinion, and knowledge sharing" (Warnick, 2007, p. 1). The fact that political blogging provides spaces, or, more accurately, many networked spaces, where commentary and political discussion can be situated, has special significance. When we consider the practice of blogging as more than something that can be simply defined in an analogy to journalism, and instead redefine it as a platform for conversations, its role in the public sphere makes more sense, and takes on new importance.

According to Siapera (2008), interactive and dialogical blogs that allow their visitors to post comments responding to the issues or opinions raised by the bloggers reflect a unique kind of "authorial subjectivity." The visitors' comments "set up a tension between the subjective position of the blogger and other subjectivities, which is resolved by the dialogue in which they are involved" (Siapera, 2008, pp. 57–58). In such a case

> the comments feature of the blog may be seen as establishing the subject as not only an authorial, positioned one, but also as emerging in dialogue and interaction through connection with other subjects.... Comments justify and validate the blogger's posts, hence providing a crucial connection between the blogger's subjectivity and other subjectivities that ends up validating them all, in recognizing and acknowledging them. This is the case even if there is no agreement or consensus, but merely an engagement with/in the blog. (Siapera, 2008, p. 58)

In discussing the role of political blogs in revitalizing online democracy, we have to also acknowledge that they have their own limitations. For example, most bloggers, particularly the ones who blog on a voluntary basis, have limited time and resources. "Indeed, some bloggers complain of 'burnout' and have given up blogging altogether.... Because of these resource constraints, it is simply impossible for top bloggers to be able to comment on or link to news stories about every issue up for political debate" (Drezner & Farrell, 2004, pp. 19–20).

Furthermore, several governments have developed new approaches and tactics to respond to political blogs. "Astute political actors can read blogs as easily as media professionals, and use that information to predict the direction of future news cycles. This also gives them the ability to develop strategies to counter or blunt the influence of blogs before media groundswell develop" (Drezner & Farrell, 2004, p. 20).

Another constraint or challenge that may hinder political blogs' influence and effectiveness internationally is language barriers among Internet users across the globe. The fact that the majority of blogs are in English may prevent many people from participating. In this context, Hall (2006) predicted that "just as English had earlier become the near-universal language of science, it may also become the root language of the blogosphere" (Hall, 2006, p. 48).

Media literacy is also an issue when it comes to blog use. The process of sifting through the vast amount of information on the various political blogs requires a nuanced understanding of the complicated issues at hand, and how those issues are handled in the world of new media. And "less 'media literate' people may take blogs as factual and 'trusted sources' in the same way they would a newspaper" (Kreutz, 2009, p. 32).

Ideally, political blogs would serve as an exemplification of a free marketplace of ideas, where participants exchange views and engage in vibrant political discussions with no inhibitions. This has been the case with the blogs that have "lower[ed] the threshold of entry to the global debate for traditionally unheard or marginalized voices, particularly from poorer parts of the world which are too often represented by others, without being given a chance to present their own accounts" (Coleman, 2005, p. 277). However, in reality, what takes place in many political blogs is "the phenomenon of social herding...whereby people cluster around sources of information and channels of communication that support their values and prejudices. [Some] people choose...[blogs] more to reinforce than to shape or challenge their beliefs. The more they read, the more certain they become that social reality is as they believe it to be—and that this reality is shared by a wider readership which comes to represent 'the public'" (Coleman, 2005, p. 278). Along the same lines, Eveland & Dylko (2007) suggested that "individuals would be more likely to participate in political discussions online because of...the ease of self-selecting into groups of similar others no matter what the rarity of one's views might be" (p. 108).

Additionally, the "digital divide," which is exemplified in the drastic gaps in the levels of Internet penetration across the globe, may hinder the Internet's potential in serving as a platform for a global public sphere (Bohman, 2004, p. 135), or a "global blogosphere." In this context, it is worth mentioning that Internet accessibility is "highest in developed countries, ranging from 65 to 75 percent, whereas developing countries average just 10 to 20 percent" (Crack, 2007). It is also worth noting that an equally significant digital divide does exist within the same country, or the same region, between the technological "haves" and "have-nots", based on multiple factors, including education, socioeconomic status, gender, geographic location, and technical skills. This, in turn, inhibits the creation of an equally accessible and universal blogosphere.

Along the same lines, Dahlgren (2009) also questioned the possibility of having one global public sphere, or one global blogosphere, online, since he believes that "the goal of ushering all citizens into one unitary public sphere, with one specific set of communicative and cultural traditions, is mostly rejected on the grounds of pluralism and difference" (p. 163). Additionally, Poor (2005), as cited in Al-Saggaf (2006), "doubted that a single online public sphere can accommodate millions of Internet users and still function properly, because deliberation on that scale would be difficult" and proposed that "it makes sense to have multiple spheres...[which] are publics within a larger public consisting of people with diverse characteristics coming together for various reasons to form a public" (p. 315).

This last point deserves further attention. It is true that the Internet has drastically lowered the cost of engaging in political discussion, since anyone with Internet connection can post a blog, as previously mentioned; however, these same low costs could also make it easy for Internet users to find information that conforms to their own worldviews. It is not safe to assume that since the Internet contains so much free-to-access information, users will take in a steady, balanced diet of different viewpoints online. We must recognize the possibility of users sticking to ideological enclaves online by joining only like-minded blogs in cyberspace.

In this context, it is worth noting that the term "blogosphere" implies that there is "one network" that all blogs are connected to. While it may be true that blogs may share some common characteristics, and that many of them may be intertwined and interconnected in some way or another, it is also true that there could be many smaller networks within this blogosphere. Liberal blogs or conservative blogs could compose their own networks, or "mini-blogospheres," for example. We should remember that part of what the public sphere is supposed to do is lead toward consensus, since it is supposed to be where divergent groups can come together and decide on policy issues (Warnick, 2007, p. 1). Therefore, if these divergent groups are not communicating with each other and, consequently, the discussions needed to achieve consensus are not taking place, then this should in turn cast some doubt on the notion that Internet-based interactions, like political blogging, could have positive implications for creating online democracy or ideal public spheres. This view is supported by researchers who argue that blogs have become sites of discussion that are only welcoming to "same-minded" individuals (Coleman, 2005;

Eveland & Dylko, 2007). If we acknowledge blogs as important sites of discussion, and these sites become "closed circles," only opening up civil discussion to those who share similar views, then the implications for the notion of the ideal public sphere and online democracy, in general, could be enormous.

In comparison to television or even magazine production, blogging has very few barriers to entry for those who are already Internet literate and have a bit of spare time, which promises to increase the ability of blogs, in theory, to create a more equal and accessible venue in the public sphere; however, there are, in practice, a number of limitations and constraints in this regard. These include the generally skewed readership of most blogs and the lack of demographic diversity, whether in terms of race, gender, or profession, in those blogs that do get heavily read. Most blogs do not attract a lot of readers, since a blog might have a limited topical scope or it might be directed at a highly localized, or even personalized, audience. As Matthew Hindman (2008) puts it, "The question is not who is posting on blogs, but who is getting read" (p. 103). Blogs that do not garner a large readership do not have a lot of sway or a significant impact. This is mainly due to the intertwined nature of the blogosphere, where blogs are not independent or isolated, but rather interconnected with other blogs.

The blogs with the most potential to reshape the public sphere are those that have become "hubs" in the social network, that is, places from which ideas, links, and information chain out to the rest of the blogosphere. The web might be a horizontal platform, and blogging might be a social network tool, but this does not mean that certain blogs have not garnered an elevated status. In fact, the website Technorati (http://technorati.com/) assigns an overall and a topical authority number to each blog, which indicates the amount of influence a blog has. Authority is a continuously recalibrated number, reflective of the constantly changing conversation within the blogosphere, but it should give us some indication of the blog's popularity and influence, as well as its readership, or online traffic, and, thus, its potential impact, within the blogosphere (Technorati authority). Most blogs do not do well enough, for whatever reason, to have a significant influence on the social network, public thought, or the public sphere. That could trouble our celebratory notion that blogging could possibly allow for equal weight for all voices in an egalitarian space.

Even more troubling is the sheer lack of diversity amongst top bloggers. Matthew Hindman, author of *The Myth of Digital Democracy* (2008), explains that few blogs ever achieve more readership than a small town newspaper. Of those that do, an overwhelming majority of those bloggers are white, male, highly educated, and have achieved a good measure of professional success (Hindman, 2008, pp. 121–123). This lack of diversity implies that there are not enough members of other ethnic, racial, sexual, or professional communities in the ranks of high-status bloggers. Due to this lack of diversity, it is quite likely that there are issues left uncovered and perspectives and opinions that are undelivered; therefore, the public sphere, as a place for the display of diverse ideas, and the examination of political issues, is left lacking in turn.

However, there is good reason to believe that, despite any possible imperfections or limitations that may be witnessed in the type of online democracy or the form of public sphere(s) brought about by the phenomenon of political blogging, the mere existence of these outlets of free speech and platforms of independent expression could be seen in itself as an educational effort that paves the way for the adoption of democratic values, through practicing the virtues of tolerance, listening to *other* opinions, and accepting diversity, especially in nondemocratic societies. For example, in her study of blogging in Malaysia, Smeltzer (2008) suggested that blogging could be a democratizing force in countries with limited freedom. Likewise, in many Arab countries where differences of opinion were not encouraged, there was little opportunity for citizens to experience the sharing and exchanging of different opinions (Lynch, 2007; Seymour, 2008; Khamis, 2008; Seib, 2007). This limited exposure to diverse opinions may lead to an unhealthy environment of intolerance and resistance to new ideas. Thus, blogging offers a rare opportunity to hear different perspectives, through opening the window on diverse national and international online communities. This, in turn, is bound to increase the universality and accessibility of these newly emerging online "virtual public sphere(s)," which are created through multiple blogs and mini-blogospheres, both locally and globally.

In this context, Nora Younis, an Egyptian blogger, talked to the authors in the summer of 2009 about the role of political blogging in paving the way for democracy in Egypt. She said, "I consider blogs to be the only public forum which cannot be controlled by anybody other than the blogger who posts on his/her own blog. Because blogs have no specific structure, it is very hard to infiltrate them. Blogs have challenged the Egyptian regime and the mainstream media, which advocate the regime's policies." According to Younis, political blogs have thrived in a suppressive political environment in Egypt, and have revitalized the Egyptian public sphere by creating "political hype, a state of mobility, community interest, and civic awareness in a free marketplace of ideas."

Along the same lines, Ahmed Gharbeia, another Egyptian blogger, told the authors in the summer of 2009 that "blogs serve as an open forum outside the realm of state control, and bloggers have forced the government media to cover issues such as torture in prisons and sexual harassment in the streets by providing firsthand testimonies, documents, and pictures of such abuses." Gharbeia also highlighted the blogs' role in promoting a democratic civil society, saying:

> In countries like Egypt, where there is no democracy, blogs are active, because they are an attempt to democratize society. Maybe when we have more democracy, the role of blogs will diminish, because we will have other means of expression.... But until we reach that point, blogs will continue to play a role in enhancing Egyptian civil society, through increasing public awareness about the regime's abuses and encouraging people to become more proactive. We, as people, are still learning how to interact and negotiate with each other in a civil society. But I think that the experience of dialogue on the Internet, which crystallized over the past few years, has benefited a lot of people by enhancing their abilities to participate actively in a democracy in a horizontal manner between and among people, rather than in a vertical manner between the government and the people.

Echoing the same thought, Nawara Negm, a prominent female Egyptian blogger, whose blog is analyzed in this book, told the authors: "I think that blogging and writing are both acts of thinking, and their role in discussing current affairs is very important. It is important to expose the Egyptian youth to different ideas and to train them on how to discuss issues and to develop their own way of thinking. It is important for every Egyptian young man and woman to read and write. This is the very first step in reforming society, through reforming people's minds."

Political Blogging: Energizing Civic Engagement and Political Participation?

A closely related angle that deserves special attention is whether political blogs can actually enable the creation of a vibrant and active civil society, through encouraging civic engagement and boosting political participation.

Kalaycioglu (2004) referred to civil society as "a social context that is determined by structures, processes and institutions which, in turn, stem from the voluntary, private actions of individual citizens. Hence, civil society connotes the lack of intrusion of the state or centralized national power in the affairs of private citizens. It is the autonomous, consenting and self-initiated actions of each individual that determine the gist of the matter that constitutes civil society" (p. 251). The Center for Civil Society at the London School of Economics defined civil society as "the arena of uncoerced collective action around shared interests, purposes and values. In theory, its institutional forms are distinct from those of the state, family and market, though in practice, the boundaries between the state, civil society, family and market are often complex, blurred and negotiated" (Lunat, 2008, p. 2).

It is important to bear in mind that civil society has been affected by the global—not just the local- political environment. This has led to the introduction of the term "global civil society," which

> can be structurally defined as encompassing all associations, excluding governments, private sector actors and families, that act transnationally. This transnational activity has been facilitated by the wider process of globalization, including easier travel and communication across borders, and by the information and communication technology (ICT) revolution, which has provided unprecedented levels of access to information. These various processes have enabled like-minded groups to co-operate and co-ordinate their activities across national boundaries. (Wild, 2006, p. 5)

In this globalized civil society, information plays a key role in coordinating efforts of civic participation. "When people are better informed, they are more likely to participate in policy discussions where they can communicate their ideas and concerns freely. Most importantly, citizens need...[to have access to information so] they can speak freely, discern different perspectives, share similar interests and concerns, and pursue what they believe is in their and the public's interest" (Kranich, 2004, p. 281). But access to information, in and by itself, will not enhance the effectiveness of civil society. In the information age, members of the public ought to have the "information literacy skills" that would activate their role in society. "To cope successfully, citizens must be able to identify, evaluate, apply, and communicate information efficiently, effectively, and responsibly. They will have to become information literate to flourish in the workplace as well as to carry out the day-to-day activities of citizens in a developed, democratic society" (Kranich, 2004, p. 289).

Citizens' access to information and their ability to utilize this information for the purpose of enhancing civil society have been affected by the Internet and other communication technologies. Therefore, we need to map some of the scholarly views that hailed the potential implications of the Internet and its multiple applications, such as blogging, in terms of bringing about actual political involvement and citizen participation, as well as those that were skeptical of such possibilities.

Today, several civil society organizations and nongovernmental organizations (NGOs) are utilizing the Internet to get their voices across to as many citizens as possible. Moreover, "many people connect to established social groups through the Internet as they receive e-newsletters from their groups or visit group websites. In addition, cyber associations have expanded rapidly as individuals interact through online forums, chat rooms and personal pages that are separate from the traditional social groups. This has led to the development of a 'virtual civil society'" (Kittilson & Dalton, 2008, p. 3). Moreover, "The dynamic and changing nature of the . . . [Internet] and its promise of inexpensive and universal access to information and communication suggest rich potential for civic uses" (Day & Schuler, 2004, p. 363).

Thanks to the Internet, civic engagement has expanded due to the fact that the average individual has a bigger say in the day-to-day issues of public concern. "Structurally, the Internet has inverted the few-to-many architecture of the broadcast age, in which a small number of people were able to influence and shape the perceptions and beliefs of entire nations. In the many-to-many environment of the Net, every desktop is a printing press, a broadcasting station, and a place of assembly" (Rheingold, 2004, p. 272).

This expansion of civic engagement due to the Internet was clearly manifested in the role played by cyberactivism in mobilizing, energizing, and improvising the Egyptian revolution. In this context, Ahmed Badawy, an Egyptian blogger and one of the cyberactivists who were camping out in Tahrir Square in Cairo during the Egyptian revolution, talked to the authors in the immediate aftermath of the revolution about how blogs and other forms of social media were the impetus or the catalyst for the revolution. According to Badawy,

> Bloggers played a big role in disseminating information about the intention to launch the revolution. Most of the work of those bloggers and of online activists, in general, has been on the Internet in the prelude to the revolution. Once the revolution started on Jan. 25, all

> bloggers and online activists started to shift their efforts from their computer screens to the streets. When you are blogging, you don't see all the immediate reactions to what you post, but when you talk to people face-to-face on the streets, you get immediate and direct feedback, which is amazing.

Echoing the same thought, Esraa Abdel Fattah, a young Egyptian woman who has been politically active on the Internet for the past three years, told the authors:

> Since 2008, new media have been playing an important role as a tool that young Egyptians and online activists used for preparing, coordinating, organizing and paving the way for their activities on the street. Recently, young activists started printing some of their online posts in the form of brochures and pamphlets that have been distributed among average people on the streets. We have recently printed more than 50,000 pamphlets for people before the revolution. That way, we made sure that our messages reach everybody, even the ones who do not have access to the Internet. This was a way of connecting the virtual world and the real world. It also helped us to get an immediate sense of the average Egyptians' feedback on the ground to what we were calling for on the Internet.

This last point reminds us that "civil society actors are increasingly using the Internet to document and share reality" and this can "lead to a profound shift in how politicians go about doing campaigning and interacting with the general public. This has the potential for an inverted 'panopticon' where citizens constantly monitor the state and document the practices of the state and those aspiring to become a part of the state" (Vatrapu et al., 2008, p. 16).

The Internet has taken civil society to another level:

> Today's [electronic] forms of civil society suggest that lives are increasingly lived in fluid relations where electronic information flows, material and virtual bodies, and physical locations are intersecting and integrating in more prolific, engaging and interesting ways.... Social relations...[engulfed in civil society] are becoming increasingly informed through emerging technologies that allow for distributed connectivity and information sharing and cooperation. (Dennis, 2007, p. 32)

Brauer (2008) argued that "the Internet seems to provide current social movements with new opportunities for restructuring their internal communication activities as well as their external media use in order to enhance their strategic potential" (p. 229). According to Fuchs (2006), the Internet has paved the way for a self-administered "grassroots digital democracy" that relies on a bottom-up "e-participation," and this "self-organized democracy is a process of self-determination and self-management that maximizes the involvement of affected humans in political discourse and decision taking and avoids the formation of political elites that constitute . . . [hierarchical] political systems that are alienated from the direct involvement of citizens" (p. 5).

Echoing the abovementioned views, Perez (2004) argued that the Internet, as a transparent and multidirectional, rather than a unidirectional, form of communication, can allow for a simultaneous presentation of "multiple forms of deliberation and decision-making structures, which could cater to different individual profiles and utilize varied discursive frameworks" (p. 89). Witschge (2004) referred to the Internet's role in promoting deliberative democracy, particularly in the political arena:

> Not only could the Internet encourage more people to discuss politics by freeing them of psychological barriers, but it could do so by offering a (partial) solution to the problems that deliberative democracy is confronted with—problems previously seen as insurmountable. The Internet makes manageable large-scale, many-to-many discussion and deliberation. (p. 110)

It also offers "netizens," defined as people who are active users of the Internet, "platforms and tools to exchange the views and information needed in order to realize freedom and self-government" (Deuze, 2003, p. 211). According to Agre (2004), the Internet, "by providing a general mechanism for moving digital information and a general platform for constructing digital information utilities," can allow for new opportunities and venues through which political interactions can be crystallized (p. 63).

Moreover, some scholars argued that the Internet, and its related applications, such as blogging, can play a critical role in enhancing social capital, which was defined by Putnam (2000) as "connections among individuals—social networks and the norms of reciprocity and trustworthiness that arise from them" (p. 19). Dahlgren (2009) states that "the more and better connected one is, the more likely one is to participate as an effective citizen—[this] captures the importance of networks" (p. 159). Social capital enhances the feeling of social accountability and trust. "Together social capital and social trust foster norms of reciprocity and of shared responsibility for the greater good" (Lerner et al., 2007, p. 5). The Internet can strengthen social capital by "[drawing] people into contact with others to create shared resources and communal concerns" (Katz & Rice, 2002, p. 337).

This holds true especially in the case of blogging, which combines the shared interests among posters on a certain blog with the interconnectedness within the closely networked blogosphere at large, as well as establishing two-way channels of communication with the larger public and with those in power. This led Siapera (2008) to claim that political blogs have the potential to "deliver more citizen participation, more political debate, more direct communication between politicians and citizens, in short, more—and better—democracy" (p. 51).

Political blogging, one of the main features of civil society activism online, can play a critical role in revitalizing, enriching, and strengthening civil society offline. This is particularly the case in nondemocratic societies still suffering under authoritarian regimes, as is the case in many parts of the Arab world, where

> an army of bloggers, intellectuals, artists, [and] political [activists], using various forms of [online] dissent, are demolishing the political immobility of governments and causing profound transformations in their societies. Everything that happens inside a country can be filmed and published online for everyone to see. A blog easily manages to avoid a regime's censorship and reports the facts. Power relations between political regimes and civil societies, once balanced in favor of the regimes, are slowly achieving a new equilibrium. (Cesario, 2009)

One could not think of a better example than the role of Internet-based activism in instigating, covering, and organizing the sweeping wave of popular revolutions in the Arab world, which led to unprecedented political transformations. It was new online media avenues, such as blogs, Facebook, and Twitter—which were extensively used by members of civil society, especially youth—that revealed the true faces of their regimes and exposed their flaws to the international community at large, that is, to the "global civil society."

Studying political blogs' potential impact on public participation and civic engagement requires making a distinction between blogs that serve as forums for political expression and those that are venues for political participation (Wallsten, 2005). In this context, Su et al. (2005) argued that "in the popular media, blogging is perhaps most recognized as an enabler for collective action. Thus, some bloggers seek to influence events in their world through blogs" (p. 4).

However, Keren (2006) argued that blogging alone cannot lead to concrete political action on the ground, because "bloggers [could be] helpless *vis a vis* the evil they experience or observe, and their helplessness is only marginally relieved by the sense of community that is emerging online.... Feelings such as fear of oppression, resentment toward authority and vulnerability...are not easily reduced by online...writing" (Keren, 2006, p. 151).

One of the main reasons behind the skepticism around the ability of political blogs to bring about actual political change or transformation has been that bloggers have been widely perceived as a disjointed group varying in purpose and motivation, and therefore their ability to organize around a singular cause or impetus is likewise perceived to be weak. In fact, Gharbeia (2007) points out that even as "the media now portrays blogging as cyber-dissent and it has become a synonym for activism," nonetheless, "bloggers generally shy away from public affairs" (p. 52), or, at best, they do not have the necessary connections and tools to link their online political activism with real-life political practices that could bring about change at the decision-making level.

Echoing a similar opinion, Dahlgren (2009) indicates that there are now thousands of discussion groups, chat rooms, alternative journalism sites, blogs, civic organizations, NGOs, and grassroots issue-advocacy sites that are active in the political realm, both locally and globally. He argues that "these 'agonistic public spheres' or 'cyber-ghettos' can be a strong sign for a healthy democratic environment that is 'based on contestation rather than consensus'.... However, they can be a hindrance to democracy if there are no structural connections and procedures between these communicative spaces and the processes of decision-making" (pp. 163–165).

Some scholars, such as Keren (2006), have argued that blogging "has made political discourse interactive and abolished etiquettes that have previously served as a means to silence legitimate voices on the edges. It has allowed private or group needs...to become matters of public concern and to expand the range of issues that require political attention" (p. 16). However, the fact remains that political blogs do not necessarily serve as automatic venues for enhancing civic engagement and political participation. They may just have a "cathartic role" in the sense that "people would sit in front of their computers and mistake typing at each other for political action" (Rheingold, 2008, p. 103). In order for the blogosphere to serve as an ideal environment for democratic practice and civic engagement, users of political blogs have to grasp "the connection between their power to publish online, their power to influence the circumstances of their own lives, and the health of democracy" (Rheingold, 2008, p. 104).

Along the same lines, Dahlgren (2001) argued that the Internet has the ability to energize and augment the public sphere, but he questioned the transformative nature of the Internet, and its related applications, such as political blogging, when it comes to revitalizing political environments and energizing political mobilization offline. He contends that "the Internet clearly offers opportunities for the motivated. The questions today are not so much how the Internet will change political life, but rather, what might motivate more people to see themselves as citizens of a democracy [and] to engage in . . . political [life]" (p. 53). He rightly claims that while some of the answers to these questions may be found online, "most reside in our real social circumstances" (Dahlgren, 2001, p. 53).

This is especially true since Internet technology, in and of itself, may not be the only answer to the problems facing civil society activists. "The Internet will always be a supplement to, not a replacement for, other connections. Those who already have power can make more effective immediate use of the technology—so those with less power have to work harder to make it effective on their side" (Calhoun, 2004, p. 241). Moreover, the Internet complements, rather than replaces, face-to-face communication. "It empowers local activists who would otherwise find it harder to reach others with similar concerns in remote locations. It enables both lateral sharing of information and better access to information" (Calhoun, 2004, p. 243).

In this context, Rheingold (2004) posed a very critical question: "Will worldwide Usenet discussions . . . World Wide Web pages, and email chain-letter petitions add to civic life, or remove people from it?" (p. 275). To put it differently, "Will the Internet strengthen civic life, community, and democracy, or will it weaken them?" (Rheingold, 2004, p. 273). According to Rheingold (2004),

> Electronic communications do not offer a utopia, but they do offer a unique channel for publishing and communicating, and the power to publish and communicate is fundamental to democracy. Communication media are necessary, but not sufficient, for self-governance and healthy societies. The important stuff still requires turning off the computer and braving the uncertainties of the offline world. (p. 276)

This last point is certainly applicable in the case of the Egyptian revolution. If it wasn't for the willingness of political activists in the real world to risk their own lives, through having the moral courage to take out to the streets in large numbers, at great personal costs to themselves, no form of cyberactivism in the virtual world alone could have brought about the desired political transformation and the historical outcome that marveled the world.

In this context, Esraa Abdel Fattah, the female online activist who was quoted earlier, talked to the authors about how cyberactivists collaborated in their efforts and organized their activities on the ground, risking their lives during the Egyptian revolution. She mentioned that

> youth from different political groups were protesting in Tahrir Square.... It was a perfect division of labor among the protesters. It was a whole life in the square. Some [activists] were assigned the responsibility of bringing tea; others would bring water; others would distribute juices and milk and so on and so forth. Some people even went out to collect the garbage. All of this was done and coordinated spontaneously without the Internet['s] help. I was responsible for bringing blankets and water for the protesters, as I expected that this protest would take a long time.

Salter (2004), as cited in Lunat (2008), argued that "the Internet is not passive but rather shaped by... 'forms of use.' To suggest that the Internet has a positive or detrimental impact on communication and discourse ignores the fact that the Internet does nothing without people doing something with it" (p. 6). In other words, as Bohman (2004) rightly points out, "electronic and computer-mediated network communication may well expand the scope of certain features of communicative interaction across space and time.... [However], it is the software rather than hardware that constructs how communication occurs over the network" (p. 132).

Therefore, without taking into account the overall political, social, economic, and cultural contexts in each society, and the accompanying factors that might either mobilize and activate the public(s) or restrict and limit the level of political activism, any discussion of online modes of communication, such as political blogging, and their ability to bring about political change will not be sufficient to provide answers or solutions for the lack of political involvement and civic engagement.

In brief, we can contend that political blogs do influence our discussions of current events and public affairs. However, the implications of these blogs on actual political engagement are still largely controversial. While a lot of scholarship on the issue are empirical studies of whether or not the Internet increases or decreases outside political engagement (such as voting, campaigning, or other "tangible" forms of political engagement), we can argue that the very act of engaging in political blogging communities online could also be considered a form of political action in and of itself. This could be attributed to the fact that a large part of the purpose behind political actions, such as gathering in rallies and protests, is to garner saliency.

Therefore, the act of writing on a topic or an event, commenting on it, and interacting with it, as is the case with political blogging, could also lead to the same result of increasing saliency and drawing attention to that topic or event. Choosing which facts to present and constructing meaning(s) around them could be considered a political activity that could indirectly shape political action through agenda setting and issue framing, which is what most political blogs do. In fact, those blogs that enjoy high "authority" ratings, or large numbers of followers, can oftentimes get their stories picked up by traditional media outlets and read by large numbers of ordinary citizens. This was certainly the case with the blogs analyzed in this book.

In this context, Wael Abbas, a prominent Egyptian blogger, whose blog is analyzed in this book, told the authors:

> I was among the first bloggers to use videos and photos, and I covered many "scoops" that nobody else covered. I am always at locations where there are no other bloggers or journalists, so I get exclusive coverage. What I post is always perceived as credible news and information. Many newspapers and wire services rely on the news I post on my blog.... My postings on police torture led to street demonstrations. Also, my coverage of the issue of sexual harassment gained so much media attention and encouraged many women to file police reports saying that they were sexually harassed. Also, blogs covering labor issues have encouraged labor unions to become more organized and to call for their rights.

Nawara Negm, another prominent blogger who was quoted earlier, told the authors:

> There is one commentator who is really against all my beliefs.... He is very different from me, yet he insists on following my blog daily and commenting on it. He is very polite. He angers other visitors on my blog. For example, during the Gaza war, he wrote that it was Hamas's crime, not Israel's crime. Other posters call him names, but he is very dedicated to my blog.... I don't understand why he follows my blog despite the fact that it completely contradicts his opinions. I find that to be very healthy and flattering for me, because he posts his comments politely, but he just wants to engage in a constructive dialogue. Despite our differences, we engage in a civilized dialogue.

The question of whether blogs, and other Internet-based political activities, increase or decrease outside political action is not yet conclusively answered. However, most of the data from empirical studies shows that there is a positive effect, albeit one that is small and subject to change over time (Boulianne, 2009). Other longitudinal-style studies found evidence of increased civic engagement and political participation over time (Shah et al., 2005; Mesch & Talmud, 2010). However, there still hasn't been an overwhelming amount of research on the topic, and the picture coming out of existing research does not indicate clear or large effects (Boulianne, 2009, pp. 198–200). Obviously, this is an area needing more research before we can more fully understand the implications of the Internet on political engagement. Yet, going beyond ideas of blog followers turning into campaign volunteers or at least voting, we need to consider the notion of political blogging itself as being a consequential activity in the civic, not just the public, sphere and to analyze its multiple prerequisites and implications as such.

Political Blogging: Reconstructing Citizen Journalism?

After engaging in a discussion of how political blogging can contribute to revitalizing online democracy and what kind of implications it may have on energizing civic engagement and political participation, we now turn our attention to an equally important dimension, namely, Could political blogging be considered a form of "citizen journalism"? If so, how similar or how different is it from other forms of journalism, both online and offline? And what are its strengths and weaknesses?

Citizen journalism "wants citizens to be conscious of themselves, informed on the issues, and ready to act on their conclusions" (Leonard, 1999, p. 85). It attempts to enhance citizens' ability to discuss the problems that are covered in the news and to contemplate solutions for these problems (Nip, 2006). In a way, the citizen press' role in this type of journalism is "not just to inform a public that may or may not emerge, but to improve the chances that it will emerge" (Rosen, 1999, p. 19). In that sense, citizen, or public, journalism, as it is sometimes called, is closely tied to Habermas's notion of the "deliberating public," where there is "a focus on topics of common concern to all citizens" (Haas, 2007, p. 39).

Advocates of public or citizen journalism have several goals. "They want to ensure that the voice of the public is heard and that not all reporting is top-down; that all communities, even marginalized ones, are listened to...and that we hear from the middle spectrum of ideas as well as from the polar extremes" (Witt, 2004, p. 51). These goals "presume a common good of some sort—providing a framework for healthy democracies, community connectedness [and] civic involvement" (Christians, 1999, p. 67).

Some scholars argue that the way we name public, civic, or citizen journalism does not matter, since, as Witt (2004) claims, "the name has never been as important as the concept" (p. 54). Since the concept of citizen journalism is relatively recent, there is not yet one formal name that can best describe it. One "might hear terms like community, participatory, or grassroots to describe it, but they all refer to the same basic concept of giving people the tools to publish their own content" (Miller, 2005, p. 23).

Citizen journalism has been subject to various criticisms. For example, Brown (2005) compared citizen journalism to traditional, or what he called "professional," journalism. In his comparison, which was critical of citizen journalism, Brown argued that while a professional journalist's priority is to be precise and correct, a citizen journalist's priority is to be "interesting." Also, while "a professional journalist has layers of editors checking his facts, a citizen journalist is usually a lone crusader" (Brown, 2005, p. 42).

The Internet has helped in crystallizing and reformulating the concept of citizen journalism. Online media have blurred "the boundary between professional and non-professional journalists by co-opting their consumers into the process of message production. Casting their lot with consumers-turned-producers, they abolish the hierarchical boundary between production and consumption of messages. The result may be communications that faithfully reflect the reactions and needs of the users" (Woo-Young, 2005, p. 926).

In referring to the Internet's role in citizen journalism, Paulussen (2008) states that it is not realistic to exaggerate the power of online journalism in a way that reflects "technological determinism," which "falls short in considering the social, cultural and economic contextual factors that influence how and to what extent journalists use new technologies" (p. 28). Paulussen (2008) also points out that recently, "technological deterministic accounts of online journalism have become outnumbered by social constructivist approaches in which the adoption of online journalism practices...is no longer seen as the result of a technology-driven process, but as the outcome of the complex interaction between professional, organizational, economic and social factors" (p. 28).

Several scholars considered blogging to be a form of citizen or public journalism because it allows for:

> a decentralized, bottom-up approach to news reporting by turning traditionally passive news consumers into active news producers....Moreover,...the interactivity of weblogs, and especially the practice of linking to and commenting on other Internet-based materials, gives rise to a radically different kind of news discourse than the one found in mainstream news media. Specifically, the practice of juxtaposing news reporting and commentary from a diverse range of sources...[on many weblogs] is seen to facilitate a "multiperspectival," "multivocal" or "intertextual" form of news coverage. (Haas, 2005, pp. 388–389)

In a way, blogs have allowed for virtual communities "where dozens—sometimes hundreds—of citizens regularly comment, offer news tips, and generally gather around these blogs just as they might meet at a local coffee shop" (Fanselow, 2008, p. 24).

In this context, Miller (2005) argued that "citizen journalism is part of a wave of new media that includes blogs and podcasts and folks with digital cameras posting their pictures on Web sites" (p. 27). Miller adds that blogs have given "people the power to contribute to the discussion in ways never thought possible before in traditional media models" (p. 27). Along the same lines, Coleman (2005) noted that blogging has led to the appearance of "a new breed of citizen-reporters [who are] utilizing mobile-phone cameras and discrete networks of intelligence, [and] are breaking down the old dichotomy between message-sender and message-receiver" (p. 274).

According to Coleman (2005), blogs serve as

> vehicles for self-presentation...[by] diminish[ing] people's need to be spoken for by others. So, journalists can reflect on their stories without checking them with editors; civil servants can contemplate policy without having to follow traditional bureaucratic paths; and civilians about to be bombed (such as the Baghdad blogger, Salam Pax) can express what it feels like to be opposed to a dictatorship as well as opposed to an invasion. (p. 276)

Given the unique role that they play, "blogs provide a channel for authentic expression that is free from the repressive controls of traditional media" (Coleman, 2005, p. 276). Domingo & Heinonen (2008) state that "by challenging the conventional understanding of what journalism is, weblogs have revitalized the voices that expect a paradigm shift in journalism in the Internet era" (p. 3). In a way, blogs have allowed "amateurs" who happen to be close to an event to record what they see, as eyewitnesses, gather information and post it online through their own lens or perspective (Allan et al., 2007). This has certainly been the case during the Egyptian revolution, as well as the other revolutions that swept many parts of the Arab world, where ordinary citizens have used their handheld cell phone cameras to record police brutality, document historical events, and make their voices heard by the rest of the world.

In this context, a young Egyptian engineer, who was interviewed by the authors in Tahrir Square on February 11, 2011—the day former president Hosni Mubarak stepped down, said, "For a long time, I have always believed that any revolution in Egypt would take place only with the help of social media because of the big gap between the government and the Egyptian youth. It is through the Internet that I have been exchanging my political views with my friends. The Internet has been serving as the only venue for expressing my views."

Another Egyptian female college student, who was also interviewed by the authors in Tahrir Square on the day of Mubarak's resignation, told the authors: "I have participated in some groups, which supported the revolution on Facebook. I also posted my opinions on several blogs, and I received several messages inviting me to participate in the revolution. Even though I did not actually go out to the streets during the protests, I felt as if I participated in them through my posts on Facebook and various blogs."

Due to all the previously mentioned reasons, the resemblance between the role played by bloggers and that played by citizen journalists led some scholars to contend that blogs are a new form of (citizen) journalism that are free of the disciplinary practices of journalism and, therefore, tend to be more authentic and independent. Thanks to blogs, regular people feel that they have their own voice and that they can set the political news agenda. "Blogging today has become an alternative platform that offers voice and contact to those outside the mainstream media.... This new phenomenon of Citizen-Generated Media..., which includes uncensored information and unmediated conversation, is considered to be the greatest strength of the blogosphere" (Hall, 2006, p. 6).

Along the same lines, Keren (2006) argued that "the channels opened up by the Internet to individual self-expression [including blogs] have raised hopes for a reinvigoration of a public sphere worn off in an age of centralized mass media.... The current diversification of communication channels.... is politically important because it expands the range of voices that can be heard in a national debate, ensuring that no one voice can speak with unquestioned authority" (p. 9).

Similarly, Ford & Gil (2001) highlighted that the Internet, and its related applications, such as blogging, can play an important role as an alternative medium. "As an interconnected infrastructure for multiple forms of communications, [the Internet] facilitates an era of convergence of media technologies. By providing for the easy transmittal of simple texts as well as the means to combine and re-combine a range of media formats and social actors, it allows for an unprecedented distribution of knowledge and resources to virtually anywhere in the globe" (Ford & Gil, 2001, p. 202).

In this context, it is important to mention how bloggers can oftentimes rely on multiple sources of news and information, including both online sources and information from mainstream media, in addition to relying on audiovisual resources, such as uploading videos and photos, and including links to other blogs and websites. This provides a clear example of one of the advantages that blogging can have over mainstream media sources: hybridization.

The previous discussion reveals that many scholars have considered blogging only in the context of a form of journalism. If they discuss ideas of blogging and the public sphere, for example, it is usually in the context of how blogging, acting differently from, but still in analogy to, journalism, can affect the public sphere. Barlow (2007), for example, compares blogging's horizontal structure to journalism's vertical structure, while Stephen Cooper (2006) examines what effect blogging might have on journalism and, therefore, the public sphere.

However, blogs do not just perform a journalistic role in society, since their main function is not simply disseminating news or being news sources. Rather, they play a multitude of other roles, such as becoming venues for public discussion and debate, as well as platforms for the exchange of controversial and/or conflicting views. In other words, it could be said that their functions fall more into the domain of commentary, analysis, and the expression of opinions, rather than objective and balanced journalism.

Sometimes what blogs produce, in terms of content, can be hard to define, since blogging can blur the distinction between the different categories of news stories, political commentary, and media criticism. Blogs can achieve a degree of fluidity much like that of the Internet itself. It is far more constructive to recognize that blogs can perform multiple roles than limit our perspective of them to one function. Furthermore, none of these roles, that is, commentary, criticism, or news coverage, are truly inseparable.

Ultimately, blogging's role might be perceived more as a shaper of news, rather than as a source of news. Blogs are the place to digest what is out there in current events. For some readers, blogs might add another layer of analysis to what they already know, whereas for others, blogs might be a place to go and discuss the news and see what others think and feel about current events. In every case, it is important to bear in mind that this fluidity and intersection of multiple functions is a distinctive characteristic of blogs that distinguishes them from mainstream media outlets.

Moreover, another distinction between blogs and mainstream media outlets is the use of community posts, which is an important aspect of major blogs. These community-building measures don't just promote readership for the blog, they also familiarize regular readers with each other, and encourage more open discussion. In other words, they help to create "online communities" in cyberspace (el-Nawawy & Khamis, 2009).

In every case, the fact remains that blogs can definitely create a forum bringing together groups of people interested in a certain issue, while reducing the associated transaction costs of that process of group formation (Faris, 2008). It is also possible to say that the blogosphere "is creat[ing] a new breed of citizen journalists who communicate what they witness like any correspondent" (Al Malky, 2008), while eliminating the high costs involved in mainstream media production and news dissemination. However, it still remains to be seen just how influential blogs can be or how many people they can reach since the fluidity of the medium makes estimating the exact size of the blogging world very difficult (Isherwood, 2008). At the very least, blogs enable individuals to express themselves and introduce unique ideas and perspectives to the Internet-savvy crowd throughout the world. That, in and of itself, is not an insignificant mission.

In this context, the relationship between blogs and mainstream media deserves special attention, since the content of popular blogs has begun to increasingly influence content that the more mainstream media report on. "Stories carried on blogs and websites not only set the tone for 'water cooler' discussions for general readers, but often show up on listservs that target specific interest groups, as well as influence mainstream media reporters" (Berenger, 2006, p. 181). This is a positive indication that the blogosphere could potentially challenge the content of mainstream news providers by purposefully covering controversial events and topics. Bloggers can also utilize mainstream media to establish credibility with readers "by selectively linking to or quoting these mainstream media sites while adding their interpretations of a news story or an issue" (Berenger, 2006, p. 182).

By influencing the agenda of mainstream media, "blogs threaten to unravel the carefully managed, state-controlled narrative which frames government policy" (Al Malky, 2008). This is especially true in the case of dictatorships, where authoritarian regimes carefully monitor the media and dictate its content. The fact that blogs are relatively low-cost and easy to maintain means that changes in readership can have very little influence over the material addressed. This, in turn, gives blogs an advantage over mainstream media, which needs its audiences and, therefore, must appeal to their tastes and interests to sustain themselves and/or have to be keen not to offend the ruling governments and not to cross the red lines set by those in power. This resulted in a greater margin of freedom for blogs, since they have more liberty to tackle sensitive, or even taboo, issues, which can set bloggers apart from mainstream news sources, through drawing the readers' attention to these issues and raising their awareness. This, in turn, puts pressure on mainstream media providers to offer more open, frank, and objective news coverage, since their credibility can suffer if they fail to keep abreast with the news covered in blogs.

In this context, Noha Atef, a young female Egyptian blogger, talked to the authors about how blogs changed the media landscape in Egypt. She said, "The [Egyptian] mainstream media are starting to use blogs as sources for news. They regard alternative media and citizen journalism as potential competitors, and so they use some of the sources used by bloggers. They are also forced to cover stories that are leaked by bloggers. For example, the case of Emad El Kebir, the bus driver who was tortured and sodomized by a police officer, was first released by a blogger, and then mainstream media picked it up afterwards."

The traditional media's deteriorating credibility in many people's eyes seems to be a main factor that has led to the increase in the number of blog visitors. In this context, Johnson and Kaye (2004), as cited in Eveland and Dylko (2007), "argued that blog readers are individuals who became disenchanted with traditional media (which they distrust) and as a result turned to blogs for political information" (p. 108).

Interestingly, however, blogs can also come under fire due to a number of factors undermining their credibility, albeit for different reasons. For example, Kaid and Postelnicu (2007) argued that

> the free and open nature of blogs for information distribution has a darker side as questions of responsibility, believability and credibility surface daily. The absence of a gatekeeping authority, combined with lack of formal journalistic education, can lead to postings of inaccurate content. For instance, errors normally filtered by the editorial process are sometimes not caught before being posted...and entries can include all sorts of inaccuracies, from spelling to facts. If such situations occur, bloggers are not bound by any legislation or editorial policy to public retractions or corrections; many of them do not go back to correct a post (p. 150).

Other scholars argued that bloggers "are more likely to point potential readers toward a narrow range of views that reflect the state of elite opinion than toward a multiplicity of competing truth claims that can be compared and contrasted" (Haas, 2005, p. 389). According to this argument, blogs are considered an "online echo chamber of mass-mediated political views...[rather than] an alternative sphere of news and views" (Haas, 2005, p. 390).

Moreover, Brown (2005) argued that while blogs serve a "watchdog" role over the mainstream media, the blogs' credibility is often questionable since there is no clear system of checks and balances governing them. "Blogs are good at finding the flaws in others' information. They're not so much seeking new facts and reporting them; they're seeking to rebut the 'facts' others report" (Brown, 2005, p. 42).

Therefore, "Rather than considering weblogs as a potential substitute for journalism, [some] scholars...suggest that the major impact of blogging and citizen journalism lies in the fact that these online media developments are challenging journalists' monopoly of the occupational practices and ethics that are at the heart of their professional identity and democratic role" (Paulussen, 2008, p. 26).

At the heart of the credibility crisis for political blogging is the fact that bloggers are not limited by the disciplinary practices of journalism. Journalists are expected to be balanced and unbiased in their presentation of the news, but it is known that they do present particular frames in covering their news stories (Jamieson & Waldman, 2004; Cooper, 2006). Blogs can openly admit to their frames, and they could even present alternative frames to those in other forms of media (Cooper, 2006).

The problem, of course, is that in liberating themselves of many of the journalistic practices that can stifle discussion and thinking, bloggers also risk losing elements of credibility. Bloggers can readily admit to using a particular frame, but this puts their credibility in question because the readers cannot wholly trust what is presented to them, since not even the pretense of balance is upheld. The standards and ethics of blogging are still very open for discussion and debate. Presuming that blogs may take over a number of the functions that newspapers once performed for the public, then questions of bloggers' responsibility and ethical blogging become even more pressing.

Of equal importance, however, are issues of reader responsibility: What should our expectations be of our fellow citizens as blogs take their place in their daily information diet? Blogs perhaps should remain supplements, rather than full meals, of information, but then questions of the limited time and energy that the average citizen might devote to politics come up. The critical skills readers need in their encounters with blogs, and the ethical practices that should bind bloggers, are still unsettled in our public discourse, but the answers will certainly have a profound effect on how people interact with political issues, both online and offline.

Concluding Remarks

This chapter provided an overview of the process of political blogging and its potential for being a venue for online democracy and, thus, a catalyst for democratization. While there is a significant amount of debate as to whether blogging currently has an influential role in promoting actual change and boosting political transformation, even the critics and skeptics agree that blogging does have a great deal of potential to influence meaningful social and political change in the future. This potential will largely depend on the ability of the blogosphere to create an atmosphere where activists could successfully organize, and controversial events could be brought to center stage. In this regard it is important to remember that the size of a blogosphere is not the key defining variable in determining its success in fueling movements for political change. It is also quite helpful to consider that not all blogospheres will be equally successful as catalysts for political change. Rather, it makes more sense to consider each blogosphere as a separate entity and a unique case that should be better analyzed within its own contextualized setting and intertwined variables.

Throughout this chapter we explored the multiple, and sometimes conflicting, roles of blogging as a new form of participatory, and potentially empowering, venue for spreading news, exchanging views, and shaping public opinion. We displayed the divided positions that scholars adopted towards this rising phenomenon of political blogging and its ability to provide an opportunity for any voice to be heard. On the one hand, some scholars have placed a lot of hope in this new phenomenon in terms of its ability to empower publics. On the other hand, other scholars were skeptical of its ability to bring about actual change in social life (Cammaerts, 2008).

In exploring these issues and discussing these various perspectives, we were careful to avoid the "technological determinism" perspective, which claims that new media technologies have unlimited powers and highly effective roles in political change. Rather, we agree with Dahlgren that "when we in verbal shorthand talk about the net's role in politics or society, we of course mean people putting the technology to social uses" (Dahlgren, 2009, p. 161). Therefore, we were keen not to overestimate, or to underestimate, the potential implications of new media applications, such as political blogging, in terms of revitalizing online democracy, energizing civic engagement, and reconstructing citizen journalism. Instead, we tried to highlight the multitude of complex and intertwined factors that might enhance, or limit, the impact of this new form of online communication and, in turn, shape its societal and communicative implications and potentials. In doing so, we were fully aware of the need for ongoing research and further investigation of this evolving phenomenon to reach a deeper understanding of its multifaceted characteristics and possible effects.

One of the limitations that must be acknowledged in studying this topic is that blogging is a relatively new phenomenon in social scientific research, due to the novelty of the Internet and its multiple applications, which have become widely accessible in the West only in the last few years. Although an increasing number of scholars in different fields are starting to study blogging, as a new social phenomenon, much of this research has mainly focused on a homogeneous segment of society, namely, white US college students (Muhtaseb & Frey, 2008). This points to the importance of expanding research about blogging to other parts of the world, in an effort to account for an array of variables stemming from local cultures and their authentic contexts. This book attempts to contribute to filling this gap in the current literature.

The scholarly arguments and debates, which were discussed throughout this chapter, illustrate that the Internet, in general, and political blogging, in particular, can "pose both new problems and solutions to democracy" (Rasmussen, 2007, p. 22). The "cyber-democratic enthusiasm" that has been exemplified through Internet-related activities, such as blogging, can reflect "the worst and the best from the point of view of rational discourse" (Rasmussen,

2007, p. 7). On the one hand, it can enhance civic engagement and political mobilization in a way that can enrich civil society, but, on the other hand, it can also be a turn-off for many participants in online discussion forums and blogs, mainly because "substantial parts of Internet interaction seem to amount to hasty, unfocused and inconsistent chat because of the expansion and democratization of access to un-edited discussion that the Internet offers" (Rasmussen, 2007, p. 7).

In this regard, more research needs to be done on political blogging, since its role as a potential facilitator of vibrant political debates online, and as a catalyst for active political participation offline, is still unclear and, thus, warrants further, deeper, and broader investigation.

Most importantly, moving our thinking and definitions of bloggers and blogging activities beyond journalistic endeavors and (re)conceptualizing them as online networks and cyber communities has many implications for how we see blogs operating in the public sphere, on the one hand, as well as how we understand their overlaps with, and divergences from, citizen journalism and other forms of online and offline journalism, on the other hand. Blogs provide a venue for information to be shared and commented and opined on, not just created and simply dispersed, as is the case in traditional, mainstream media outlets. Blogs act as nodes in the broader, intertwined network, which is referred to as the blogosphere, and their importance rises or falls depending on whether people come to them to share information and exchange views, or whether they choose to go elsewhere.

Moreover, bloggers oftentimes play the "watchdog" role over traditional media, through criticizing their coverage of particular stories or revealing certain flaws or gaps in this coverage. Yet, the common purpose of most blogs remains to be reaction to, and digestion of, current political events. Therefore, blogs are not typically instigators in our media cycle. It could be said that they function more as our "news digestive system," rather than our "news meal." Although it is true that blogs may sometimes break a story or obtain some original quotes from news sources, thus giving their posts a more "news-like" feel, the fact remains that the sweeping majority of posts on blogs are almost entirely commentary, opinions, and reactions to others' posts. While we can certainly challenge the notion of bloggers being citizen journalists and blogs as news sites, we also have to acknowledge the important role played by blogs, whether in the public sphere, the civic sphere, or the news sphere, through providing virtual spaces where online communities and cyber networks could be created to discuss what is being said elsewhere, to digest the content of mainstream media outlets, and to form opinions and post comments on it.

The transformations that political blogs are introducing in our public interactions and discussions will inevitably result in transformations in our overall political culture. In the new media age, one of these transformations could be that the online public sphere(s), as exemplified in political blogs, will carry the implications of freedom and renewal found in online discourses alongside the freedom to pull into separate political discussion communities and fragmented mini-public sphere(s) in cyberspace. Understanding these transformations requires a completely different vision, one that encompasses fragmented communities and their competing discourses, in an effort to produce a healthier democracy. Indeed, these fragmented groups might actually be useful in terms of fostering extreme positions that can lead to change in society and providing "an important step in building alternative visions of life before contributing to opening the boundary of dominant discourse through more explicit forms of contestation (publicity, protest, activism, etc.)" (Dahlberg, 2007, p. 837).

Historical moments of political transformation, such as the current wave of "Arab Awakening," necessitate a deeper reflection on new forms of communication, such as the phenomenon of political blogging, and its multiple implications, both online and offline.

CHAPTER 3

The Arab Political Blogosphere: The Case of Egypt

Introduction

This chapter, as its title suggests, is divided into two sections. The first section provides an overview of the introduction of the Internet and its multiple implications on the Arab world, with a special focus on the phenomenon of blogging, especially political blogging, in this important and volatile region. In doing so, it sheds light on the Internet's prevalence in Arab societies, its multiple roles and functions, as well as its potential for acting as a catalyst for democratization and radical transformation in the Arab region. It explains why and how there is a significant amount of debate as to whether blogging has an influential role in promoting social and political change, and its potential for continuing to do so in the future. It also sheds light on some of the most important challenges confronting bloggers in the Arab world.

The second section of this chapter deals with the role the Egyptian blogosphere played in paving the way for the 2011 revolution by giving a general overview of how and why blogging started in Egypt, identifying the needs political blogging meets in the case of Egypt, providing a brief description of the different types of blogs, the challenges Egyptian bloggers face, as well as elaborating on the potential the Egyptian blogosphere may have on influencing meaningful social and political change in Egypt's future.

Section One: The Transformative Arab Cyberspace

The Internet in the Arab World: An Overview

The Arab world began to use the Internet as a credible and efficient news source in the early 1990s. The Internet has an empowering and liberating potential in Arab societies due to its ability to defy boundaries, to provide an alternative voice to traditional media, and to challenge autocratic regimes by resisting governmental censorship. Since the introduction of the Internet in the Arab world, the number of Arabs with Internet access has more than doubled each year. "It was reported in April 2007, that there were 20 million Arabs daily logging on to the Internet. This access to the cyberworld provides an avenue for millions of Arabs to express views and opinions that are otherwise censored by the government in more traditional media sources" (Khalid, 2007).

However, these numbers have been increasing steadily on an annual basis. In fact, "Between 40 and 45 million Internet users were found in 16 Arab countries surveyed in late 2009, including Arab nationals and non-Arabic speakers in the region, according to the Arab Advisors Group, a research and consulting firm based in Amman, Jordan. The Arab Knowledge Report 2009 placed the number of Arabic-speaking Internet users at 60 million" (Ghannam, 2011, p. 4). It is expected that one hundred million Arabs will be online by the year 2015 (Ghannam, 2011, p. 4).

The proportion of Arabs with Internet access is generally small; in June 2010 "about 3.32% of the world's Internet users" were "from the Middle East" (Rinnawi, 2011). However, these figures and percentages have to be perceived with caution, taking into account the challenging infrastructure in a number of Arab countries, in addition to the very high illiteracy rate in this region, which is considered the highest globally. Interpreted within this context, we can appreciate the steady and remarkable increase in Internet access and usage in this part of the world, despite the multiple challenges, which will be discussed later in this chapter in more detail.

Internet use is increasingly more prevalent among certain groups within the Arab world, such as youth, the highly educated, urban dwellers, and middle and upper middle class segments of society. It is reported that the 20- to 30-year-old age group uses the net more avidly compared to the rest of the Arab publics. This is of special significance, taking into account that those younger than 20 years old are the group growing most rapidly in the Arab world today (Hofheinz, 2005). This point is clearly connected to the central role played by young cyberactivists in igniting the Arab Awakening, or Arab Spring, that swept the Arab world, in which social media played a crucial role in terms of mobilization, organization, and coordination. In other words, similar to Western cultures, the use of the Internet became a way of life for the young, educated Arabs, and they started to use it effectively to achieve their own political goals and aspirations.

Although in the Arab world the Internet is used for many reasons besides gaining news and information, such as browsing search engines; establishing social connections; discussing taboo topics; and accessing entertainment, sports, and religious guidance, the fact remains that it has become an increasingly popular alternative for news and information, especially political information and commentary, in the Arab world. This is mainly because when people get their news from online sources, they are generally able to ask questions, provide feedback, engage in discussions, and communicate with the author and other readers. This increased level of interactivity and engagement is certainly among the top advantages of blogging.

In fact, through online-based discussions, like those found on bogs, "Not only can they offer their opinions, but the Internet creates the opportunity for the consumer to become the producer" (Al-Saggaf, 2006, pp. 311–312). This explains why "journalists and non-governmental organizations (NGOs) were among the first in the Arab world to use the Internet professionally" (Hofheinz, 2005, p. 84). We can also add to this group political activists and dissidents who found in it a safe haven not only for self-expression, successful mobilization, and effective organization, but also for making their voices loudly heard regionally and, most significantly, globally.

This last point is particularly significant since the Internet creates a global community that no other media source has been able to establish before, due to its capacity to significantly reduce national and international boundaries. Even with a minor presence in the Arab world, in comparison to Western countries, the Internet has created a viral global community unmatched by other sources. Therefore, it provides a space for greater integration of the Arab community into the global community (Seib, 2004–2005, p. 81), as well as enabling Arab voices to be heard by a wider international audience. In addition, Arabs all over the world can retrieve news about the Arab world easily and efficiently with the help of the Internet. "For the Arab communities scattered over the globe, the internet really can provide an Arab 'global village'" (Khazen, 1999).

Censorship by the government of media sources had been a continuous struggle in almost every Arab country. "Before the Internet, non local newspapers especially, could be censored by being stopped at the borders of the country. Now with the Internet the distribution of the content has a far greater reach" (Lynch, 2003, p. 62). Censoring the Internet has created a challenge for autocratic regimes in the Arab world and has proven to be quite difficult. Years ago, some Arab countries felt threatened by fax machines and kept a close eye on people that had them; it is nearly impossible to do this with the Internet. Even if only a small percentage of the Arab world has access to the Internet, it has spread to homes, universities, and cyber cafes in a number of Arab countries (Khazen, 1999) to an extent that makes it difficult, if not impossible, for the governments to effectively censor it.

A number of Arab countries attempt to filter certain sites that are inappropriate for moral and political reasons. This has been a very common practice in countries like Saudi Arabia, Syria, Yemen, and Tunisia, before its recent revolution. Other Arab countries that do not block sites may monitor Internet traffic through police and security organs. Even though censorship is a great concern to some, it has not been able to stop the increasing use of technology to strengthen communication and opposition. Banning sites will not be able to stop those that really want to communicate; there are ways around censorship, as the events in Tunisia, Egypt, and Syria clearly revealed. Those with the needed financial and technical resources can always find ways to circumvent governmental restrictions and censorship efforts in order to access the Internet. Therefore, it can be safely assumed that "the introduction of the Internet has opened doors and expanded what can be said in public and made it easily accessible to all" (Hofheinz, 2005, p. 79). Since "the Internet proves to not be totally censored, it can still act as a catalyst for change for those so empowered" (Walters & Barwind, 2004, p. 157). This prediction was certainly fulfilled, as the radical transformations in the Arab region revealed.

Political Blogging in the Arab World: Facts and Functions

The Arab world could be said to be engaging in a conversation that is taking place over the Internet, namely, blogging. Internet discussion forums, similar to those found on the newspaper websites with each article, are a very popular characteristic of Arabs' use of the Internet. According to Hofheinz (2005, pp. 92–93),

> No other language group debates as avidly on the internet as Arabic speakers. Individuals that use blogs hold all different political opinions. In the Arab world, when the blogs were novel, fierce discussions surfaced between the Islamists and their secular opponents. During the year 2005, the first annual Best Arab Blog Awards were voted on and the press started to pay attention to the phenomenon that was sweeping the viral community. These blog users in the Arab world

> tend to develop an increase in self confidence and belief in one's own potential. Arab internet users become aware of their own individuality when they separated from the traditional worldviews.

Since Internet access in the Arab world is relatively low (ranging between 10% and 17%), blogging is somewhat limited to the socio-economic elites who try to share their political views, which are often highly critical of the governments (Beckerman, 2007). Only a tiny portion of the approximately 33 million Internet users in the Arab world have launched their own political blogs. "Given that, it may seem that with such small numbers, the potential impact of the bloggers is limited. But has that not always been the way of political dissent?" (Seymour, 2008, p. 62). "The small size of the Arab blogosphere forces people with contrary opinions, or even more mildly divergent viewpoints, to engage each other. As one [Arab] blogger said, 'We're not big enough to preach to the choir yet. There is no choir'" (Beckerman, 2007, p. 19).

One of the main functions of blogs as an online application is that they create an opportunity to have the readers post their own comments, read other people's comments, and give their feedback on the posted stories. This function turns these blogs into "virtual public spheres" (el-Nawawy & Khamis, 2009), as discussed in chapter 2, bearing in mind that "a public sphere is the formation of a public body by individuals. It is open to all citizens and deals with matters of general interest. It provides a place where all citizens can be included in the conversation with equal chance to be listened to" (Al-Saggaf, 2006). In such cases, the vibrancy and significance of the discussed issues and the debated topics become of central value and they overshadow the fact that the number of participants may be limited.

In relation to the last point, Lynch (2007) undermined the argument that political blogs are limited to a small number of users in the Arab world and, therefore, their potential impact could also be limited. He compared the Arab blogs' impact to the effect of salons and coffee houses that were highlighted in the Habermasian public sphere. "How many people actually attended literary salons in Habermas' idealized eighteenth century[?] (few)....What matters is the arguments themselves, and the political identities, commitments, and ideas they generate. Blogs give young Arabs [who are] frustrated with the [political] status quo an outlet to voice their concerns and ideas in spaces where they will be taken seriously and where results are possible" (Lynch, 2007, pp. 21–21). According to Lynch (2007), "Volume might not be necessary for political influence. Since much of the new energy in Arab politics comes from relatively small groups of activists, a technology which empowers their efforts could have a disproportionate impact even if it does not reach a mass base" (p. 5).

Therefore, it can be argued that although of the estimated total number of Internet users in the Arab Middle East, only a small fraction publish blogs and, of these, political blogs contribute probably only a few thousands (Seymour, 2008, p. 62), neither the size of the Arab blogosphere nor the number of politically-motivated bloggers is relative to its potential for organization and empowerment. As Ajemian (2008) rightly states, "Despite the relatively low level of Internet infrastructure in the Arab world, much of the new energy in Arab politics comes from a relatively small group of activists, and a technology that empowers their efforts could have a disproportionate impact." Indeed, this impact was clearly evidenced in the midst of the radical wave of transformation in the Arab region and the Internet created the suitable environment that gave birth to these transformations.

In a region where there are so many red lines, taboos, and restrictions on freedom of expression and political activism, political blogs can serve as "a chance to contradict, to undermine, and to assert" (Beckerman, 2007, p. 20). Lynch (2007) also argued that Arab blogs exemplify a "counter-public" platform that generates innovative ideas and fresh perspectives outside the realm of state control. They can also serve a multitude of other functions. For example,

> The ability of blogs to expose a Kuwaiti parliamentary candidate's vote buying, or to publicize the mistreatment of ordinary Egyptians in local police stations, could be only the cutting edge of new ways of enhancing political accountability and transparency. The dialogues and interactions on blogs...may contribute to the rebuilding of transnational Arab identity by creating "warm" relationships among otherwise distant youth (Lynch, 2007, p. 3).

In this context, Lina Bin Mhenni, a young female Tunisian blogger who was active during the course of the Tunisian revolution that took place in January 2011, told the authors:

> Blogs helped break the media blackout that the Tunisian authorities had enforced on the country. In 2008, we had a social movement in the south of the country, but the government succeeded in controlling it because we were not really familiar with blogs and other forms of social media. So, the government was successful in hiding the atrocities that it did in suppressing this movement. But now, the government

> could not succeed in suppressing this revolution because we covered the events using the Internet and social media. These media were also useful in mobilizing the people. Many demonstrations were organized through blogs, Facebook and Twitter. The government tried to control the Internet and social media and arrested several bloggers. However, the other bloggers continued to work and got around the government censorship.

Connecting with an Arab youth who has always been skeptical of the political message requires a political blogger with special qualities. A recent study conducted by the Berkman Center for Internet & Society at Harvard University coded more than four thousand Arab blogs, and revealed that the majority of Arab bloggers are young and male (Etling et al., 2009). In this context, the Egyptian political activist Saad Eddin Ibrahim was cited in Whitaker and Varghese (2009) as saying that "[Arab] bloggers are nearly all young people under 30, and that is not to belittle or to underestimate them, because as a constituency, they make up 60 percent of the population" (p. 10).

As for the contents of the blogs that were analyzed in the Berkman Center's study, "those that write about politics [in their blogs] tend to focus on issues within their own country and are more often than not critical of domestic political leaders. Foreign political leaders are discussed less often and most commonly in terms more negative than positive.... The one political issue that commands the most attention of bloggers across the Arab world is Palestine, and in particular the situation in Gaza" (Etling et al., 2009, p. 4).

One group that seemed to have particularly benefitted from political blogging is Arab women. In fact, many courageous political blogs in the Arab world were launched by young, motivated Arab women. The percentage of women using the Internet in the Arab world jumped, in a matter of years, from only 4% of the Internet users to around 50% of the users by the year 2005 (Hofheinz, 2005). "With the [Arab] mainstream media populated mostly by Arab men, young Middle Eastern women have turned to blogging to express their views publicly. While initial enthusiasm that this might lead to their emancipation has died away, the outlet for women, hitherto unheard from in some societies, remains" (Seymour, 2008, p. 63). Saudi women are a case in point in this context. They "are using blogging as a form of 'electronic unveiling.' So even though Saudi women are veiled from head to toe, through blogging and electronic media, they are unveiling, they are exposing, they are talking, and they are getting their voices heard. And that is a very welcome sign" (Whitaker & Varghese, 2009, p. 11).

Although most Arab blogs are written in Arabic not English (Beckerman, 2007, p. 18), it would not be erroneous to deduce that English-language, and especially "pro-western," blogs receive a disproportionately large amount of attention based on that qualifier alone. This could be linked to the fact that some western journalists may "mistakenly think that only those sharing a Western vision of modern society can freely exchange ideas and take part in engaged debate online" (Weyman, 2007), and that the West, in general, may be more likely to cater to those blogs which reflect its objectives, that is, secular and liberal blogs (Weyman, 2007). However, as the events leading up to the Arab revolutions, and the role that social media played in them, showed, this is a faulty assumption, since the outcry for political change, democratization, and social reform came from diverse voices representing different, and sometimes even clashing, ideological orientations.

In relation to this last point, it can be noted that even in the short period of time that blogging has taken hold in the Arab world, there has been an evolution in the nature and goals of Arab bloggers. The first generation of bloggers were classified by direct Western influence, and they were mainly "writing in English and politically unengaged" (Hunt, 2008), while the second generation "write in Arabic and are 'more organically embedded in the political realm'" (Hunt, 2008). This change over a single generation of bloggers indicates that the movement toward a more politically-driven Arab blogosphere is already in place. However, Western optimists and critics will have to accept that not all political movements, both online and offline, will necessarily endorse secularism and/or represent Western policies. A good example is the level of political online activism demonstrated by members of the Muslim Brotherhood in Egypt, as will be discussed later in this chapter.

A key question in studying the Arab political blogs is whether they have formed a unified Arab public sphere, or whether it is even possible to talk about one single Arab blogosphere in the first place. According to Lynch (2007), "There is less of an 'Arab blogosphere' than a series of national blogospheres loosely linked at key nodes in each" (p. 22). This is based on the assumption that blogging in the Arab world differs so much between Arab countries that it is better to consider it as a series of "national blogospheres [that] can create a space in which citizens are able to engage in sustained, focused political argument" (Lynch, 2007, p. 25).

Within the small population of Arab bloggers, most are accurately described as part of the elite (Lynch, 2007) due to their predominantly urban, educated, upper middle class profile, as previously mentioned. However, in spite of the relatively analogous profile of bloggers, their areas of discourse and their expressed political and ideological views online are highly factional. There are many unique voices in the world of Arab blogs: political and apolitical, personal and activist, secular and religious, liberal and conservative, to mention only a few. In fact, it can be safely assumed that "blogs in the Arab Middle East have empowered pro-American liberal secular voices, and they have also empowered those whose primary political reference is Islam" (Weyman, 2007).

Therefore, it would be misleading to deem the Arab blogging world as capable of providing a unified voice, since blogging has become a forum for individual expression. It would also be inappropriate to suggest a unified purpose in the Arab blogosphere. For example, in examining just three female bloggers from around the Arab world, Basilio G. Monteiro (2008) shows the range of purposes that blogs can have: "the Egyptian blog was analytical and political, the Jordanian blog was literary and expressive, and the Saudi Arabian blog was political and referential (there was no analysis of issues)" (p. 47).

However, despite all of the acknowledged differences and admitted diversities among Arab blogs, it is safe to say that political blogs, in particular in the Arab world, despite their different ideological orientations and political loyalties, predominantly shared one common goal, which is fighting corrupt, autocratic regimes and fueling resistance and opposition against them.

Moreover, despite their differences, there has been continuous collaboration and cooperation among Arab bloggers, particularly during the Arab Spring that started in late 2010. In this context, Malek Khadrawi, a popular Tunisian blogger, told the authors that "there has been a strong relationship between Egyptian and Tunisian bloggers. We have been exchanging ideas through our blogs. We have been sharing information through various forms of social media. We have also been meeting the Egyptian bloggers at international seminars."

To better understand the defining characteristics and functions of Arab blogs, Lynch (2007) developed three classifications for Arab political bloggers, namely, activists, bridge, and public sphere bloggers. Two of these classifications—activists and public sphere bloggers—were discussed in chapter 1. Activists use their blogs to organize political activities on the street and to disseminate information about political campaigns (Lynch, 2007). In this context, Hamdy (2009) argued that activist bloggers generally enjoy high visibility in the Arab street. "This visibility has led some bloggers to feel secure and protected particularly because of the recognition, help and support that they receive from international organizations such as Reporters without Borders" (p. 105).

As for Arab bridge bloggers, they attempt to use their blogs (which are mainly in English) to reach out to a Western audience by talking about their own societies and trying to provide context and explanation for the political events taking place in these societies (Lynch, 2007). These bloggers would, therefore, "be more identifiable to Western media and would receive more attention as they are written in English" (Lynch, 2007). They could be said to play an important role in terms of closing the cultural gap and expanding the discourse between the Arab world and the West.

Whether bloggers choose to write in English or Arabic can be a very significant decision. Taking into account the fact that many bloggers may not be bilingual, the choice of language often reflects the target audience the blogger is trying to reach and is symptomatic of the blogger's relationship with his or her country. In this context, bridge bloggers' use of the English language signifies an attempt to reach a wider, global audience in the West, in an effort to bridge the cultural gap and to fight misinformation about cultures, religions, and even nations. But the downside to this phenomenon is that writing in English can often reflect a sense of alienation between the blogger and his or her country, since "using a language other than the mother tongue for expression indicates a degree of alienation from the mother culture" (Monteiro, 2008, p. 47). In other words, there is always a risk that "as bridge-bloggers focus on addressing foreign audiences, they often stand aloof from their own national politics" (Lynch, 2007, p. 17).

Lynch's third category—public sphere bloggers—refers to Arab bloggers who "tend to not be directly involved in a political movement, but are deeply engaged with public arguments about domestic (and often Arab or Islamic) politics" (Lynch, 2007, p. 11), as mentioned in chapter 1. Unlike the general assumption that Arab blogs have to use the Arabic language to formulate "a genuine [Arab] public sphere, many of the best of...[Arab public sphere blogs] are in fact in English" (Lynch, 2007, p. 19). A good example of this type of blog would be *The Rantings of a Sandmonkey*, which is a blog in English by Mahmoud Salem that is analyzed in this book.

The first two categories of political blogs emphasize domestic politics. Only bridge-blogs are not limited, by definition, to domestic issues. This division of political blogs supports the movement to consider "national blogospheres," rather than a single, unified Arab blogosphere. Adopting this classification suggests that in order to truly appraise the value of blogs as catalysts for change, one should examine blogospheres in Arab states individually, taking into account the unique political, social, and cultural context in each country, as well as deeply analyzing the specific characteristics and functions of each type of blog simultaneously.

Moreover, while Lynch's classifications have been useful in highlighting the differences among Arab bloggers and what they do, some scholars argued that political bloggers may not often fall under one specific category. "Given the opaque nature of blogging, a blogger's political affiliations and associations are not always ascertainable" (Hamdy, 2009, p. 95); therefore, we can argue that a blog like the abovementioned *Rantings of a Sandmonkey* could be considered both a good example of a bridge blog, as well as a public sphere blog, taking into account the fact that it is in English and therefore addresses an international, rather than only a domestic, audience, while at the same time tackling important political issues that are of high relevance to the Egyptian public.

Another important function of Arab blogs has been shaping public opinion during times of war and conflict, both regionally and globally, through enabling daring messages and images to be proliferated online. Blogs have provided close to real-time, realistic depictions of warfare. Both the war in Lebanon in 2006 and the Iraq war of 2003 provided startling depictions of how blogs can change the perceptions of war in the Arab world. Lebanon experienced a substantial growth in the number of blogs as the crisis erupted and created "a surge of interest and activity in the blogosphere, underlining its unique potential for direct, interactive grass-roots journalism" (Haugbolle, 2008). This surge was made particularly significant by "the large international audience that was able to access the blogs and appeal for aid for the Lebanese civilian population" (Haugbolle, 2008). In this case, the outbreak of war created a secondary surge in blogs "fuelled by the urge to speak out and describe what was happening" (Haugbolle, 2008). Information about the consequences and suffering of the Lebanese war was instantly accessible online.

Blogging during the war in Iraq, a young Iraqi woman who uses the pseudonym Riverbend, created her own blog, *Baghdad Burning*, exemplifying the fresh and unique perspective that blogs can offer in times of war and crisis. Riverbend was not making a political statement, or purposefully reaching out to the West; she simply utilized her blog to describe the hardships experienced by Iraqi civilians during the war (Hunt, 2008). It is clear that while both examples of blogging during wartime suggest that blogging can bring the reader closer to the experience of living through war and help others understand the nature of war, they were clearly different types of blogs intended to perform different functions.

While the Lebanese blogging community was able to garner international aid and support through blogging about the hardships of war, Riverbend's blog, *Baghdad Burning*, did not aim to inspire political action. Rather, it provided a detailed and rich description of the day-to-day horrors of war. Therefore, examining the experience of blogging in war clearly suggests that there is nothing inherent about the blog medium that allows it or denies it the ability to encourage political change; it is the blogger who determines the blog's potential.

Interestingly, the fact that blogs have played a large role as a news media source during wars and conflicts meant that "the coverage of the gruesome images of the dead and injured civilians was so powerful, to the extent that traditional media sources were piggybacking stories off the research and posts conducted by the bloggers covering the war" (Ward, 2007). This was clear evidence of a maturing relationship between blogging and traditional media sources. The line between bloggers and mainstream media sources became blurry, and more audiences were able to be reached, which attests to the increasing credibility that these blogs developed almost overnight. "In the last few years, blogs have increasingly made their way into mainstream press in both the Arab world and internationally. It is a large accomplishment for blogs to be able to influence the agenda of traditional media coverage" (Ward, 2007, p. 2).

This evolving relationship between the Arab blogosphere and mainstream media is worthy of discussion. Perhaps the Arab blogosphere's greatest impact has been in this area. Covering the war in Lebanon in 2006, the Iraq war of 2003, or even the sexual harassment of women on the streets of Cairo, as will be discussed, can set bloggers apart from mainstream media sources, by attracting more readers and raising greater awareness. This puts pressure on mainstream media outlets to catch up with the coverage in blogs, by covering controversial, sensitive, and bold issues, which they ordinarily wouldn't have covered had it not been for the fierce competition from blogs. This competition became more pressing with the greater privatization of Arab media in the post-1990 era that has meant that mainstream Arab media need their audiences more than ever before and must, therefore, appeal to the public's tastes and interests to sustain themselves.

The Challenges Confronting Arab Bloggers

The Arab blogosphere faces many complex challenges that may hinder the role of Arab bloggers, especially political bloggers, as potential active contributors to the public sphere. These challenges include, but are not limited to lack of needed infrastructure, limited Internet accessibility, very high illiteracy rates, lack of unity and cohesion, and, most importantly, significant interference from autocratic and dictatorial regimes in Arab countries, who continuously impose restrictions and constraints on freedom of expression, both online and offline.

One such challenge is many Arab governments' surveillance and crackdown on any form of online political activism. In a study conducted by Reporters Without Borders, several Arab countries were described as "enemies of the Internet" (Salama, 2007). In many of these countries, "harassment and intimidation are common, and imprisonment of bloggers is a growing trend" (Salama, 2007). Even in Arab countries where there is no blocking of political sites that seem opposed to the government, the Internet traffic, in general, is subject to heavy monitoring by state police (Hofheinz, 2005).

According to Ghannam (2011), the advances in the realm of social media in the Arab world came with

> considerable limitations and challenges posed by authoritarian regimes. Arab governments' reactions to social media have given rise to a battle of the blogosphere as proxies or other means are used to bypass government firewalls only to have those efforts meet further government blocking. Government authorities in the region also have waged widespread crackdowns on bloggers, journalists, civil society, and human rights activists. Hundreds of Arab activists, writers, and journalists have faced repercussions because of their online activities. (p. 4)

"[Political] bloggers, by their nature, can be more isolated and, thus, more vulnerable to attack than their counterparts in other media. They often work on their own and do not have the organizational resources—including lawyers and money—that can help shield them from harassment" (Abdel-Dayem, 2009). Despite the Arab political bloggers' vulnerability, most of them are more likely to identify themselves by using their real names, rather than using pseudonyms, according to the Berkman Center's study of Arab bloggers (Etling et al., 2009). Here, it is worth reminding the reader that four of the five bloggers whose blogs are analyzed in this book chose to use their real names on their blogs. The only exception was Mahmoud Salem, who blogged under the pseudonym "Sandmonkey," but who also chose to reveal his real name after the Egyptian revolution, as previously mentioned.

Echoing the same thought, regarding Arab political bloggers public visibility, Hamdy (2009) noted that many Arab bloggers "give interviews, respond to email and appear on talk shows. They contribute to academic panels and meet with university students. In fact, they are also providing a role model for a generation of young Arabs who are impressed with their courage" (p. 105). In this regard, they could be given credit for their "behind-the-scene" role of contributing to creating a healthy environment for political change in the Arab world.

The crackdown on bloggers deemed as opposition is prevalent in many parts of the Arab world. For example, "Bahrain...has taken to summoning bloggers for questioning, and tries to make them register with police....Saudi Arabia, which blocks thousands of websites, has silenced many web critics with quiet warning" (*The Economist*, 2007, p. 54). Moreover:

> In Syria, 19-year-old Tal al-Mallouhi was said to be the youngest Internet prisoner of conscience in the region and in December 2010 marked her first year in prison, mostly incommunicado, for blogging through poetry about her yearning for freedom of expression. In Bahrain, a social networking campaign has called for the release of blogger Ali Abdulemam who has been imprisoned for allegedly posting "false news" on his popular site *BahrainOnline.org*. They are just [two] of the scores of Arab Internet users across the region who have faced arrest and incarceration and other repercussions stemming from their online writings. (Ghannam, 2011, p. 5)

Other governmental challenges and impediments, such as "notably low broadband high-speed Internet penetration rates as a percentage of population, stand in the way of wider and faster Internet access. According to the Arab Advisors Group, the top three countries in broadband adoption in the region as a percentage of population are the United Arab Emirates at 14 percent, followed by Bahrain at 12 percent, and Qatar at eight percent as of late 2009" (Ghannam, 2011, p. 5).

However, the growth of the Internet and its rapid proliferation in this region, on an annual basis, may impede these efforts, or at least limit their effectiveness. This argument is supported by the unsuccessful attempts by governments in several parts of the Arab world to curb or halt cyberactivism through repressive measures that, in the case of Egypt, reached the level of completely shutting down the country's Internet for an entire week during the 2011 uprising. Also, the steady increase in Internet-based activities and applications, such as blogging, offers concrete evidence in support of the same argument. In fact, it is reported that "in 2009, the Arab region had 35,000 active blogs and 40,000 by late 2010" (Ghannam, 2011, p. 5).

In other words, it is safe to contend that, regardless of the Arab governments' attempts to silence political bloggers, "the evolution of the Internet has proved too rapid for governments to keep up with[,] and the drivers of that development often find themselves a step ahead of the authorities" (Seymour, 2008, p. 63). Arab visitors to political blogs have not been dissuaded by their governments' attempts to block or ban access to some of these blogs. They have found ways to get around government censorship (Hofheinz, 2005). They even found methods to get around the total disruption of Internet access that took place during the Egyptian revolution.

Another challenge facing Arab political bloggers is the high illiteracy rates in the Arab world. According to United Nations estimates, more than 65 million people in the Arab world are illiterate (Salama, 2007). This has a negative impact on the level of political awareness in general, as it reduces the number of average Arab citizens who can access the Internet, in general, and political blogs, in particular, and interact with the online political sphere.

The language barrier is another challenge that "prevent[s] most from easily tapping into the full range of ideas available online. Furthermore, effective engagement in the field of ideas requires technical skills and media savvy, which are not uniform even among those with regular access to the Internet" (Etling et al., 2009, p. 49).

Because of the abovementioned challenges, political blogging, by itself, may not be enough to create a major change or reform on the ground. The grassroots civil society groups that exist in many Arab countries have to take action and to mobilize their efforts to be able to assist and complement the bloggers' efforts in expanding the circle of political participation (Kraidy, 2007). The Internet, as a technology tool, can help civil society agents in the Arab world by providing them with a venue through which they can express themselves and call for collective political action. Political blogging, in particular,

> can empower political movements in the [Arab] region, since it provides an infrastructure for expressing minority points of view, breaking gatekeeper monopolies on public voice, lowering barriers to political mobilization . . . and building capacity for bottom-up contributions to the public agenda. . . . [Overall], the Internet lays a good foundation for a battle of ideas, but it does not necessarily favor a winner. (Etling et al., 2009, p. 10)

Interestingly enough, the real winner in the intensive struggle between political bloggers and Arab governments turned out to be the Arab citizen, who was able to take advantage of these new means of communication, as a tool through which to make his or her voice heard internationally, as well as an effective weapon to be deployed in the struggle for democratization, freedom, and dignity. "While the wish for greater political participation in decision-making [was] certainly great, a large part of Arab Internet users remain[ed] skeptical regarding the short-term likelihood of seeing real political change.... Internet users [saw] their regimes glued to power for the sheer love of it due to nepotism and the fear of being held accountable by democratically legitimate successors" (Hofheinz, 2005, p. 89). However, the authors of the Berkman Center's study, which is cited above, were rightly optimistic about the future of the Arab blogosphere, and they were hopeful that it would create "a space populated with a broad diversity of views, many of which promote common international values such as free speech and human rights" (Etling et al., 2009, p. 50). The wave of Arab Awakening, or the so-called Arab Spring, certainly attests to the existence of this space, and its continuous expansion, in many parts of the Arab world.

Section Two: Blogging and Revolutionizing the Egyptian Landscape

A discussion of political blogging in Egypt ought to be preceded with a general overview of the Egyptian political environment and the relationship between the Egyptian government and civil society. Such an overview would help contextualize the role of political bloggers in the Egyptian public sphere.

Egypt under the former regime of Hosni Mubarak was subject to a dominant party system, with the government party, known as the National Democratic Party, at the forefront and a variety of small right-wing, left-wing, and centrist opposition parties, in addition to a large Islamist movement, which was represented by the Muslim Brotherhood (El-Masry, 2006).

Egypt had been subject to the Emergency Law since the assassination of President Anwar Sadat in 1981. This law, which was in violation to the Egyptian Constitution and international human rights organizations' bylaws, gave the government unlimited powers that allow it to infringe on basic political freedoms (El-Masry, 2006). Under this law, "police powers [were] expanded, constitutional rights suspended, and censorship legalized. The law sharply circumscribe[d] any non-governmental political activity: street demonstrations, non-approved political organizations, and unregistered financial donations [were] formally banned" (Agati, 2007, p. 58).

In addition to the Emergency Law, Egypt, like most other Arab countries, has a restrictive law that governs the operation of nongovernmental organizations (NGOs). Law 84/2002 makes it mandatory for any "group who[se] purpose includes or that carries out any of the activities of associations and institutions to operate with a permit [or a license] from the Ministry of Insurance and Social Affairs.... Foreign NGOs are not allowed to operate in Egypt without securing the [abovementioned] permission. The Ministry's decision is based on unspecified factors and not subject to any court appeal" (Elbayar, 2005, p. 8). The broad and vague provisions included in this law have been used by the government to control the functioning of civil society, and the NGOs that were licensed through the law have been subject to many restrictions and constraints. What is worrying about this law are the severe prison sentences and hefty fines that are imposed on NGOs' members if they do not comply with it (Elbayar, 2005). This law was not widely discussed in the Egyptian Parliament, and it did not receive much attention from the Egyptian state-owned media. It was "justified in the parliament, despite its deficiencies, on the grounds that it 'balances freedom and social peace'" (Agati, 2007, p. 61).

Despite the restrictive measures included in the abovementioned laws, "Egypt has one of the largest and most vibrant civil society sectors in the entire developing world" (Elbayar, 2005, p. 7). Under the Mubarak regime, particularly starting in the mid 1980s, Egyptian civil society was expanded. "Several types of civil society organizations have evolved...charities, service providers, environmental, and human rights organizations. This development represents a part of what the government has propagated as 'step-by-step democracy'" (Agati, 2007, p. 59).

A grassroots group that emanated from civil society and played an important role in increasing the Egyptian people's awareness of their political rights is Kefaya (Arabic for "Enough"). Kefaya, which surfaced in the wake of the presidential elections in Egypt in 2005, included journalists, intellectuals, and civil society activists representing various political inclinations. The group called for several political reforms, such as ending the Emergency Law; the direct election of the president in a competitive election; limiting the presidency to two terms; separating the legislative, executive, and judicial powers; allowing for freedom of association; and "free and fair parliamentary elections under full judicial scrutiny at every stage" (Jones, 2007, p. 16).

Mubarak seemed to have met one of Kefaya's demands when, in April 2005, he asked the parliament to amend the constitution to allow for direct, multiparty presidential elections for the first time in the country's history (Jones, 2007).

While political restrictions and bureaucratic constraints have a negative impact on the political environment and the functioning of civil society in Egypt, other factors play a role in this regard, such as "low levels of public spiritedness and trust, as well as poor socio-economic conditions, such as rising poverty and unemployment. Further, persistent social problems, such as high levels of illiteracy, have presented significant hurdles for the growth of civil society" (*Civil society index report for the Arab Republic of Egypt*, 2005).

In Egypt, like in many other societies in the Arab world, religion plays a critical role in civil society and the political sphere. That is why it is worth shedding some light on the growing role of the Muslim Brotherhood group in Egypt. Although *Shari'a* (Islamic Canonical Law) is established by the Egyptian regime as the main source of legislation, the Muslim Brotherhood had been considered an outlawed group under the Mubarak regime. This status did not change except after the Egyptian revolution of 2011. However, prior to the revolution, Brotherhood members were allowed to run for parliamentary and professional syndicate elections as independents. In fact, in the 2000 parliamentary elections, the Brotherhood members won 17 of the 454-member parliament. And in 2005, they captured 88 seats (approximately 20% of the total parliamentary seats). Members of the Brotherhood group are also allowed to play a role in social charity organizations (Mustafa, 2006). While it is hard to assess the real political weight of the Muslim Brotherhood, given the secrecy that surrounds its size and operations, "it is safe to assume that . . . the Muslim Brotherhood does not have the potential to overthrow the regime or take over the political system entirely" (Mustafa, 2006, p. 4). During the 2011 revolution, the Brotherhood was just one actively participating group, among many others. Its members did not give themselves credit for instigating the revolution, and they did not try to emerge, or to take over, as its sole leaders.

The Muslim Brotherhood have recognized the potential that the Internet, in general, and the blogosphere, in particular, holds for their organization, mobilization, and coordination efforts. This was evident in the fact that they engaged in a number of Internet-based activities, such as launching web-based campaigns to help their members who had been arrested in governmental crackdowns, rather than protesting in the streets (*The Economist*, 2007, p. 54), in addition to starting their own blogs. Examples of blogs launched by proponents of the Muslim Brotherhood ideology include *Waves in the Sea of Change* (http://2mwag.blogspot.com/) by Mostapha El-Naggar and *Arwaya* (http://arwaya.blogspot.com/) by Arwa El Taweel.

It is worth mentioning in this context that some of the younger members of the Muslim Brotherhood, who launched their own blogs, started "writing unprecedented, blunt public criticism of certain aspects of the Brotherhood. These are not ordinary bloggers idly chatting and surfing online, but rather rebels, freed from ideological and organizational constraints. They resent their political and social situation, and disagree with their organization's rhetoric and jurisprudential stances" (Al-Anani, 2007, p. 29). This is considered a revolutionary trend inside the Brotherhood, and it may affect the political future of the organization. The Brotherhood's leadership seems to be divided when it comes to how to react to these bloggers. While some leaders call for an outright end to these blogs, others are open to discussing the matter more deeply. The latter group believes that "blogging is an expression of a new spirit flowing in the veins of the Brotherhood's base that needs to be absorbed and strengthened" (Al-Anani, 2007, p. 37).

It goes without saying that the Egyptian media system is affected by civil society. Egypt has a strong press that is pioneering and widely popular in the Arab region. Moreover, there are many prominent Egyptian writers and syndicated columnists, who often speak their mind and were openly critical of the government, before the revolution, and of SCAF (The Supreme Council of the Armed Forces), after the revolution. However, the Egyptian media under Mubarak were subject to several restrictions, since "journalists often censor[ed] themselves on certain sensitive issues, mainly avoiding direct criticism of the president and his family, the army, security forces and human rights abuses" (El-Masry, 2006, p. 51).

The Egyptian government, under Mubarak, introduced a draft for an audiovisual law to regulate "all aspects related to broadcasting, especially its content and the distribution and receiving of transmissions.... It also technically allow[ed] for severe punishment of violators, not just through fines but also by imprisonment....[T]his law..., in comparison to penal codes, intensif[ied] punishment of bloggers rather than protect[ed] them" (Hamdy, 2009, p. 100).

The role of new media, particularly the Internet and blogging, is becoming more visible on the Egyptian media scene. Egypt had an Internet penetration of close to 15 percent, and the number of Egyptian blogs has risen from 40 in 2004 to approximately 160,000 in

July 2008, according to a study conducted by the Egyptian Cabinet's Information and Decision Support Center (IDSC) in 2009. Close to three-fourths of Egyptian bloggers write in Arabic only, 20 percent write in both English and Arabic, and 10 percent write in English only. The majority of Egyptian bloggers are between the ages of 20 and 30 years, and just over one-fourth of the bloggers are female (*Internet filtering in Egypt*, 2009).

The Egyptian government's policy toward the Internet has been ambivalent. While Egypt was one of the first Arab countries to allocate its resources toward information technology, Egyptian bloggers are often arrested, harassed, and prosecuted by the authorities. Moreover, many bloggers are detained without charge under the provisions of the Emergency Law (Carr, 2010). Moreover, a new government unit called the "Internet Police" was created under the Department of Information and Documentation in 2001 to monitor the work of Internet users and bloggers. In addition, the government "has blocked access to certain sites, shut down offending sites, monitored personal emails, and used Internet chatrooms to ensnare deviant citizens" (Radsch, 2007b, p. 21). The Egyptian government also required owners of Internet cafes to take their customers' national ID numbers, before allowing them to access the Internet (Mehanna, 2008, p. 13).

However, it is worth noting that, just like in the case of the Arab world at large, the repressive measures and restrictions by the Egyptian government on online activities did not succeed in curbing or halting cyberactivism. For example, "Although Egypt's interior ministry maintains a department of 45 people to monitor Facebook, nearly 5 million Egyptians use the social networking site among 17 million people in the region, including journalists, political leaders, political opposition figures, human rights activists, social activists, entertainers, and royalty who are engaging online in Arabic, English, and French" (Ghannam, 2011, p. 5).

According to Radsch (2007b), blogging has blurred the line between private and public spheres in Egypt, since the bloggers' "personal experiences, thoughts, and feelings become the grist of public discussion" (p. 45). She contends that the impact of blogs on Egyptian political life has been profound, mainly because

> the barriers to entry [to blogs] are low, but the potential audience enormous. Like the colonial pamphlets of early America, blogs in Egypt disseminate information, adding to the diversity of the public sphere by creating a counter-hegemonic discourse that usually revolves

> around government abuses. But unlike pamphlets, which took time and money to produce and distribute, the production and dissemination of blogs is virtually free. (Radsch, 2007b, p. 42)

The role of political bloggers in Egypt has started to surface in 2005 thanks to their coverage of the demonstrations and protests organized by the abovementioned Kefaya movement. Bloggers' coverage of one protest in particular (a May 2005 protest organized by Kefaya activists) granted them more prominence since they seemed to be the only source reporting on it. "Bloggers broke the story [on that protest] four days before the Egyptian press took it on.... So blogger accounts were critical to spreading information" (Lynch, 2007, p. 13). "A natural symbiosis between Egypt's early core bloggers and the emerging protest movement helped popularize the Egyptian blogosphere as a site of protest as Kefaya grew in popularity during 2005" (Radsch, 2008, p. 3).

In addition to their exclusive coverage of the Kefaya protests, Egyptian political bloggers were the first to expose other critical stories that took place in Egypt over the past few years. For example, the sexual harassment incident of a group of women that occurred during a public holiday in downtown Cairo in 2006 was first covered by Egyptian bloggers, who happened to be at the location where the incident took place. As a result of the bloggers' coverage of this incident, "the Egyptian media, individuals, religious figures, civil society organizations and now Parliament have championed the rights of Egyptian women in relation to the commonly practiced [sexual] harassment" (Hamdy, 2009, p. 102).

Those who perceive blogging as a medium capable of encouraging change now and in the future cite legitimate examples to support their views, such as the successes of Egyptian bloggers in covering sexual assaults and the arrests of several fellow bloggers (Radsch, 2008). These blogging optimists point toward coverage of these kinds of events as confirmation that bloggers have become, or are at least capable of becoming, political activists.

Another story that was covered exclusively by Egyptian bloggers was the violation of prisoners' human rights and their torture behind bars and in police stations. One blogger, Mohamed Khaled, posted on his blog a video showing two police officers sodomizing a bus driver at a police station. This video was picked up by independent and opposition press, leading to a public outcry. Eventually, the two police officers involved in this case were convicted and sentenced to three years in prison after a fair trial. Moreover, the bloggers' coverage of this incident "gave momentum to human rights . . . and civil society organizations that for years had been accusing the Egyptian Ministry of Interior of using uncouth techniques of interrogation against suspects. Once again, this example shows that blogging's influence on media and the public can intensify impact on wider circles" (Hamdy, 2009, p. 103). The abovementioned incidents covered by blogs exemplify the ability of the Egyptian bloggers to "fill the news vacuum left by national newspapers and local television stations" (Nelson, 2008), which have been owned and tightly controlled by the Egyptian government for many years.

Such examples clearly show that the Internet, in general, and blogging, in particular, have had some significant successes as a social organizing tool in Egypt (Faris, 2008). Indeed, Egyptian bloggers present an excellent case for this, since "their fervent belief in truth-telling and fact-based reporting is encouraging, and it propels them, sometimes like moths to a flame" (Franklin, 2008, p. 40).

Thanks to their exclusive coverage and journalistic scoops, many political bloggers in Egypt are close to becoming "celebrities." Some of them are enjoying influence and wide-scale popularity, not only inside Egypt, but also among foreign human rights organizations. "Unfortunately, however, such attention is a double-edged sword, as growing interest brings more intimidation" (Radsch, 2007a).

Today, it is a common practice that regular people send videos of torture, abuse, and corruption to political bloggers to post on their blogs (Radsch, 2008). So, in a way, political bloggers in Egypt have derived part of their power and influence from their use of visuals, such as photos or videos. "Blogs have arguably been most effective when they post pictures taken on mobile phones, pictures which in earlier days would never have been taken, let alone seen the light of day. In the blogosphere, these pictures have indeed been worth a thousand words. They represent undeniable evidence" (Hardaker, 2008, p. 7).

This use of video on the Internet has been widely utilized in blogs in Egypt by ordinary citizens and political activists alike. Taking into account the fact that "seeing is believing," videos, which are more "real" than just reading print, are usually the most shocking when it comes to troubling news. It also allows us to better understand what situations are like by seeing, for example, footage of a war, torture, or police brutality against unarmed civilians. The so-called "'You Tube effect' enables the Arab masses to communicate with each other, exchange ideas about politics and values, express their deepest hopes and fears with a freedom that only technology makes possible and even government censors are powerless to restrict" (Khalid, 2007, p. 9). This is very closely linked to the notion of citizen journalism, which will be discussed and analyzed in the rest of this book in relation to the five political blogs under study.

The abovementioned study conducted on Arab bloggers by Harvard's Berkman Center categorized political bloggers in Egypt under the following clusters: "Secular reformist, wider opposition, Egyptian youth, Egyptian Islamic, and Muslim Brotherhood" (Etling et al., 2009, p. 15). According to the study, many of those bloggers do not just cover politics in their blogs, but they actually participate in political activities. For example, some bloggers "frequently use pictorial badges on their sites to show support for various campaigns, such as for freeing [fellow] bloggers, calling for reform, or promoting social issues such as combating HIV/AIDs stigmas" (Etling, et al., 2009, p. 15).

Because of its crackdown on political bloggers, Egypt was listed by the Committee to Protect Journalists (CPJ) as one of the "ten worst countries to be a blogger in 2009" (*Internet filtering in Egypt*, 2009). According to the CPJ report, the Egyptian authorities "monitor Internet activity on a regular basis. Traffic from all Internet service providers passes through the ... [government]. Authorities regularly detain critical bloggers for open-ended periods. Local press freedom groups documented the detention of more than 100 bloggers in 2008 alone.... Most detained bloggers report mistreatment, and a number have been tortured" (Committee to Protect Journalists, 2009).

A case in point in this context is the blogger Abdel Monem Mahmoud, a former member of the Muslim Brotherhood that used to be outlawed under the Mubarak regime, and one of the five bloggers whose blog is analyzed in this book. Mahmoud, who was detained several times and was last released in June 2007, was cited in Rifaat (2008) talking about his experience in jail, saying,

> I stayed for 13 days in a two-by-three meter cell. I spent five full days in it sleeping, praying and using the WC while I was handcuffed behind my back.... I was obliged to remain on this cement terrace all the time, including performing the prayers because the floor was not clean. My interrogation ended after eight days, but I was held for five more days in my cell to increase the psychological pressure. I also heard the screams of my colleagues, and they hear mine, while they were [being] beaten by the guard. (p. 59)

In a personal interview with the authors, Mahmoud said, "I don't think that people should be sentenced to prison for their ideas. This opens the door for the government to exercise all kinds of pressure on people for just expressing their views. That is why, I was against imprisoning...[several other bloggers], despite the fact that I totally disagreed with [their] ideas."

It is worth noting that the majority of Egyptian bloggers were arrested as a result of their offline activities (e.g., organizing a protest or participating in a street demonstration), rather than for what they wrote or covered on their blogs (Isherwood, 2008). However, the first Egyptian blogger to be imprisoned for his online activism, rather than street activism, was Abdel Kareem Nabil Soliman, who was known as Kareem Amer. He was sentenced to four years in prison in 2007 for using his blog to insult the former president Mubarak and to incite hatred against Islam. Amer "has since become the symbol of online repression for the country's bloggers" (*Internet filtering in Egypt*, 2009).

"The majority of political bloggers in Egypt had come to Amer's defense, and they [continued] to work on a campaign calling for his release" (Radsch, 2008). In fact, it could be said that "the one ray of hope was that bloggers of many different positions came together to support him and to bring global attention to his case" (Weyman, 2007). Amer "was released in November 2010 after more than four years in prison and alleged torture" (Ghannam, 2011, p. 4). He "returned to writing his blog shortly after his release" (Ghannam, 2011, p. 5).

A more recent incident of a political blogger imprisoned for his online activism was that of Maikel Nabil, one of the five bloggers whose blogs are studied in this book. Nabil was sentenced to four years in jail following a military trial in April 2011, three months after the Egyptian revolution, on charges of insulting the Egyptian military, as mentioned in chapter 1. Here again, Nabil's case attracted wide support from his fellow bloggers, as well as from political activists at large, who called for his release and created a Facebook page entitled "We are all Maikel Nabil" to demand justice for him.

In addition to harassment and imprisonment of several political bloggers, the Egyptian government has employed other tactics, such as "character assassination." A case in point is Wael Abbas, one of the most influential political bloggers in Egypt, whose blog, *The Egyptian Awareness* with an English title *Misr Digital*, is also one of the five blogs analyzed in this book. Abbas was "publicly accused [by the government] of being a homosexual, a Christian, a man with a criminal record and an agent of US/Israeli influence, when none of the above were true" (Hardaker, 2008, p. 16).

All the above examples clearly show how the Egyptian government maintained a record of suppressing political bloggers using multiple methods, such as threats, arrests, imprisonment, and even defamation. Therefore, it is safe to conclude that "the maltreatment, lack of transparency, protracted procedure and threat of a legal precedent... [are negatively] affecting the [Egyptian political] blogosphere" (Gharbeia, 2007, p. 55).

Similarly, there has also been an official crackdown on the political activists who use Facebook. A case in point is the government's arrest of the leaders of what came to be known as the "April 6 Movement." Members of this movement formed a group on Facebook on April 6, 2008, calling on the Egyptian public to join textile workers, who were complaining about their work conditions and low salaries, in a general strike. More than 70 thousand people nationwide joined that strike (Hamdy, 2009). In addition to the movement's leaders, several political bloggers were arrested the night before the strike. This movement "exemplifies the convergence of new media platforms and political activism but also the necessity of linking online movements to offline organizing" (Radsch, 2008, p. 10). Commenting on the April 6 movement, Ethan Zuckerman, a research fellow at Harvard's Berkman Center, was cited by Shapiro (2009) as saying that this movement exemplifies a "cute-cat theory of digital activism.... Around the world, dissidents thrive on sites, like Facebook, that are used primarily for more mundane purposes (like exchanging pictures of cute cats)."

It can be argued that political bloggers in Egypt are "opinion leaders" in the sense that they "have challenged the privileged role of professional journalists by giving ordinary citizens platforms for mass dissemination, whether for a moment or a lifetime" (Radsch, 2008, p. 10). The question that needs to be addressed in this context is: What is the extent of political change that can be expected of political blogs in Egypt? According to Isherwood (2008), political blogs have "indeed changed the way politics [are] conducted in Egypt. However, in most cases, [they] have done so not by dramatically altering or revolutionizing politics, but rather by intensifying and speeding up trends that had already begun with satellite media and the opposition press" (p. 10).

Along the same lines, Hardaker (2008) argued that "the Internet has high impact, but low penetration. Satellite television, on the other hand, has high penetration, but a relatively low impact as a medium of social protest. Together, though, the two media multiply each other's impact" (p. 8). Thus, it can be argued that between traditional media sources, satellite television channels, and the Internet, the information readily available to the Arab world transcends the boundaries created by censorship.

In this context, Eltahawy (2008) argued that bloggers and "generation Facebook might not be able to change their regimes today, but in building communities and support groups online, they are creating the much-needed middle ground that countries like Egypt desperately require" (p. 77). The events that took place in 2011 in Egypt certainly proved the accuracy of this prophecy.

Access (or lack thereof) seems to be a major concern of blogging's impact on the Egyptian public sphere. Blogging, "while allowing some to engage in counter-hegemonic discourses…, continues to be the privilege of a limited number of Egyptians.… [This] can prove to be an elitist exercise that further marginalizes people who don't have access to this digital technology" (Rifaat, 2008, p. 67).

However, the recent events that led up to the Egyptian revolution clearly showed that there is an increasing "trickle-down" and "spill-over" effect from the virtual realm of the Internet and Internet-based applications, such as blogging, tweeting, and posting on Facebook, to the wider realm of on-the-street activism and on-the-ground organization.

Concluding Remarks

The Internet is a growing and ever-evolving phenomenon in the Arab world. As Internet sources continue to gain credibility, there will be limitless opportunities as to the next great Internet application. The Internet proves to be a valuable media source because of its timeliness, its global reach, and its alternative voices. With its inability to be censored effectively in the Arab world, the Internet will continue to defy traditional boundaries, in both the political and the cultural spheres. The wave of the so-called Arab Awakening or the Arab spring that spread all over the region proved that there is ample evidence for the ever-growing and expanding role of Internet-based communication to transform both the political and the communicative landscapes.

One of the most significant Internet-based functions that helped pave the way for this new wave of political change in the region is the phenomenon of political blogging that played a number of important functions, including, but not limited to providing platforms for free speech and uncensored expression of individual and collective opinions; enabling the formation of virtual public spheres, where ideas and views could be freely discussed and openly deliberated; as well as helping the voices of dissent and opposition from within the Arab world to be widely heard in the rest of the world.

Commenting on the bold, courageous, and controversial nature of the topics covered in the Egyptian blogosphere, Nelson (2008) stated that the Egyptian bloggers were clearly "altering the nature of dissent in Egypt.... The precise outcome is impossible to predict, but the impact will surely be profound." This profound impact was certainly witnessed in Egypt's historic, popular revolution of 2011 and the events which led up to it, as well as the radical transformations that followed it, on the political, social, legal, and communication fronts. Here, it is important to highlight that "before the Internet enabled self-publishing and dissemination, there were really no mass media through which youth and minority groups could get their message out. But politically entrepreneurial uses of digital and social media by young Egyptians helped bring down a president who vowed not to give up and to die on Egyptian soil" (Radsch, 2011).

While we are careful not to establish a relationship of "causality" between social media, in general, and blogs, in particular, in terms of instigating the wave of Arab Awakening that swept the Arab region, it is not unreasonable to give them credit for paving the way or for being one of the main factors for this radical transformation, through enabling the exchange of political discussions and deliberations online and, most importantly, through exposing the governments' many dysfunctions and malpractices. By doing so, they created a favorable public opinion for change among the small, but influential, circle of opinion leaders online, which then effectively "snowballed" and "trickled-down" to reach the much wider popular base of supporters and activists on the Arab streets, who were able to translate cyber-activism in the virtual world into on-the-ground activism in the real world. In this context, it is useful to bear in mind that

> in authoritarian regimes the spread of information is an inherently subversive act. Twittering, Facebooking and blogging are all about spreading information and communication. And indeed the information revolution has helped bring about political revolutions in a region of the world considered "exceptional" by so many in being inherently incompatible with democracy. The contours of the information society have made citizen journalism, social networking and other forms of digital activism one of the most potent and politically charged manifestations of power in societies where citizens lack access to the political arena and the media sphere is dominated by state interests. (Radsch, 2011)

Looking ahead, the possibility that the Arab blogosphere, in general, and the Egyptian blogosphere, in particular, will successfully continue to promote political change and to put pressure on authoritarian, autocratic regimes to meet the demands of their peoples in the future is quite reasonable. Despite the many challenges that the Arab blogosphere faces, it could potentially create an atmosphere where activists could successfully organize, and controversial events could be brought to center stage. While we have to consider the limited number of blogs that actually address political issues, or provide space for groups to organize and grow membership online in the Arab world, taking into account the many pressing challenges that confront Arab bloggers, it is important to remember that the size of the blogosphere is not the sole defining variable in determining the success of movements for political change. It is also quite helpful to consider that not all national blogospheres will be equally successful as catalysts for political change, as the different experiences of Arab countries in their struggle for freedom clearly reveal.

In every case, it is certainly useful to avoid a "technologically deterministic" approach that privileges the medium over the context within which it functions, through reminding ourselves that blogs, just like any other communication tool, are whatever the bloggers make of them. Therefore, we have to always bear in mind that these tools can only be effective when used by successful actors within suitable contexts to achieve attainable goals.

CHAPTER 4

Blogging on Violations of Human Rights and Limitations on Freedom

Introduction

Violations of human rights and limitations on freedom were among the most serious problems under the rule of ousted Egyptian president Hosni Mubarak. "Basic to the concept of human rights is the notion that human beings have the inalienable right to respect for their intrinsic dignity. This means that people must be treated in accordance with certain basic standards. The recognition of the dignity of the human person implies that human beings cannot treat each other however they see fit" (Hamelink, 2004, p. 72).

A major factor behind the deterioration in the condition of human rights and freedom in Egypt was the 1971 Constitution that gave the president an "enormous amount of authority comparable to that of a tyrant. Even when the constitution was amended in May 1980, the pivotal role of the President was further enhanced" (Hassan, 2010, p. 327). What worsened this situation was the seemingly unlimited and unmonitored power of the state police, their continuous efforts to protect the Mubarak regime, and their intervention in the minute details of Egyptian citizens' everyday lives. Although there were apparently many opposition parties and several media outlets voicing their criticism against the government, in reality the regime obstructed any type of serious opposition, particularly when it had anything to do with the president. Many political activists, especially those belonging to the Muslim Brotherhood, were imprisoned and tortured. Elections were often rigged, and many voters were not allowed to reach the ballot boxes (El-Mahdi & Marfleet, 2009a).

Torture practices by the police forces at detention centers "included extremes of abuse: prisoners were stripped and blindfolded; suspended from ceilings or doorframes with feet just touching the floor;

beaten with fists, whips, metal rods or other objects; subjected to electric shocks; doused with cold water; and sexually assaulted" (Seif El-Dawla, 2009, p. 132). All of these human rights violations were committed under the auspices of the Emergency Law, which provided unlimited powers to security forces to arrest and detain any suspects without charge or warrant. This law was renewed by the Mubarak regime several times, despite continuous demands to abolish it (El-Mahdi & Marfleet, 2009a). Mubarak often used the threat of global terrorism as a justification for the continuation of the state of emergency in Egypt. "Ending the state of emergency, which the government had once again extended for another two years in 2010, was one of the central demands of the protestors" in the January 25, 2011, revolution (Gelvin, 2012, p. 58).

Addressing the deteriorating situation of human rights under the Mubarak regime, Gamal Eid, director of an Egyptian NGO called the Arabic Network for Human Rights Information (ANHRI), told the authors in a personal interview in Cairo in 2009:

> Every year, the human rights situation in Egypt gets worse than the year before. In 2007, we had more than 500 cases of human rights violations. In 2008, human rights violations were more. I think the prosecutors are generally biased against journalists and bloggers, and that is why they expedite cases that involve a journalist or a blogger and they move on to trial courts. However, if the case involves a police officer, the prosecutors refuse to expedite the case by moving it to the trial court. This is because the regime is opposed to freedom of expression.

This "Pharonic Egyptian State" (Hassan, 2010, p. 327) had led most political activists during the last decade of the twentieth century to resort to blogging to report about and highlight the political authorities' infringement on human rights and the breaches of freedom of expression. In an environment characterized by a high level of state intervention in people's lives and where the president "enjoyed unlimited authority that border[ed] on deification" (Hassan, 2010, p. 319), blogging seemed at one point to be the only breath of fresh air and was utilized by activists and proponents of change to break away from the political status quo. In a way, the bloggers' role in this regard had made up for the absence of a truly free and independent press that would have had the ability to highlight human rights' violations whenever they occurred. In this context, the prominent Egyptian blogger Wael Abbas told the authors in a personal interview in Cairo in 2009: "The bloggers have worked hard to create a margin of freedom for themselves. If there was true democracy in Egypt, blogs would not have existed. These blogs have surfaced because there are no true political parties, civil society is not carrying out its role, and the press is not free."

This chapter will analyze a number of threads selected from the five blogs under study that deal with human rights' violations and limitations on freedom. It will shed light on whether they reflect effective civic engagement, citizen journalism, and the functions of a vibrant civil society, in an attempt to assess the role of the five blogs in enhancing democratization and contributing to popular participation in Egyptian civil society.

The analyzed threads in this chapter will be divided into three main categories based on the primary function they are attempting to perform, namely, mobilization, documentation, or deliberation. In other words, whether the main objective of the thread is to mobilize people by urging them to take a certain action or to engage in a specific activity; to document the atrocities and wrongdoings of the regime in power and its security apparatus; or to provide a platform for the exercise of online democracy by engaging in deliberation, brainstorming, and useful exchange of ideas.

Section One: Threads Urging Public Mobilization

"How Can You Help Bloggers?"

This thread was selected from Maikel Nabil's blog. It was posted in Arabic on July 26, 2008—two and half years before the January 25, 2011, revolution erupted. This shows how Egyptian blogs had paved the way for the revolution and created an environment that was fertile for political awareness, mobilization, and civic engagement. In this thread, Nabil proposed some "practical steps" that ordinary citizens could take if they wished to create their own blogs or to support other bloggers.

In the thread, Nabil wrote:

> If you access a blog that you like and you want other people to benefit from its content, here is what you need to do: 1) Post a comment expressing your opinion about what you read, whether you agree with it or not; 2) Send the link to your friends and to all the groups and discussion forums that you are a part of; 3) Click on the ads in

> that particular blog since most bloggers are in need of financial support and advertising is a viable source of revenue that will help them sustain their blogging efforts; 4) Create your own blog. Currently, bloggers are subject to so much harassment by the state, and having more bloggers would help create a critical mass of bloggers that can initiate change; 5) If you have your own blog, include in it links to all the other blogs you like; 6) Join the online groups and the mailing lists of the bloggers whose blogs you like, as this helps widen their circles of supporters; 7) Make your favorite blog the homepage on your computer; 8) Bookmark your favorite blogs on your computer; 9) If you happen to be fluent in foreign languages, particularly English or French, make sure to translate the contents of the blogs you like. This helps spread the message of those bloggers to a worldwide audience; 10) If you notice any mistakes made by the bloggers in the way they reported the news or the sources that they used, you can politely highlight these mistakes to them so that they can avoid making them in the future; 11) If you happen to own a company, a newspaper or even an online forum, you can place an advertisement on your favorite blogs. That way, you would be contributing to the financial resources of the bloggers whom you like.

Nabil's steps initiated some comments, mainly praising and supporting him. For example, Farouk (only first names are given in the comments section) wrote: "Bravo Maikel! I will take this opportunity and publish these steps in a bloggers' magazine that is distributed through regular mail."

Mounira wrote: "Thank you for your proactive approach Maikel. Imagine if there are 30 million proactive people like you. Definitely Egypt would be much better."

Ahmed wrote: "This is excellent Maikel. Believe it or not, this is the first time that I ever posted in a blog. The topic that you raised has motivated me."

Vera wrote: "Your steps are marvelous Maikel. I have my own blog, which I use to express my views as you mentioned. I will wait for you to be released [from prison] to tell me your opinion about it.... As per your advise[sic], I will include a link to your blog on mine."

This thread is a good example of "civic engagement," as it tries to get people to *act* and *do* something to make their voices heard, and to spread their opinions through blogs. It captures several of Larry Diamond's (1999) civil society functions, such as "stimulating political participation"; enhancing "education for democracy"; "structuring multiple channels...for articulating, aggregating, and representing interests" (pp. 242–244); and spreading "new information and understanding" (Diamond, 1999, p. 247). By helping achieve the functions mentioned above, this thread reflects what Diamond described as "the ideological marketplace," through which creative ideas and autonomous information are formulated and circulated by civic groups, away from the hegemony of the state. Bloggers can be an integral component of those civic groups that "seek (in a nonpartisan fashion) to improve the political system and make it more democratic (for example, working for human rights, voter education and mobilization, election monitoring, and exposure and reform of corrupt practices)" (Diamond, 1997a, pp. 7–8).

In this context, Maikel Nabil told the authors in a personal interview in Cairo in the summer of 2010, "I think that based on the feedback from the posters on my blog, I have affected many of them. I provide different perspectives, and I have the ability to write in a way that attracts readers' attention. Whenever I write about how the regime is suppressing people's rights, this contributes to improving civil society because it enhances people's awareness about the rights that are taken from them and that they need to fight to get back from the regime."

It can also be argued that the thread discussed above reflects another civil society function, that of "recruiting and training new political leaders" (Diamond, 1999, p. 245). The posters' comments to Nabil's steps suggested that they were willing to be proactive civil society pioneers who would follow what he recommended and who would make sure that they used the Internet technology to initiate change. They were united in their endorsement of Nabil's suggestions and steps to support bloggers. In this context, Diamond (1997a) referred to the process of "democratic consolidation, [which] occurs once there emerges a 'consensually unified elite' that shares a common commitment to the rules of the democratic game, a broader set of norms about the rules of political conduct, and a dense structure of interaction that fosters personal familiarity and trust" (p. 1). The unity of the posters in the thread mentioned above could promote what Putnam (1993), as cited in Diamond (1997a), referred to as "social capital," which is "the features of social organization . . . that can improve the efficiency of society by facilitating coordinated actions" (p. 12). The posters' unity around Nabil's message was a form of civic engagement "in which citizens are drawn together as equals in intense horizontal interaction" (Diamond, 1997a, p. 12). It is a coordinated civil society effort that is initiated by the blogger and "driven from below" through his supporters (Diamond, 2001, p. 7).

"They Reconnected the Internet, but Not Facebook or Twitter: Please Spread Widely."

This thread was taken from Nawara Negm's blog and was posted in Arabic on February 2, 2011, a few days before former president Mubarak announced that he would step down. This thread included a call for action made by the blogger herself, asking the posters to take action by spreading the word about the disruption of online forms of communication.

In her post, Negm wrote: "Despite Mubarak's promises for reform and his claim of lack of interest in power, his regime is still cutting off Twitter and Facebook. Only the Internet service was restored to make sure it serves the interests of the business people[sic] who support the regime. . . . We have to remain united and persistent in our efforts to bring down the regime. If this regime is able to suppress us once more and to convince us to leave the streets and go back to our homes, it would never go away, and it would make us pay a dear price for what we did so far. We are going through our last fight against this suppressive regime. Freedom is knocking on our doors, and our only weapon now is to stay out on the streets in the millions until we see this regime go. We warn the regime and all its supporters that we will prevail and we will hold them accountable for their actions."

Some comments were very critical, and even insulting to Negm. For example, Yehia wrote: "You are an agent."

Hamed wrote: "Please stop. You got what you want. You weren't dreaming of 0.01 percent of this [achievement] a week ago. We got what we want or 90 percent of it. Let's not let our greed push us to ruin our country. We must be rational and seize this now. If [Mubarak didn't do what he] promised, we know our way to the streets. Let's give him six more months. . . . We waited for thirty years. Also, let's not remember ONLY the bad things for this guy. He did also a lot of good things, and he is also a war hero."

Hoffman wrote: "I am not with you. We have to wait. Anybody with a political project should not seek to achieve it by force, but through negotiations. We should not be opportunists, and we should give this regime another chance."

Tamer wrote: "I don't have a Twitter account, but my Facebook account is working fine, and it is not blocked. Despite my disagreement with the Mubarak regime, we have to give it another chance. We have to give people a chance to catch their breath. I call on all the people who are protesting in Tahrir Square to listen to this advice so as not to lose the public's support. Don't be stubborn[,] and remember that Mubarak . . . [once] carried a weapon and defended this country."

Amal wrote: "Thank God, Facebook and Twitter services are restored. Mubarak has promised us that he would leave, but for the sake of his image and our dignity, we should not insult him in the cartoons and in the global newspapers. He might not be a perfect leader, but he is a war hero who deserves to leave with dignity, rather than humiliation."

Mona wrote: "I am really scared of the future. I am scared to see more deaths and casualties as a result of this revolution. I am worried and concerned that the more pressure we put on the Mubarak regime, the more destruction we will see around us. The military people are telling us to leave the streets and go back to our homes; if we don't listen to them, we will be on our own without the military people's support. We need to listen to the voice of logic and realize that Mubarak's latest speech included promises that would satisfy our demands. If he breaks any of his promises in the future, we can always go back to Tahrir Square."

However, other comments were supportive of Negm's post. There was a call for action by many posters on this thread, from both inside and outside Egypt, in both English and Arabic. For example, one poster sent Negm a link that could be used to overcome any blocking of online websites. Another poster, named Sorrayya, wrote: "I am writing to you from Syria. If I can be of any help, please let me know. You can contact me through my Twitter account or through email, both of which are listed below."

Amgad, an Egyptian living in Denmark, wrote:

> I'm an Egyptian living abroad. My heart is with you, and I do all that I can by writing to newspapers and talking on the radio, asking people to support the Egyptian revolution and asking governments to stop supporting Mubarak. I urge you to continue until he is out. I would like to suggest to you, the youth who started this magnificent movement, forming a committee or even the nucleus of a political party, for example you can call it 'the youth party for change,' and appointing from among you those who can participate in negotiations and the formation of a transitional government after Mubarak leaves office. This will give you more international and national weight and will help you to better organize yourselves. You can start collecting names for those who could be members. Your political program will be developed in the process. Your demands now are clear, simple and just. I'm sharing these thoughts because without a figure from you who can address the media and without a mandate that represents your

> demands and your plan for action, many people out there will remain skeptical. . . . Just a suggestion.

Om Hagar wrote: "I live in England. My sister and I have organized several protests in Manchester against the Mubarak regime, and we were joined by hundreds of Egyptian and British citizens. This has given us hope for change, and has provided us with a sense of pride and confidence in our cause."

Samer wrote: "Long live the Egyptian revolution. Salute from North America."

Shaker wrote: "I am an Egyptian living in the UK. We support you [the youth behind this revolution] as much as we can. You are in a very critical situation. We feel like you are targeted by a very wicked plan to divide you. Please stand strong. The thugs of the government will never be able to defeat you. DON'T BE FOOLED BY MUBARAK'S PROMISES. How can we support you?"

Noha wrote: "Dear Nawara; I will post your message on my Facebook page. This is all I can do, but my heart is aching for this great nation and for the lives that were lost in this revolution."

Gouda wrote: "My friend Nawara: Please let me know if there is anything that we, the Jordanian bloggers, can do to help you and your people in your fight against the regime. We feel helpless and ashamed that we are not able to do anything for you. May God support your cause."

Samy wrote: "I am a Syrian citizen living in the United Arab Emirates. Since the beginning of the Egyptian revolution, I haven't been able to do anything other than follow the details of what has been going on in Egypt and praying for the Egyptians to achieve their noble cause."

Mohannad wrote: "You are right in calling for and insisting on removing Mubarak. Next Friday is not too far, but we should be organized for this day and the weeks to come as the protests will continue. We need LEADERS to take the lead and speak with the army. We need to prepare someone to talk on our behalf before Friday."

Amira wrote: "This is a plea to all the Egyptians. Be courageous and leave your homes to join your fellow Egyptians in Tahrir Square. Join the fight against the horrible Mubarak regime."

Hussein wrote: "The police are trying to save the head of the Egyptian regime by using their thugs and by bribing people to leave the streets and go back home. But this is not going to work. Mubarak will have to leave before we leave."

As the comments mentioned above show, there was a deep polarization among the posters who commented on this thread. Some were supportive of Negm's position, while others had reservations about it. While some observers may consider this polarization to be a negative phenomenon that may curtail civic engagement and harm citizens' efforts to achieve unity behind a national cause, others may see it as a natural and healthy occurrence that is better than political apathy or indifference, particularly during times of political crises.

We contend that it is important to acknowledge both the pros and cons, or the opportunities and threats, posed by such polarization. This is in line with Diamond's (1997a) argument that

> when organizations in civil society become intensely and enduringly politicized along partisan lines of division, society may polarize, as the cross-cutting bonds of solidarity and civility dissolve. Such polarization may be creative and advantageous for social justice and democracy at moments of political crisis, bringing the downfall of an authoritarian regime, the reform of a decadent and occluded democratic system, the permanent expansion of participation and enlargement of civil liberties, and impeachment and removal of a corrupt president from office, the cancellation of a fraudulent election. But democracy cannot function indefinitely on the basis of crisis, polarization, and pervasive civic and political mobilization by every type of organization imaginable (pp. 11–12).

Interestingly, the polarization that was reflected in the thread mentioned above did not stand in the way of exercising some sort of citizen journalism. This was reflected in Negm's post, as well as in the posters' comments. Most posters in this thread felt that they had a voice, and they were mobilized further by Negm's words. This echoed the "problem-solving" model, which was discussed in chapter 1. According to this model, the citizens are provided with mobilizing information on how to act in any given context, and then they ought to decide whether they need outside intervention or whether they are capable of handling the issue at hand on their own (Lemert, 1981 as cited in Haas, 2007). In this thread, the posters generally adopted the citizen journalists' role, and they felt that they could topple the Mubarak regime on their own by sticking to their places on the streets and the squares; finding ways to circumvent the regime's blocking of online social media outlets, such as Twitter and Facebook; and spreading the word about the revolution and mobilizing support for it nationally and internationally.

In other words, this is an example of a situation where ordinary citizens utilized blogging to engage in citizen journalism. This clearly shows how blogging can "help members of the public come to see themselves as citizens, and hold them accountable for grappling with the full complexity of issues and become participants in civil society rather than mere spectators of it" (Nichols, et al., 2006, p. 78). It also reveals that "what blogging, citizen journalism and social news sites yield are new possibilities for citizen participation at various points along those chains of sense-making that shape news—not only new possibilities for citizens to 'break' news" (Goode, 2009, p. 1291).

Acknowledging the mainstream and ordinary nature of her blog's visitors, Negm told the authors in a personal interview in Cairo in 2009: "I am very happy that it is not the elite who like my blog. I know that from the comments I get. It is ordinary young individuals. They are university graduates, but they are ordinary; they are not involved in any political party. They are not very elitist in their thinking." According to Negm, it is not the bloggers' job to solve problems, as much as it is to provide ordinary citizens with a venue to express and exchange ideas. "I think that blogging is like a stage of 'mind training.' Right now, we are thinking about our lives. Everybody is angry and they don't know what the real solution is. Bloggers also don't have the solution, but we brainstorm and exchange ideas with our readers. We have to figure out our route together."

Addressing the meaning of citizen journalism and how it has been practiced and exemplified through Egyptian blogs, Amira Howeidy, a political editor at *Al-Ahram Weekly* newspaper in Egypt told the authors in a personal interview in 2009:

> Citizen journalism means that you don't have to be a professional journalist. You can just write your random thoughts on a blog. Or you can report on what happens around you in your life with a certain political perspective or view. It is citizen journalism in the sense that it doesn't have to meet deadlines. You go to the blogger, and the blogger doesn't come to you. Newspaper editors dictate what the readers get, but the blogger dictates what his followers receive. And you go to the blog knowing that this [is] the specific view of x or y, and they are not censored or regulated. And that is citizen journalism; it is the freedom to express your thoughts regardless of any pressures.

The thread mentioned above reflected a strong and evident sense of civic engagement through which the posters expressed an "active and collective commitment to achieving the common good for their society…[and] to contribut[ing] to problem-solving in their community" (Ibrahim, 2005, p. 5). This civic engagement was evident at both the local and global levels, since the posters were not just Egyptians, but they came from other countries too. Moreover, they engaged in a thread that was "horizontal... [or] peer-to-peer in nature, [where] citizens share, discuss, provoke and argue with each other" (Goode, 2009, p. 1294). An interesting observation in the horizontal nature of this thread was the balance between male and female posters. One of the positive results of the January 25 revolution in Egypt was the inclusion of the female citizens in the political process—a phenomenon that has further strengthened collective civic engagement in postrevolutionary Egypt.

In addition to its reflection of citizen journalism and the problem-solving model, the thread mentioned above illustrates an important civil society function, as explained by Diamond (1999), which is "the transition from clientelism to citizenship" (p. 244). The posters' sense of citizenship, as exemplified in their calls for resistance to the Mubarak regime, enabled them "to advance their interests and... sever[ed] the psychological and structural bonds of clientelism that have historically locked them in a dependent and subordinated status, isolated from one another and unable to rally around their common material or cultural interests" (Diamond, 1999, p. 244).

"Urgent to the Youth: Leave Downtown and Go to Other Places to Be Decided upon Later"

This thread was posted in Arabic by Nawara Negm on January 26, 2011, just one day after the eruption of the revolution. In it, Negm is trying to mobilize protestors and guide them to safe places to avoid the state's security forces.

Negm wrote: "We will not allow anybody to suppress our protests. We will just strategically change our spots and stay away from downtown Cairo, which has been transformed into a war zone where live ammunition is being used by the police against the protestors. You need to go to neighborhoods, such as Heliopolis, Abbassya, Manial, Zamalek, Maadi, 6th of October[,] and Haram. If you read this message, please send SMS to other people and encourage them to go to these places[,] which have no police forces, since all the police forces are concentrated downtown. That is why you have to leave downtown as soon as possible."

Negm's message had a great impact on the posters in this thread who shared some other detailed and step-by-step instructions for the protestors in order to make the revolution successful. For example,

Safwat wrote: "This is a message from a Tunisian citizen to the brothers and sisters in Egypt. In order for your revolution to succeed, you have to do the following: 1) You have to protest in the evening so that you can avoid getting arrested, kidnapped or getting identified by the police through the video cameras; 2) You should not commit suicide. If you are going to die, let it be by a police bullet, not by your own hands; 3) Make use of the media to get your message across to the outside world; 4) [S]pray the police cars with black paint to stop them from moving. May God help you."

Akmal wrote: "Nawara: I hope your post is read by as many protestors as possible."

Youssef wrote: "I would stay away from the neighborhood of Maadi. It is packed with police cars and state security forces right now. Even on regular days, police forces are in Maadi to protect the embassies and the ambassadors' residences which are concentrated there."

Sherif wrote: "Nawara: You should not have posted this message since it may provide some hints to the police forces who may read it and act accordingly."

Negm responded to Sherif by saying: "We don't have any secret plans. We should not be afraid of the state police. They are the ones who should be afraid of us. This is our country, and we are taking it back from them."

Ayman wrote: "Currently, the protests don't have leaders who can guide them. That is why I think there should be some operations' centers created by the protestors to help provide some guidance and organize their movements in the city, and each one of these centers should be supervised by one of us. I have also posted this message on my blog and my Facebook page. If you have any comment or opinion on this idea, please send it to me through my blog."

Fathi wrote: "Nawara: I think you need to draw maps of the locations where the protestors need to go and post these maps on Facebook and on your blog. This may encourage the people sitting at home to leave their homes and join us. It will also help the protestors decide what locations they can head to and how to flee from a location if they get cornered."

Yasser wrote: "I just came across a news item on Facebook regarding a group of protestors in the Boulaque neighborhood who were able to trick the police officers by putting them under siege. The protestors then beat some officers up, and the rest of the officers fled the scene in disgrace."

Zaher wrote: "History tells us that dictators do not grant freedom to their people voluntarily. The Egyptian people have to take freedom by force from the despots. Currently, the Egyptians are sacrificing their blood and their lives to regain their dignity. Keep the pressure on the regime."

Zaki wrote: "I would like to share with you how to access a blocked site on the Internet by using Firefox. You need to change your Internet profile by selecting 'options' from the 'tools.' From the scroll down menu, choose 'advanced' then 'network.' Then, from another scroll down, choose 'manual proxy.' It will open several lists; under the first list http, enter the number 121.97.59.11, and under the second list titled port, enter 3128. Then press OK and you will be in. If this technique does not work, we can then change the numbers, but so far it has been effective in accessing all types of websites. Nawara: Please make sure to disseminate these instructions, since I know for a fact through a friend of mine who works for the communications company, Vodafone, that the government will soon instruct all the communication companies to block all the Internet sites, including Google."

Feras: "To brother Zaki who posted the message about how to access the blocked Internet sites. We have tried using the technique you suggested here in Sinai, but it didn't work. The Internet in the Sinai peninsula doesn't work most of the time, and so we would appreciate it if you can provide more clarification so that we can access the Internet. And we would like to thank Nawara for her great blog."

This thread provides an excellent example of how political blogs can play a vital role in aiding the process of civic engagement and boosting public mobilization. It will be commented on along with the next thread, which provides another example of the same phenomenon.

"Urgent: Go Immediately to the Lawyers' Syndicate"

Like the previous thread, this thread was also posted in Arabic by Nawara Negm on January 26, 2011, one day after the eruption of the revolution. In this thread, Negm offered a minute-by-minute update on activists, journalists, and lawyers who had been arrested, beaten, captured, or cordoned by the police forces. Negm wrote: "The reporters have just started heading toward the lawyers syndicate in downtown Cairo. Please join them in large numbers. The lawyers' syndicate could be a take-off point for us, but we cannot do so unless we have enough protestors. Yesterday, we had martyrs, whose blood is precious. Today, we have to mobilize more than yesterday; otherwise, nobody is going to respect us, and the regime will look down on us and will take us lightly. I am invited to appear on Al-Jazeera at 8:30 tonight. Please let me know if you want to send a message through me to the whole world. You are the best and the most noble nation."

In response to Negm's message, posters, both inside and outside Egypt, offered their help, advice, and support. Some provided their phone numbers from outside Egypt, while others narrated their personal experiences of going down to Tahrir Square and what happened there. Others provided useful tips and links to overcome any blocking of online websites. Here are some examples of such posts:

Saeed wrote: "Yesterday, I was very proud of myself as I went out with four of my friends, and we joined a group of approximately 1,000 protestors at El-Galaa' bridge. We tried to cross over the bridge, but we were prevented by the police, and so we changed our direction to [the] October bridge, and we managed to cross over to Tahrir Square, where we were joined by three thousand protestors in front of the National Democratic Party building. I am extremely happy and proud of what I did."

Karam wrote: "I am writing from Dubai. Here is my telephone number. I would like to help in any way I can."

Shadia wrote: "I just came back from a protest, and I have to tell you that there are several groups of protestors in downtown that need more people to join to create a critical mass. Nawara: Please make sure to write about the fact that the authorities cut off the Internet and are arresting protestors right and left. The world needs to know that our police forces are not as civilized as they have been trying to portray themselves."

Amr wrote: "Nawara: Please let Al-Jazeera folks know that they are not doing enough to cover the Egyptian revolution and the street protests."

Sameh wrote: "You need to click on this link to access Twitter and Facebook."

Ramy wrote: "Nawara: You need to focus as much as you can during the Al-Jazeera interview tonight, and speak in colloquial, rather than classical, Arabic, so that it can be easier for you to express your ideas."

Alaa: "Nawara: Encourage more people to join the peaceful protests. Remind them of the problems in health care, education[,] and the environment. Also, remind them of the human rights' abuses and the beatings at the police stations. Let them know that they need to set the Tunisian revolution as a model."

Akram: "Let's make next Friday a huge 'rage day' to provide a spark for the ousting of Mubarak. Let's make sure that protests will come out of every mosque in Egypt. We are starting to see the regime lose its grip and we have to make sure we finish the job."

Tarek wrote: "Nawara: I think we need to schedule a big protest on Sunday at 3 p.m., as this will give us time to attend a training session on how to protest and how to deal with the security forces. This will also allow the folks who haven't had the chance to check your blog or access their emails, Facebook[,] or Twitter accounts to see this notice. Let the regime know that we are patient and persistent in pursuing our demands, and that we will not give up until we see the regime go."

Abo-Ali wrote: "We should not compare the Tunisian revolution to what is happening in Egypt, since every country has its own unique political circumstances and context that are different from other countries. In Tunisia, the ousted regime was a closed dictatorship that did not unite with any political parties, while the Egyptian regime adopts an open dictatorship style that has tried to attract some political trends in society to create the illusion that it is a democratic regime and to extend its stay in power. What best characterizes the Egyptian revolution is that all the opposition parties have united under one banner, and this united front has succeeded in breaking the barrier of fear. This united opposition has created a new, more open political environment that is being nurtured by the free flow of information enabled by new means of communication."

Adel wrote: "We have to make sure to continue our protesting to achieve the following demands: Mubarak and his son have to leave power; the constitution has to be rewritten to prevent the president from running for office for more than two terms; the parliament that was formed as a result of rigged elections in 2010 has to be dissolved; the state police forces have to be reduced, and they have to be used as a tool to serve the people, rather than terrorize them; the emergency law has to be stopped, and people should be given the right to protest peacefully with no restrictions; the national resources have to be redistributed, and the minimum wage should be increased; new development projects have to be launched in all fields, particularly agriculture and education; and a transitional government has to be formed to pave the way for a new legislative system and new presidential elections in the year 2012."

The two threads mentioned above from Nawara Negm's blog provide excellent examples of public mobilization, civic engagement, and call for action. This sense of collective mobilization and proactive engagement emanated from the Egyptian protestors' lack of trust in the "system efficacy, [or] the belief that the system is capable of solving the basic problems confronting the country," and their increasing confidence in their "individual political efficacy, [or] the sense that one's own individual participation can make a difference" (Diamond, 2001, p. 1). In other words, the protestors felt that their only hope for reform and for the improvement of their conditions would have to be initiated by them, not by the regime, which totally alienated them. The protestors' own will, determination, and desire for change were translated to "a constructive readiness and hopefulness to campaign for institutional change" (Diamond, 2001, p. 9).

The posters' collective determination, as exemplified in the two threads mentioned above, is a component of the concept of "social capital" that was referred to earlier in this chapter. The posters expressed a strong desire toward "voluntary cooperation—to pool resources, to engage in exchange, to organize for common ends....[This] voluntary cooperation is greatly facilitated by interpersonal trust and norms of reciprocity, and these cultural orientations in turn are fostered by (but also deepen) 'networks of civic engagement'" (Diamond, 1997a, p. 12).

Negm's original posts in the two threads mentioned above and the posters' reactions to them elevated citizens' social capital by "educating...[them] about their rights and responsibilities, and building a culture of tolerance and civic engagement; incorporating marginal groups into the political process and enhancing the latter's responsiveness to societal interests and needs; providing alternative means, outside the state, for communities to raise their level of material development; [and] opening and pluralizing the flows of information" (Diamond 1997b, as cited in Makumbe, 1998, p. 306).

It was the pluralization of information flow through blogging and social media that had made all other aspects of social capital possible with regard to civic engagement in the context of the January 25 revolution in Egypt. Putnam's concept of social capital was criticized on the grounds that it did not explain "how group involvement affects citizen behavior or attitudes so as to influence government performance or enhance the prospects for democracy" (Booth & Richard, 1998, p. 782). This is to say that effective civic engagement and organized group involvement need a venue and an impetus to help operationalize them and to provide them with momentum. In other words, "civil society needs an enabling environment of...infrastructural supports. It cannot operate where public order or the state is collapsing or operating well below capacity" (Bratton, 1994, p. 5).

New forms of communication, such as blogging, can help provide an environment where civil society can thrive and civic engagement can flourish. In this context, Bratton (1994) realized the important role of media technologies in civil society, almost a decade before the advent of social media. He argued that

> in order to be politically active, citizens require means to communicate with one another and to debate the type of government they desire for themselves. Civic discourse can take place in various fora, the most important of which are the public communication media.... Civil society is always stronger where there is a diversity of media outlets and political views. New technologies of personal communication...can strengthen civil society by empowering citizens to communicate independently of state supervision. A healthy civil society is a multi-stranded web of cross-cutting channels of communication (Bratton, 1994, pp. 2–3).

In the Egyptian context, it was blogging that served as a platform where collective civic engagement was crystallized and stimulated. The Mubarak regime felt the mounting pressure of the public's anger and massive protests through social media. The Egyptian political activists used blogs and other forms of social media to organize their activities on the streets and to exchange ideas about how to deal with the security forces and how to make their protesting more effective. The two threads mentioned above were a case in point. It was the impact of blogs and other forms of social media that made the Mubarak regime decide to cut off the Internet during the revolution.

Commenting on how blogs had prepared the Egyptian citizens for the Egyptian revolution, Nawara Negm told the authors in a personal interview in the summer of 2011, "Before the revolution, blogs played an important role in brainstorming and exchanging ideas about the future of this country. There was a general state of public anger, but there was no crystallized idea or vision for the future. During that time, blogs also broke the taboos and helped pave the way for the revolution."

Echoing Negm's thought, Gamal Eid, director of the Arabic Network for Human Rights Information, told the authors:

> Blogging has, to a large extent, enhanced the Egyptian civil society. For example, the blogs that drew attention to torture inside prisons have contributed to increasing the public's awareness about torture and the fact that it is not something abstract, but rather something concrete which happens everyday at police stations. This awareness level has made things easier for human rights organizations functioning

> in Egypt. Bloggers have no red lines, and they don't negotiate their stands or ideologies like some organizations do. Bloggers are also technology-savvy, and they know how to utilize technology to serve the public's interests. If we compare that to many civil society organizations, we will find that such organizations still use primitive tools to communicate with their target audience. So, the bottom-line is that these bloggers are complementing, and even strengthening, the work of civil society organizations in Egypt.

Overall, we can contend that all the previous threads have in varying degrees and different forms called for some form of action to be taken by the blog's visitors, whether it is knowing how to help bloggers; spreading the word about the interruption of online modes of communication and social networking sites; leaving one place and moving to another one to avoid being caught by the police and to ensure their personal safety; or going to a certain destination, such as the lawyer's syndicate, to demonstrate their support for a certain cause. This clearly demonstrates that

> the opportunities to apply considerable political pressure for reforms are now available through digital media networks. Perhaps those networks could be dedicated to the task of political reform. The next social movement may well launch demonstrations from desktops and cellular phones. It may write its own news and gain large audiences for it. Indeed, early efforts to mobilize large-scale protests targeting particular governmental actions...have shown the power of networks in action. The question is whether generations as distant from government as recent ones will find the time, energy or relevance to reform the system (Bennett, 2008, p. 20).

In the Egyptian case, it could be said that young people were able to find the time and energy to engage in the challenging task of reforming the political system through the use of digital media networks, which acted as catalysts and supplements for on-the-ground political organization and action. It was this unique combination of both online and offline mobilization that ultimately paved the way for the 2011 revolution.

The concept of mobilization that manifested itself in the above threads is also in line with the notion of empowerment that David Crocker (2009) states is related to that of agency and could be seen as "those conditions and processes that enable individuals and groups to strengthen and exercise their agency" (p. 19). Amartya Sen (2000), who has written extensively on the idea of agency, describes an "agent" as "someone who acts and brings about change, and whose achievements can be judged in terms of her own values and objectives, whether or not we assess them in terms of some external criteria as well" (p. 19). Agency is arguably key to human dignity and control over one's life because actively bringing about change according to one's own goals (i.e., exercising agency) leads to a life where the individual is in control, rather than passively being acted upon by others.

In light of the above definitions, it is safe to argue that both the political bloggers and the active participants and posters on their blogs could be described as "agents" for social change, who strive to take advantage of these online discussion forums in cyberspace to empower themselves and others in the hope of bringing about positive and effective change on the ground. By doing so, they have, in fact, chosen to be in control of their own political reality and destiny, rather than being passively acted upon by the regime in power, through exercising their agency, asserting their public will, and enacting their mobilization, both online and offline.

This notion of agency best manifests itself in the fact that "young people can better learn how to transfer skills they are already using in other online experiences to more conventional arenas of politics. They can also be encouraged to acquire additional skills that actively enable the formation of public voice both in their social networks and in more explicitly political contexts" (Bennett, 2008, p. 20). Moreover, as Bennett (2008) rightly points out, "Given even minimal learning opportunities…citizenship concerns seem strong enough among young people to motivate the continued creation and growth of impressive youth engagement networks focused on issues such as environment, global justice and human rights" (p. 20).

In this context it is also important to bear in mind that "from a liberal perspective, citizens are free agents, and just civic norms are those that do not seek to impose upon individuals' collective notions of what is good. In contrast, the communitarian perspective places greater emphasis upon the common good than upon citizens' self-determination, and, therefore, justifies policies intended to shape civic behavior at the expense of individual agency" (Coleman, 2008, p. 190).

The "push" and "pull" dynamics between these two contrasting perspectives, that is, liberalism and communitarianism, reveal that "the policy of 'targeting' young people so that they can 'play their part' can be read either as a spur to youth activism or an attempt to manage it. Indeed, the very notion of youth e-citizenship seems to be caught between divergent strategies of management and autonomy.

Although these two faces of e-citizenship represent ideal types, and should perhaps be understood as opposing points on a spectrum rather than mutually exclusive positions, they differ sufficiently in their contrasting conceptions of the status of young people, the affordances of digital technologies, and the authenticity of 'actually existing democracy'" (Coleman, 2008, p. 191).

This ongoing struggle between the two poles of "management" and "autonomy" is best exemplified in the fact that

> in contrast to the conception of e-citizenship as socialization, proponents of autonomous e-citizenship refuse to see themselves as apprentice citizens, arguing that, despite their limited experience or access to resources, they possess sufficiently autonomous agency to speak for themselves on agendas of their own making. Autonomous e-citizens regard youth itself as a reflexive project in which narratives of emergence, socialization, and engagement can be renegotiated by each new generation.... In this sense, not only the objective conditions facing youth, but the subjective experience of what it means to be a young person becomes a matter for politicized discourse (Coleman, 2008, p. 191).

The level of civic engagement, agency, and political mobilization exhibited in the above threads is highly indicative of the existence of a high level of genuine, autonomous ecitizenship among Egyptian youth, who were able to put forward their own agendas and to make their voices heard on salient issues of special relevance and importance to them. To do so, they were able to take advantage of the Internet, which "appeals to autonomous e-citizens, who see it as a relatively free space in which untrammeled creativity and acephalous networks can flourish" (Coleman, 2008, p. 192).

The next group of threads performs a different function, which is documenting police brutality, the regime's violations of human rights, and the limitations the regime imposes on various forms of freedom.

Section Two: Threads Documenting Brutality, Violations, and Limitations

"The Martyr of Suez"

This thread was taken from the blog of Wael Abbas and was posted in Arabic on January 26, 2011, a day after the launch of the January 25 revolution. The thread included a video shot from inside the morgue in the city of Suez in Egypt. The video showed a young man who was shot to death by the police forces. The voice-over was by one of the nurses who was asking for help in handling the body of this man. Abbas wrote that he received the video through his mail, and that it was accompanied by a message asking him to upload it on his blog. The video elicited several comments by posters inside and outside Egypt, expressing their disdain with the Mubarak regime. Some of the comments included rhetoric and poetry attacking the regime and asking Mubarak to leave.

Doaa wrote: "May God bless his soul. A really heart-breaking video."

Shawkat wrote: "I would like to share with your visitors the following telephone numbers to call in cases of robbery, theft or any kind of emergency. I am a member of the Life Makers Youth Committee. When you dial any of these numbers, you will be transferred to the committee chapter in your governorate. I would like to take this opportunity to thank Wael Abbas for his efforts in enhancing our political awareness."

Roberto wrote: "Hi Wael. This is Roberto. I work for *O Globo* newspaper, the largest daily paper in Rio de Janeiro, Brazil. I co-edit a magazine for youngsters that *O Globo* issues every week and I'm looking for young (16 to 23 year old) bloggers who are in Egypt and could talk to us about what's going on in the country from their own points of view. Do you know any young people who can do so? Could you recommend some names to me? You may contact me by e-mail (it's above) or phone, if you like. I appreciate your time and attention in advance. Thank you so much."

Haroon wrote: "Dear Wael: I think it could be very powerful if you and others could lead a charter for non-violence—across all sects, parties, ages, male and female—and encourage its adoption by all protestors—like Martin Luther King did—only according to Egyptian values, principles and words. This could serve to unify people when opposition leadership is blocked or elusive. It could serve to prevent some outbreaks of violence. It could serve to protect the integrity of the popular movement from those who try to paint it as a conspiracy, as a threat to those last vestiges in the regime, as a threat to your neighbour(s) in the region who are trembling and could become aggressive. It could also serve as a tsunami against all of the conspiracies and conspiracy theories. Take it in your own hands—wipe them all out. This is your charter—it is about peace, it is about freedom, it is universal . . . no? Good luck and God Bless"

Mazen wrote: "Don't cry on the martyrs. But follow their steps in the battle to achieve victory so that this revolution can succeed. Egypt's revolution is the ray of hope for the rest of the Arab world."

Faiza wrote: "Hi dear Wael: I would like to ask you to publish your posts in English because, as I know, your blog has too many international visitors. Your friend from IRAN."

Ismael wrote: "We need to communicate the following information to the Egyptian youth who are protesting in Tahrir Square as soon as possible: 1) They need to select a group of eloquent speakers who can appear on the Arab media channels and try to draw the 'silent majority' to their cause; 2) Try to reach out to some prominent personalities and famous people to ask them to speak on their behalf; [and] 3) Explain to the world that the reason for your refusal to leave the square is not stubbornness or disrespect to anybody, but the desire for freedom and dignity, and protest is your only option right now."

Salem wrote: "This is a nice and informative blog. I will be visiting it regularly. Thanks for posting some great ideas. I'll try to return back with a completely different browser to check out things! Also, I put a link to your blog on my site. Hope you do not mind."

The thread mentioned above exemplified the concept of citizen journalism, through the posting of the video by the blogger, in an attempt to document police brutality, as well as civic engagement by involving both local and global audiences. Abbas often receives videos by ordinary people to upload on his blog, given his prominence and the high popularity that his blog enjoys. In this context, Abbas told the authors in a personal interview in 2009: "I often get participation from ordinary people. In fact, many people send me videos and pictures of things that they have seen and did not like and they wanted me to post on my blog to draw the public's attention to such crimes."

The posters in this thread adopted a proactive approach and came up with some concrete solutions to reduce the pain of the Egyptian protestors and to publicize their case regionally as well as internationally. This can be an exemplification of the problem-solving model discussed in chapter 1. Despite the abundance of rhetoric and poetry in the Arabic blogs under study in this book, the participants in this thread provided a pragmatic type of civic engagement—one that called for "discuss[ing] issues, not just on the basis of emotion, but on facts about how things work" (Meyer, 1995, p. 21).

The pragmatic nature of the posters' contributions to the thread mentioned above dovetailed nicely with several of Diamond's civil society functions, such as "stimulating political participation," "recruiting and training new political leaders," "mobilizing new information and understanding," and "widely disseminating information . . . [to] empower citizens in the collective pursuit and defense of their interests and values" (Diamond, 1999, pp. 245–247). Information was a main key in mobilizing people and raising their awareness through the thread mentioned above. The video that was posted by Abbas made people realize how brutal the regime was in dealing with the protestors. Additionally, some posters tried to mobilize the general public by providing several concrete steps to stand firm in the face of the regime and to spread the word about the noble cause of the protestors.

In an interview with the authors in Cairo in the summer of 2009, Abbas commented on the value of providing information and spreading awareness through his blog. He said,

> Through my blog, I address issues that haven't been discussed publicly before, such as political change and torture by the police. I don't claim that blogs have caused a big difference, but at least they have drawn people's attention to issues that have gone uncovered for a long time. People have become more aware of their political rights thanks to my blog and to other blogs. People are ready for political change anytime, but it all depends on the level of their awareness. That is why there has to be a higher margin of freedom in a way that allows different political factions to express their views and help the average person form a sound political opinion. And that freedom was made possible by blogs.

"The Al- Qatta Prison Massacre and the Truth Behind the Killing of General El-Batran"

This thread was also taken from Wael Abbas' blog and was posted in Arabic on February 8, 2011, three days before Mubarak announced that he was stepping down as president. In this thread, Abbas posted a series of recordings that he made over the phone with prisoners and their families. In these recordings, the prisoners accused the police forces of torturing and killing prisoners and also murdering a police general for refusing to open the prison's doors to let the convicted criminals out. "Setting the prisoners free was part of the plot to create chaos and terror in the country as part of Mubarak's regime's plan of counter revolution" (El-Gundy, 2011). The police forces, according to these recordings, killed him and claimed that he was killed by the prisoners.

In one of the recordings, a prisoner from Al-Qatta prison explained to Abbas over the phone how he and his fellow prisoners were not given any food for days during the revolution, to the extent that he had to kill a cat and eat it to satisfy his hunger! The prisoner also mentioned that two prisoners were killed by police forces for no reason while they were lining up to get some water. He told Abbas that the prison officials refused to let the paramedics in to treat the sick prisoners and left them to die. The prisoner also explained that a group of thugs, in collaboration with some police officers, shot General Mohamed El-Batran to death during the early days of the revolution for his refusal to open the jail's doors to let the prisoners out. Then, according to the recorded testimony of that prisoner, El-Batran's body was transported to another prison to cover up this crime.

Another prisoner from Al-Qatta prison explained to Abbas in another recording how he saw a sniper shoot General El-Batran. He also said that several of his cellmates were killed and their bodies were left on the ground until they rotted. According to that prisoner, more than 25 prisoners were shot to death on January 28, 2011, for no clear reason. He also said that all prisoners were deprived of food and water during the revolution.

A woman, in another recording, said that her father and her husband, both imprisoned in Al-Qatta prison, told her that the prison authorities had not given them food or water for several days, and that several prisoners were dying. There was also no electricity inside the prison. She also said that the prison authorities were shooting live ammunition at prisoners' families who were trying to bring in food to their imprisoned relatives at Al-Qatta prison.

In a different recording, a father of one of the prisoners who was killed in prison mentioned how he was informed by one of his son's cellmates that his son was shot to death by one of the police officers. He expressed his worries about the state of lawlessness that existed inside the prisons during the revolution. He also said that during a phone call, his son told him that the prison officials had locked him up with no food or water.

In commenting on all of these recordings, Abbas expressed sympathy to the prisoners and their families, and told them that he was hoping the situation would get better, particularly with the appointment of a new minister of interior, who will be in charge of the state police and the prisons' affairs.

Several posters expressed their shock after listening to these recordings. Galal wrote: "This is the Managing Translator at @AliveInEgypt, and we'd like to add English subtitles to the recordings. We want to show the entire world what happened, and we would like to get your approval for translating and subtitling these recordings."

Manal El-Batran wrote: "I am General El-Batran's sister. My brother was killed by a fellow police officer on January 29, 2011 for refusing to open the doors of the prison. He is a martyr. The Egyptian Organization for Human Rights announced that it will investigate the details of what happened on the 'Friday of Rage' which fell on January 28, 2011, the day which witnessed attempts by several police officers to open the prison doors and let the prisoners out to create a state of chaos on the Egyptian streets and to pressure the protestors to leave the streets and go back to their homes. On this sad day, General El-Batran was killed while attempting to perform his noble duty of maintaining security."

A number of posters called for a free and just investigation into the incident to determine who really killed General El-Batran.

Citizen journalism was exemplified in the thread mentioned above through Abbas' recorded interviews with several inmates from Al-Qatta jail and their families. In these recordings, the prisoners recited the difficult, inhumane treatment that they were receiving from the prison's officials during the days of the revolution. They also provided their testimony regarding the killing of a senior police general, El-Batran, as a result of his refusal to open the prison's doors to set the prisoners free. In this context, Abbas adopted the citizen journalist role by reaching out to these important sources, but, unlike previous examples of citizen journalism in this chapter, Abbas did not provide a solution to the problem of prisoners' mistreatment or the problem of covering up for the killing of El-Batran.

According to Haas (2007), citizen journalists need to "carefully consider which particular kinds of intervention would be required to adequately address given problems before they promote any public problem-solving activity" (p. 42). In this thread, neither Abbas nor the few posters who participated in the thread thought about a particular type of intervention or provided a concrete solution to the problems or issues at hand. There was sympathy toward the prisoners and their families on the part of Abbas and the few posters in this thread, but there was no clear call for action. It is a possibility that the state of lawlessness and confusion that Egypt was going through during the revolution obstructed thinking reasonably about an appropriate intervention method or solution to the human rights' violations that were taking place at Al-Qatta prison. It was only Manal El-Batran, the slain general's sister, who alluded to the investigation that was to be launched by the Egyptian Organization of Human Rights to look into the circumstances that led to the killing of her brother.

Despite the absence of a call for action in the thread mentioned above, Abbas had brought to the surface an issue that might have gone unnoticed had he not addressed it through his blog, and he succeeded in documenting it and raising public awareness about it. This in itself can be considered a positive and healthy approach in the context of citizen journalism, since a citizen journalist's main responsibility should be "to help bring into being a deliberating public by creating and sustaining an open-ended, unbounded public sphere to which all citizens have access and in which all topics of concern to citizens and all opinions available can be articulated, deliberated, and critiqued" (Haas, 2007, p. 47).

"I Am Prohibited from Covering Obama's Visit by the President's Office"

This thread was posted in Arabic on June 4, 2009, and it was taken from the blog of Abdel Monem Mahmoud. In his post, Mahmoud wrote: "The Egyptian newspaper, *Al-Dostour*, has sent the names of five of its reporters, including myself, to the government press office to get clearance for covering the speech that the U.S. President Barak Obama will give at Cairo University. The clearance was provided to my four other colleagues, but not for me. When I inquired at the press office, I was told that I was only allowed to cover the speech from the press center that faces the auditorium where Obama will give his speech. I was hoping to know what risk do I represent as a reporter in this context. Is this the democracy that this country has to offer its citizens?"

All posters were sympathetic to Mahmoud's situation. They tried to console him, provided him with moral support, and shared his bewilderment as to why he was not allowed to attend Obama's speech.

Maged wrote: "It is a big problem if you still believe that there is true freedom or democracy in our Arab countries."

Gaafar wrote: "I can share your pain, but you have to remember that God has a reason for everything."

Kamal wrote sarcastically: "Freedom for terrorists is a big mistake."

Mamdouh wrote: "You are not the first citizen to be stripped from their rights and freedoms. Anybody with a noble cause and true intentions has suffered in this country. Since you love your country, you were imprisoned and banned from travel. But people with a strong faith like you and me should never give up."

Farag wrote: "You are blacklisted since you belong to the Brotherhood. You have to be patient."

The thread mentioned above, despite its brevity and the few posters who participated in it, strongly reflected collective commitment to the cause of freedom, but without any proactive or concrete steps to achieve it. The posters were kindhearted in their support of Mahmoud's situation, but none of them provided any specific plans or strategies to enhance freedom in the Egyptian civil society. Devising ways to attain freedom might have been an easier-said-than-done objective under the Mubarak regime in Egypt. This was due to the severe restrictions that the regime imposed on political dissidents and the opponents of state policies.

In this context, Diamond argued that it is easier for an active civil society to strengthen an already existing democratic environment, rather than create it anew. Diamond, as cited in Encarnacion (2000), noted that "a vibrant civil society is probably more essential for consolidating and maintaining democracy than for initiating it" (p. 10). According to Diamond, civil society facilitates a democratic environment by "stimulating political participation and stimulating the efficacy and skill of democratic citizens, and by aiding citizens in the collective pursuit and defense of their interests and values" (Encarnacion, 2000, p. 10).

Social media have been the main driving force behind civil society's ability to stimulate political participation in the Middle East and North Africa. This has been particularly the case in a country like Egypt, where blogging has allowed political activists such as Abdel Monem Mahmoud to express their views and frustrations with the regime's infringement on human rights. Mahmoud, whose Brotherhood ideologies limited his opportunities for freedom of expression under the Mubarak regime, utilized his blog to share his ideas with others and to even generate collective interest. The thread mentioned above is a case in point.

Commenting on the impact of his blog, Mahmoud told the authors in a personal interview in Cairo in 2009:

> What we have in Egypt is not democracy, but it is a margin of freedom that we, the bloggers, were able to take by force from the regime. Blogs, in general, have helped increase the general political awareness of the young people. Before 2005, most political activists in Egypt were in their fifties and sixties; today, we are seeing young people in their twenties interested in pursuing political activism. I think the blogs have played a big role in that regard. My blog has caused some difference. It has encouraged some other young members of the Muslim Brotherhood to express themselves more openly online. It has also encouraged other Brotherhood members to try to humanize and personalize their identities as members of the Brotherhood. It also has encouraged constructive criticism for improving the Brotherhood.

> Moreover, I believe my blog has contributed to changing some of the old ideologies that were prevalent inside the Brotherhood movement. For example, we used to believe that all leftists were infidels. Now, thanks to my blog as well as other blogs launched by Brotherhood members, we exchange ideas online in a way that has melted the ice and has paved the way for us to engage in constructive dialogue with people from different factions and ideologies. Also, I don't believe that blogging has stopped torture in prisons, but at least it has forced the government to be more accountable in its actions out of fear that bloggers maybe monitoring these actions and writing about them.

Echoing Mahmoud's comments with regard to how the Internet, in general, and blogging, in particular, has provided a venue for suppressed voices, such as the Muslim Brotherhood's members under the Mubarak regime, Zayani (2011) argued that "the Internet shook off the sense of isolation and enabled many to be part of the information revolution and to ride the wave of globalization. It was an alternative space for engagement and relative freedom in a suffocating environment marked by tight control and heavy censorship" (p. 3). According to Zayani, social media have been an integral component of the "evolving dynamics which reinvented political engagement among a seemingly depoliticized young generation.... The sphere and terms of political action as such are reconfigured in the age of social media" (p. 2). Along the same lines, York (2012) argued that "blogs allowed ordinary Arabs to re-engage with politics, hone their analytical and argumentative skills, and escape the state-driven red lines which even the most independent of Arab media are forced to acknowledge" (p. 36).

Despite their lack of proactive ideas, the posters in the thread mentioned above were provided a venue, through Mahmoud's blog, to share their frustrations with the lack of personal freedoms and the violations of human rights that were epitomized by denying a reporter the right to cover an important event without providing any reason or explanation. Their ability to express their views about this and other situations was, in and of itself, a form of political engagement that was made possible thanks to social media, in general, and blogging, in particular. It was this political engagement and collective activism, exemplified through almost a decade of blogging, that awakened a dormant public and planted the seeds for the success of the January 25 revolution in Egypt.

The previous threads provided clear examples of the process of documentation, whereby the blogger uses the blog as a venue for providing evidence of governmental atrocities, violations, and limitations by offering real-life examples, through audio and video recordings and images and supplying the needed facts and figures, for the purpose of raising the public's awareness about these issues, both locally and globally.

They also provided clear evidence that some Internet "users treat personal Web logs (or 'blogs') . . . as alternative news sources. Moreover, there is a growing industry of alternative media production that relies on the efforts of solitary individuals equipped with handheld computers, digital cameras, and wireless technologies to bear witness to political violence that established media consider too controversial for their prime time viewers" (Howard, 2004, p. 7).

This fits neatly with the argument made by Mohamed Mustafa, an Egyptian political activist and the coordinator of the National Coalition for Change in Egypt, who was interviewed by the authors in Cairo in the summer of 2011, that

> the role of social media in the Egyptian revolution did not just exemplify itself through the actions of the organizers of this revolution, who used their hand-held mobile devices, especially cell phone cameras, to document any incidents of arrest or police brutality and to upload them immediately to Facebook and tweet about them, thus attracting attention and rallying support. Rather, it started well before the eruption of the 2011 revolution, through the diligent efforts of some social media activists, such as the famous blogger Wael Abbas, who used their blogs and other online forums as platforms for documenting the Mubarak regime's crimes against its own citizens, through its corrupt security apparatus, thus raising public awareness about such atrocities and paving the way for effective change.

The phenomenon of "youth-led citizen journalism" (Rheingold, 2008), which manifested itself in the above threads, clearly shows that youth

> who do express an interest in using participatory media to do journalism have unprecedented access to both the tools of production and the means of distribution: digital audio and video production via laptop computer today is equivalent to expensive professional equipment of only a few years ago, and while Internet publishing does not guarantee that a worldwide audience will pay attention, it does provide inexpensive access to it on a scale never before possible (Rheingold, 2008, p. 112).

Most importantly, the fact that some of the stories that were covered by these young citizen journalists, such as incidents of police brutality and torture, for example, were later on covered by mainstream media in Egypt is a clear indication that "opportunities for eyewitnesses to introduce their stories, and especially their pictures, into mainstream media abound" and that "although it is unlikely that purely citizen-created journalism will replace mainstream journalism, it is already clear that a niche exists" (Rheingold, 2008, p. 112).

The next group of threads concerns a third equally vital aspect of cyberactivism, which is opening platforms for online deliberation and electronic democracy through the useful exchange of knowledge and brainstorming between the blogger and the posters.

Section Three: Threads Providing Platforms for Online Deliberation

"Lest You Forget"

This thread was posted in English on September 8, 2011, and was taken from the Sandmonkey blog, which was created by Mahmoud Salem. In this thread, the blogger tried to remind people who were disappointed or dismayed with the situation after the January 25, 2011, revolution about the gains that were accomplished in that revolution.

Sandmonkey wrote:

> "There is a general feeling of malaise and melancholy affecting the January 25 protestors, for they feel as if they have accomplished nothing: that the Supreme Council of the Armed Forces has halted the revolution, and that it was all for nothing. This kind of talk infuriates me, not because of its self-pitying whiney nature from otherwise strong people, but because it's categorically not true. Let me count the ways:
>
> 1. I've been in this since 2005, from the blogosphere old guard, and for six years, me [sic], alongside the other bloggers I've worked with, were simply trying to get the people to get one idea into their heads: If we all, as people, get together in big numbers, and go to a public square protesting, we will bring down the president. The president is not the inevitable, immovable, God-like figure we made him up to be. And we accomplished that, pressuring Mubarak enough to bring him down. This is the first time in 7,000 years of continuous tyrannical rule that Egyptians managed to depose their ruler by their own hands.
> 2. Historically, Egyptians have always succumbed to the violent actions of whatever internal security force that runs Egypt, foreign or domestic. Up until the revolution, people were discounting the notion that Egyptians, even if they are out in numbers, would ever

win a face-off with the police. The January 25 revolution has also reversed that trend forever, as the protestors were able to beat up the police every single time they have faced them, to the point that in order for the police forces to take back Tahrir Square from the protestors, they had to be there in the protection of the military. Now we pity the police more than anything. This, historically also, has never happened in 7,000 years.

3. Being under tyrannical rule for this long, Egyptians also grew apathetic to whatever it is that the government does, and got used to not being part of the decision-making process. Now, they are embedded with the idea of democracy, voting, and having their voice count. I don't think any of you realize how many people will head to the polls this election, with some estimates pointing towards up to 80% voter turnout. This is unprecedented, and unlikely to go away. The days of voter apathy are over. We did that.
4. Also, in the history of this great nation, never was there an incident where Egyptians held their rulers accountable. Now, we have not only removed the president, we have also put him on trial. It doesn't matter if it's a Kangaroo court; the historical precedent is there, not just on a local, but on a regional level. This has NEVER happened before. We are now the people that removed their president and put him behind bars on trial. Think about what that means before you discount it. We not only created history, but we have changed the narrative of this country forever.

This revolution is only the start, and it won't end until the equation is balanced, even if we lost steam for now. And we should also know that we will get there, but we just won't do that at our time table. We were overly ambitious, hoping to change 30 years of corruption and institutional disintegration in a few months. It doesn't work like that, but we managed to get the country to take the big leap forward in the right direction. Please understand, this is not an invitation to stop protesting. This is your country, and protesting is your blood-earned right. So don't let anyone dissuade you from exercising it if you believe that it's necessary. This is an invitation to give yourselves some credit. Our generation, for better or worse, has forever changed the history of this country. Be proud of that.

Sandmonkey's message instilled some energy and confidence in the posters to this thread. Thunderstorm wrote: "Good Sandmonkey. This world is changing—and all those who are living now have to change their part for the better. That takes persistence. When people become disheartened, and everything seems too complex or overwhelming—focus on your part in the whole goal. Preserve yourself for the long run. Learn what you can about how things work while not allowing yourself to be diverted from too many things."

Aisha wrote: "Thank you! I needed to hear exactly what you wrote! Ashamed of myself for letting negativity take over my beliefs."

Sandra wrote: "I agree, that's what I believe too. Thanks a lot! These words were needed. I'll spread them around. You are my confirmed favorite blogger."

Shamel wrote: "You always manage to make me feel more positive. WE changed history damn it!"

Alice wrote: "You Egypt have pulled out the foundations of your faulted government system and now start from scratch. You haven't lost steam; it's just phase two: a different process and procedure required and produced. Phase one was very physical and used a different part of your mental state to survive it. Phase two needs all your mental alertness for it will be filled with negotiations and manipulations. Phase three will be adaptation—The Revolution didn't fail. You won!"

Samuel wrote: "Sandmonkey man—Very, very, well said indeed. Cowboy Up and hang in there. I am from Cheyenne[,] Wyoming[,] USA."

Toby wrote: "There is a Chinese proverb that says: a journey of a thousand miles begins with one small step. Egyptians have taken that small step, and then some. You are on the right path. Believe that! Keep taking those small steps and one day you'll look back and be amazed at your journey!"

Sayyed wrote:

> Good points Sandmonkey and you are right about being proud for what has occurred earlier this year. Something needs to be said about the feeling that we have not accomplished our goals. Have we thought about what the appropriate actions are in order for these goals to be accomplished? Can demonstrations in the square ever resolve the problems of traffic, housing, education or health care in Egypt or anywhere else for that matter? Do we really expect these problems to be solved by yelling at officials?
>
> What are the appropriate actions for these problems? If not shouting in the street, then what? No one is asking not to shout in the street but at least one should be honest to recognize that it is as effective as jumping in the Nile.
>
> Look at how Japan is rebounding after its devastating earthquake. Hint: they did not do it by demonstrations. Japan also rebounded after losing a war and being hit with atomic bombs in WWII. Different goals require different actions. Building requires different thinking.

Salma wrote:

> I agree with you, Sandmonkey, that so far some progress has been made. We dared to demand the ousting of a long-standing despot. But more importantly, we dared to do this in vast numbers, with peaceful determination and persistence and we have succeeded. This is unprecedented. But, we have seen, again and again, interlopers hijacking the revolution, under many banners, and with varying agendas. We are also now swayed in different directions with a multitude of matters that have risen to the surface as a consequence of the revolution, the religious aspects, the trials or absence of such, the neighbors, the economy, the prime minister, constitutional changes, presidential elections or parliamentary elections first, the military trials of civilians...etc. With a little levelheadedness, we need to avoid being distracted by these diversions, we need to stop finding every single excuse on earth on why this wonderful revolution is stalling[,] and we need to proactively regroup under common demands and remain on track. These demands should address next steps such as stability, growth and social justice.

Jim wrote: "We Americans are anxiously watching Egypt. In the best circumstances, the picture is muddy with many conflicting sources. I pray that the secular democrats triumph in the long run."

The thread mentioned above provided a strong example of civic engagement, along with collective optimism and pride in the Egyptian revolution, even by non-Egyptian posters. The type of civic engagement that was showcased in this thread is "value-driven" and "provides the human resources necessary for a vibrant civil society.... It emanates from the idea that citizens have rights to social participation and obligations" to enhance their society and improve its conditions (Ibrahim, 2005, p. 5). Moreover, the thread reflected an indigenous and foreign civic engagement, as exemplified by the Egyptian and non-Egyptian posters. One could feel the passion of the foreign posters and their willingness to share their conceptual resources with their Egyptian counterparts for the purpose of taking the Egyptian revolution to another level. The strongly felt sense of optimism on the part of Sandmonkey blew confidence into his followers and his blog visitors and drew their attention to the positive aspects and the achievements of the Egyptian revolution. In a sense, Sandmonkey's post had an emancipatory tone that elevated the spirits of his followers and overcame the barriers of culture and geography (Meyer, 1995). Sandmonkey's dose of optimism was highly needed since several Egyptian protestors and revolutionaries were starting to get frustrated with the unfelt or delayed results of their revolution. What he tried to do was to encourage them to follow through with their demands and to finish the journey that they started. He realized that "positive attitudes...should precede behavioral change" (Nichols et al., 2006, p. 79).

Sandmonkey's positive message and the posters' enthusiastic acceptance of it reflected several civil society functions as envisioned by Larry Diamond. The message encouraged political participation by enhancing the Egyptian revolutionaries' appreciation of their political worth and the value of what they had achieved on the ground (Diamond, 1999).

Sandmonkey's message also touched on several aspects that empowered the Egyptian protestors in their "collective pursuit" of political demands. The information that he conveyed to them through his analysis of the situation gave them hope in the future. This was reflected in several of the posters' comments. In this context, Diamond (1999) argued that "[w]hile civil society groups may sometimes prevail temporarily through the raw political power of their numbers (e.g. in strikes and demonstrations), they generally cannot be effective in contesting government policies or defending their interests unless they are well informed" (p. 247). Sandmonkey's analysis of the revolution's achievements helped the protestors reach a new level of understanding about what they had done. That is why his post could be considered a good example of online deliberation.

Moreover, it can be argued that Sandmonkey's post helped "strengthen the social foundations of democracy...[through] build[ing] social capital by bringing citizens together to cooperate as peers for their common advancement" (Diamond, 1999, p. 249). The "voter apathy" that Sandmonkey referred to, and that, according to him, used to exist before the revolution, turned into a high voter turnout after the revolution. This is a case where civil society has taken democracy to another level "in two generic ways: by helping to generate a transition from authoritarian rule to (at least) electoral democracy, and by deepening and consolidating democracy once it is established" (Diamond, 1997a, p. 25). This is a case where citizenship was revived, civil society was "resurrected, and a general mobilization is likely to occur, or even to snowball into a popular upsurge that pushes the transition further than it otherwise would have gone" (Diamond, 1997a, p. 26).

Through his post, Sandmonkey tried to get the Egyptian revolution back on track and to revive the revolutionary spirit that had started to fade away. He used an optimistic, mobilizational approach to revitalize the Egyptian youth, who took to the streets and the squares, demanding the overthrow of the regime. Sandmonkey's message and the posters' positive interactions were a testament to how a blog can possibly reenergize a civil society.

Explaining the role of his blog in this context, Sandmonkey, or Mahmoud Salem, told the authors in a 2010 interview in Cairo: "Bloggers create awareness but change has to come from the people. Our problem in Egypt is that we give up too easily. I believe that the bloggers' main job should be to provoke people. I will promote certain points of view and fight for them, so I can provoke people to get a debate going and get people to think."

"Tahrir: An Exercise in Nation-Building"

This thread was also taken from Sandmonkey's blog and was posted in English on July 16, 2011, six months after the January 25 revolution. In this thread, Sandmonkey tried to provide a snapshot of the protestors' life at Tahrir Square through his own eyes as a political activist and a blogger who had spent an extensive period of time at the square during the course of the revolution. Since Sandmonkey's post was too long, we included sections from it to provide the gist of what he wanted to communicate.

Sandmonkey wrote:

> A couple days ago, a friend of mine asked me what I was doing at the Tahrir sit-in. When I asked him what he meant by that, he commented that I was acting differently this time; that instead of analyzing and taking a macro view of things, I was actually on the ground, not writing, but doing things all around the square instead. He simply found this to be out of character. I explained that I was there because I believe in the [protestors'] demands. The 'Tahrir dance' we have been doing—going to Tahrir to get the government to take action—has gotten tired, and in order to ensure that they continue taking action on critical matters, it's better to simply stay in Tahrir. But that was only part of the truth: that's why I went there, but what intrigued me and got me moving around, doing things and staying there, was the fascinating social experiment that the sit-in was creating. In essence, Tahrir was very quickly becoming a miniature-size Egypt, with all of its problems, but without a centralized government. And the parallels are uncanny. And that's when it hit me—I was facing a unique opportunity here, one that very few people get; the opportunity to create a new nation, alongside everyone else, from scratch. We were in a space without a centralized government or arbiter, where all the political movements and parties of Egypt had presence, and were free to duke it out or to work together to create the best nation possible. It was

a chance to create the 'Free Republic of Egypt' that I spoke about before. So immediately I went to work promoting and helping to facilitate ideas...bringing in [singers] to do a free concert [at Tahrir], and discovering great talents...thus creating education, art and culture. And naturally everyone loved them, worked on them, cooperated and financed them...and some wrote about them, and it seemed like we were really creating a utopian society, forgetting that there was no utopia. But how very quickly this utopian society turned into a parallel miniature Egypt, with all of its problems, took everyone by surprise, although in hindsight it may all seem very predictable. Paradise was found, and lost, predictably, but the lessons and insights it gave me made the whole thing invaluable.

Sandmonkey goes on to draw the parallels between what has been taking place in Tahrir Square and its resemblance to the overall situation in Egypt. He recalls,

We, at the square started realizing the need for some sort of decision-making body, so attempts to create one started in earnest, by holding meetings at which at least one representative of every tent set up at the square (whether for individuals or movements) met up to figure out what were are going to do....We also have 12 stages in Tahrir now, set up by various groups and parties, which are all loud and trying to drown each other out, all playing the same patriotic music...[complaining about] the abuses of the military and chanting for the rights and the blood of the martyrs. They have varying degrees of eloquence and ignorance, on and on and on, making us sick of hearing about them and wishing for some different music or silence. Naturally, they represent the current state of the media in Egypt. And in order to make the resemblance more eerie, while some of us manage to get on one of those stages every once in a while, the only true media outlet we have is Tahrir Radio, which is an online radio, broadcasting maybe twice a day from there.

Sandmonkey points out other parallels. He adds:

Or how about the fact that we lose electricity in the morning, because the government started shutting down the electricity circuits and then turning them on at night, so we have to go buy generators (i.e. mini power plants), which require gasoline to operate. Every single gas station—all of which are outside our borders—nearby has 'instructions' not to sell it to so we have to get it elsewhere and incur higher costs of transportation, and yet still face power-cuts when a generator runs out of fuel (Egypt's energy issues)? Or that our main focus every day in the sit-in is to get more people from outside of our borders to come to Tahrir and join to make us stronger and having them bring supplies with them, which causes more trash, more street vendors, and more 'crime' and thus making everything uglier (Egyptian tourism and its side-effects)? Or that many of the new tents are now occupying areas of the circle used for sidewalks and many people have closed the entrances next to them and created the equivalent of backyards or terraces that they are imposing on everybody (illegal construction and settlements)? All the while, there are those who are camped next to the Mogamaa [the big government building at the center of the square], and they have the natural fence protecting them and a security guard at every exit. Are you noticing the similarities [with the society at large]?

In summing up his Tahrir Square experience, Sandmonkey notes: "For some people, what I just recounted will be heartbreaking, but to me it's brilliant, because it's a learning experience in governance unlike anything the world has ever seen, and it gives all of those new parties and movements that aim to rule the country a chance to take a much closer look at the issues facing us and figure out the limitations of their solutions and cracks in their organizational structure.... We might never control this country or rule it, but that may not be our role. Our role is to frame the debate and the demands, and push and advocate for them by explaining to people how they relate to them and benefit them directly. We get to frame the debate, and whoever frames the debate in a democracy has a huge effect on it and its future. And in reality, if we are not dictators, that's all that we should aim to achieve, because our people, despite what you may think, are not stupid people, and if you are persistent enough, they get it."

Sandmonkey concludes his interesting post by stating:

But as an ending note, here is some food for thought: If Tahrir is a microcosm of modern-day Egypt with all its issues, and it managed to get there in a week, then being there for the next few days is crucial to understand what might happen in the next few years and how to prevent it. The lessons that we will learn from being there now, about our problems and the proposed solutions to solve them[,] are invaluable for a nation that is seeking a new beginning like ours, not one that we created from scratch like Tahrir was. All of those people with ready[-]made solutions should go and try them out there before proposing them nation-wide. All of those people from outside who know how to best solve our problems should come and help us solve them, because as a nation we will also need this help from Egyptians who live abroad, whether we like it or not. Basically[,] if you are interested in figuring out the problems facing our society and the best ways to solve them, Tahrir is where you should be heading to right now. And you must stay

> with us, and help us in every way you can if you choose that responsibility. We no longer want tourists who want to have fun and give advice from afar; we want people who love this country so much that they are willing to get their hands dirty, even if it means standing at a security checkpoint for two hours a day, and spending the rest with your friends there. Let's go, and try, and fail and learn [collectively] there, because that's better done in Tahrir than in Egypt. It's really simple: If everything is hazy, and you want to know what's going to happen next in the country, Tahrir, right now, is the place to be.

Sandmonkey's insightful post was generally well-received by the posters in this thread, as the following comments clearly show.

Maha wrote: "Let me tell you something. I have been watching you for a while, and I have noticed that you only write motivational posts when things on the ground aren't in favor of the January 25 group."

Amina wrote: "Interesting. I am coming to Tahrir now. Would love to meet you."

Marwa wrote: "A GREAT post as usual, Monkey. A great comparative analysis, view and perspective from inside the training camp."

Francesca wrote: "The only problem for me is that I live in Rome! I already wrote you thanking you yesterday, but now, my THANK YOU is bigger!!! I really hope that this article will be read all around the world. If I can do something, from here, let me know."

Aliaa wrote: "Keep the good work up man!! I have to admit I enjoyed reading your magnificent piece!! You took me to the square life. Let me know if I can be of any help!"

Mark wrote: "Well, you destroyed my utopian vision of Tahrir, but strengthened my understanding. What a keen piece of writing. It is this spirit that will overcome and lead Egypt to its new self. Democracy is hard work and you are doing it; the people are doing it. And not only are you learning, but you are teaching the world how to be a better place. Long live Tahrir!"

Andy wrote: "Thanks for this thoughtful and true-to-life report from the microcosm that is Tahrir Square. Often, I think that we'll never really come to a full answer, but perhaps that answer is really missing the point. To test, to try, to explore, to learn, and to navigate—these are the things that allow us as human beings to function with ourselves and with others. Building and sustaining a society isn't about getting to the answer, but about always moving and looking for new ways to make things work in harmony with one another. Let us not forget that, no matter what country we live in."

James wrote: "Your analyze[sic] is excellent by the way. Coming from an old democracy (Norway), I really never thought about all the things I have taken for granted before I moved to Egypt a year ago."

A German from Berlin wrote: "All you revolutionaries have to keep on pushing and pushing your whole country in the direction you want it to go. That's your job. Most of the time, people are against changing the current state and the current system. But if you keep telling them about your ideas and about the benefits, they will start thinking and moving. You just have to be persistent and you will succeed."

Glen wrote: "I am so in awe of the power of your writing! In this article, you have made Tahrir come alive to your readers, giving those of us who can only sit on the sidelines and marvel a chance to feel the realities of this revolution instead of simply believing the utopian fantasy that is too easy to create. I've posted a link to this on Facebook, and will post it on my blog as well because I believe people should read this, and learn from it. What a unique situation you all are in as you learn, grow, and develop new perspectives about your country and your place within it. Thank you for sharing your insights! I eagerly look forward to learning more as New Egypt emerges."

Esmael wrote: "Your descriptive talents are OUTSTANDING to say the least! I propose starting an official online magazine by the bloggers participating in the sit-in to serve as an alternative media outlet for the public. Up until I read your piece, I was aggressively against the sit-in, but now I am seriously having second thoughts! I salute you!"

Jessica wrote: "I live in the United States, and have been reading your blog since you started it. I am now following you through your tweets and posts. The analysis in this one is not only very important but is also mind blowing. It should be picked up by the media."

Mostapha wrote: "Amazing analysis and constructive criticism. Simple enough for everyone, educated or not, to understand, yet so complex it presents issues that politicians, academics and authorities on governance and social studies will struggle to suggest solutions to."

Reem wrote:

> I suggest it's time to apply all this amazing knowledge outside Tahrir square. It is good that you are talking to the other parties. It may be time to make an election alliance with some of them. In my opinion, you should organize marches and protests at other locations during the day. News interviews and [T]witter articles should be written about some of the leaders of the revolution: who they are, what they

stand for, what are the important parties, who are the election candidates, electoral platforms.

It would be nice to see that revolutionaries are getting more organized (you can use the AIESEC (economic students association) organization structure as a starting point for example (or any other existing organization). It seems from the above that you are doing a lot of things instead of just writing. I suggest you set up a private TV station broadcasting the truth about the revolution. It could be Internet only and the quality of the signal does not have to be good. Freedom of speech and exercising it is an important human right. Try to exercise all other human rights and identify which are the laws or other obstacles in achieving human rights and democracy.

Zaghloul wrote: "This was a fantastic article—so realistic of life in Egypt. I have been there at Tahrir, though not enough and I have not contributed anything. But the hats off to all of you people at Tahrir. Even at this young age of yours, you have become our leaders in so many ways. I salute you sir, and your comrades. Egypt will overcome."

Mariah wrote: "Excellent analysis and a brilliant, vivid imagination making this resemblance between Tahrir and Egypt. It's interesting to think that a few weeks in Tahrir symbolize[s] the future of Egypt, well thought really. I specifically like the lessons learned as they symbolize what's missing in Egypt to make it a modern developed country: respect for law/rules, respectful leader and role model figure, citizen responsibility, and proper advocacy."

Omneya wrote: "Excellent piece Monkey and rest assured a lot of us are for the continuation of the sit-ins. P.S. Kindly admit that anyone who goes to Tahrir, even if just to contribute some supplies, is as patriotic as the campers, but in his/her own way. Not all of us can physically withstand the long sit-ins…and…some of us also believe that by going to work and keeping the wheel turning they are contributing to the prevention of a total economic collapse, so…be kind…remember, we don't want a prejudiced Egypt either!"

Tahrir tourist + Egyptian abroad wrote:

I enjoyed your analysis and yes, I do believe that Tahrir is a perfect place to create a study on democracy-building. It is every Ph.D. student's dream to have such a controlled environment where they can monitor the variables. That being said, I was extremely turned off by your passing and somewhat scathing judgments of the Tahrir 'tourists' as well as Egyptians abroad. As an Egyptian abroad, who spent my entire life abroad and moved to Egypt in recent years, Egyptians abroad have often fought and worked harder than Egyptians [at home] in bringing about change in their home country. Also another quick note on the 'tourists'—at the end of the day revolutionaries are calling for people to come out in masses to the protests, yet at the same time you're disparaging of them. This actually stops people from going. I was someone who was active in the square from January 25 until February 11 and continue to, as much as I could. However, I have a job and an important role in an NGO in Egypt that is working with a coalition of NGOs with expertise to bring about change in various sectors (increase civic participation, women's rights, education, income-generation and employment projects, etc.). Working in the NGO requires traveling and working on the ground in places like Fayoume, Minya, Beni Soueif, Qena, etc. Many of these places didn't have protests, yet these people are Egyptians, who have grievances that are not being addressed and they feel they're being ostracized and not heard. With all due respect, the people who are constantly camping in Tahrir for the most part (and I know there are exceptions) are unemployed people, students (high school, university, post-graduate), freelancers, and people with flexible work schedules. We are not all as privileged to have such flexibility and furthermore we are also working in our own way to rebuild Egypt. So please do not diminish the role of these 'tourists' and Egyptians abroad in the rebuilding of Egypt, otherwise you will alienate yourself from a large community of people, who work behind the scenes to recreate a country that we all love and are proud of.

This long thread and the interesting array of comments it triggered provide more great examples of civic and proactive engagement. The intellectually stimulating and insightful post by Sandmonkey and the equally engaging reactions by the posters, most of whom were either Westerners or Egyptians living abroad, reflect a key civil society function that is "education for democracy" (Diamond, 1999, p. 243). Sandmonkey provided a succinct dissection of the various groups that existed at Tahrir Square, along with a detailed description of the roles that they undertook or that were delegated to them. Then, he went on to critically analyze these roles by comparing the little or micro scene at Tahrir Square to the big or macro scene in the whole country. In fact, he argued that Tahrir Square could serve as a "microcosm"—using his own term—to describe Egypt at large. Sandmonkey argued that all Egyptians needed to come to Tahrir Square to gain some knowledge of this democratic scene, with all its pitfalls, nuances, and intricacies. According to him, this scene was not ideal or utopian, but more a reflection of the realities of the society at large.

The uniqueness of Sandmonkey's post emanated from the fact that it was critical, yet upbeat; realistic, yet motivational. In a way, his message included a call for action, but one that was grounded in the process of learning from the current situation. That is why Sandmonkey received several complimentary notes from his followers. He also succeeded in eliciting some pragmatic suggestions with concrete steps as to what the protestors out at Tahrir Square ought to do. In his message, Sandmonkey also provoked the Egyptians living abroad by accusing them of not contributing much to the Egyptian revolution, maybe to elicit their interest and to make them more involved in the domestic situation in Egypt. He was successful in this context as well since a couple posts came from Egyptians living abroad, one of whom challenged his position and critiqued it.

Addressing this issue of provocation, Sandmonkey told the authors in an interview:

> I play the devil's advocate, and it is always very effective. I am not claiming to be a teacher through my blog, but I am claiming to be the person who will push your buttons and throw arguments against you to get a discussion and a debate under way. On my blog, it is OK and acceptable to engage in clashes; this doesn't bother me as long as I push for provocation which makes people think.... I think that blogging, as a phenomenon, has reduced dogmatism. When I started blogging, some people accused me of being pro-American and even pro-Zionism. And so now, I sarcastically post on my blog that I am a Christian, Zionist, American, imperialist. Are we done? Let's get over that and engage in a debate. My goal is to provoke the visitors to my blog. Provocation is the ultimate means to an effective debate on my blog.

In addition to its exemplification of education for democracy, the thread mentioned above epitomized another civil society function that is the "transition from clientelism to citizenship" (Diamond, 1999, p. 244). Sandmonkey's post was an eye-opener and a wake-up call to many Egyptians who were not involved in the political process to undertake their responsibilities as citizens by joining forces with the protestors at Tahrir Square.

What a country in a stage of political transition, like Egypt, goes through during and after a revolution usually poses many threats and vulnerabilities that require the unification of people from all walks of life and backgrounds. Yet, Sandmonkey's post did not quite reflect a unifying spirit, as it assumed a bias—intentional or not—toward the protestors who were camping out at the square. That assumption on the part of Sandmonkey did not go unnoticed by some posters on this thread, who urged him to give credit to the square visitors who did not set up tents at the square, but whose patriotism is the same as the square campers. Sandmonkey's bias toward the "full time" protestors at the square underlies a bigger issue that had started to surface in postrevolutionary Egypt, which was the perception by some members of the Egyptian public that some protestors spoke and acted as if they "owned" the revolution, and that they monopolized many of the discussion forums about the revolution in both the virtual and the real worlds. In other words, they exhibited a sense of entitlement that made them come across as the official representatives of the revolution, which alienated and marginalized the rest of society.

In this context, Diamond highlighted the importance of pluralism and diversity for a healthy civil society and a functioning civic engagement. He said, "To the extent that an organization...[or a group] seeks to monopolize a functional or political space in society, crowding out all competitors while claiming that it represents the only legitimate path, it contradicts the pluralistic and market-oriented nature of civil society" (Diamond, 1997a, p. 9). Moreover, according to Diamond (1997a),

> No organization that is civil can claim to represent all the interests of its members. Still, within various sectors and issue arenas, there is an obvious tension between strength of combined members and the vitality of diversity....To the extent that advocates of particular interests unify into a single organization or confederation possessing..."strategic capacity" to define and sustain a course of action independent of immediate member preferences, as well as outside pressures[,]...they will be more powerful actors, and...will produce more stable "partial regimes" of interest mediation..., [However], civil society serves democracy best when it is dense in the sheer number of associations. The greater the density of associational life, the more memberships the average citizen is likely to have, and the wider the range of societal interests and activities that will find organizational expression (pp. 23–24).

Furthermore, we have to bear in mind that pluralistic political environments, where all civil society organizations contribute equally to the political process, can lead to more political tolerance "because multiple memberships reflect and reinforce cross-cutting patterns of cleavage that expose citizens to a wider array of interests, backgrounds, and perspectives" (Diamond, 1997a, p. 25). It might not have been Sandmonkey's intention to undermine the value of the support or contributions of members of the society who were not camping out at Tahrir Square permanently, but his post touched a highly sensitive subject that struck a cord with several posters, such as Egyptians living abroad and part-time Tahrir Square visitors, which put them on the defensive, especially in discussing their support for the Egyptian revolution.

"The Centrality of the Brotherhood and the Security Pressures of the Mubarak Regime"

This thread was taken from Abdel Monem Mahmoud's blog and was posted in Arabic on October 28, 2009, a little over a year before the January 25 revolution in Egypt. In his post, Mahmoud included a report prepared by one of the leading figures inside the Muslim Brotherhood—Essam El-Erian—shedding light on the organizational structure and activities of the Brotherhood, as well as the pressures that they had been subjected to under the Mubarak regime. El-Erian is a former member of the Guidance Bureau of the Brotherhood and a former member of parliament. As of this writing, El-Erian holds the position of the Chairman of the Brotherhood-affiliated Freedom and Justice Party, succeeding his predecessor in that position, Mohamed Morsy, who became Egypt's elected president in June 2012. Here again, since the post was too long, we selected sections from it that would provide the gist of what he was trying to communicate.

In his post, Mahmoud wrote:

> This report, written by Dr. El-Erian, is considered one of the most important studies conducted on the Brotherhood by a critical figure from within the group. The following is the report, which was published in Al-Dostour newspaper: There is no doubt about the existence of a political team behind the security and media campaigns that have been launched against the Brotherhood for 17 years. The consequences of these fierce campaigns, some of which were unexpected, can be summarized as follows: 1) The Brotherhood influence has grown over the years in a way that allowed them to win 20 percent of the Egyptian parliamentary seats in a semi-free election in 2005; 2) The voice of a more extreme 'Salafi' form of Islam has been on the rise, confronting the more moderate Brotherhood voice, and this has led to several socio-religious tensions regarding the women's[sic] face cover (niqab) and the men's[sic] beard. These issues have distracted attention from more serious issues, such as reform, freedoms, justice, fair elections and the transition of power; 3) The presence of the state police has been felt in all facets of life in Egypt, including political,

> social, economic, scientific and educational aspects, turning Egypt into a 'police state.'

Mahmoud adds in his post that El-Erian's report highlighted many hardships and challenges that the Muslim Brotherhood faced over time, yet it continued to survive and thrive thanks to its members' patience, sacrifice, and persistence, and also because "the Brotherhood's experience in dealing with political crises in the past, particularly under the rul[e] of the late Egyptian President Gamal Abdel-Nasser, has helped the group in its dealings with political tensions and pressures under Mubarak. The Brotherhood has always believed in the following principles: 1) The futility of violence, particularly as a tool for change; 2) The need for continuous work in the open, rather than secrecy and hiding; 3) The need for reaching out to other political groups, even the ones that differ ideologically with the Brotherhood; [and] 4) The importance of communicating with the youth and channeling their efforts in a useful manner."

However, according to Mahmoud, the report acknowledges several defects that characterized the internal organization of the Brotherhood over time, such as

> 1) Dogmatism and conformity and lack of readiness or courage for innovation and creativity; 2) Continuous organizational confusion due to the absences of key figures in the group's leadership, as a result of imprisonment; 3) Partial failure in achieving short-term plans, particularly when it comes to social and educational work; 4) The regime's efforts to dry [up] the financial resources of the Brotherhood by closing down the companies of the group's businessmen and making it hard for them to carry out their business and investment activities; 5) launching an organized media campaign to frame the Brotherhood negatively as the 'banned group' and to instill unjustifiable fear among people against the group—all this while preventing the Brotherhood's members from appearing in all the state and privately owned media to defend themselves or to explain their group's philosophy; 6) Isolating the Brotherhood's leadership and preventing it from forming any coalitions with other political trends or parties in society; [and] 7) Secluding the Brotherhood from the international community and preventing its members from traveling to participate in forums and conferences abroad or appearing on television shows in foreign countries.

Therefore, in an effort to aid the Brotherhood to overcome many of these obstacles and hardships during this critical time in its modern history, Mahmoud wrote that El-Erian's report called on the group to abide by the following suggestions: "1) Reduce the internal organizational bureaucracy and allow for easier streamlining of ideas; 2) [Pay]...more attention to the individual efforts of the group's members; 3) [Train]...individual members of the group on how to raise political awareness in the community; 4) [Encourage]...the young members of the group to get involved in critical thinking, innovativeness and creativity; and 5) [Encourage]...the young, talented cadre of bloggers and social media users from among the group members." This last point was particularly emphasized by Mahmoud, due to its salience and relevance to his own role as a blogger.

The post mentioned above elicited several positive reactions from Mahmoud's followers. For example, Ziad wrote: "I think that this well-written report is worth sharing with all the members of the Brotherhood, particularly the group's senior leadership."

An Egyptian engineer wrote: "I think this is a very reasonable report. I hope the Brotherhood would carefully study it as a group."

Abdel-Rahman wrote: "This report can mark a new era for the Brotherhood, if they decide to study and adopt the suggestions that were included in it."

Ehab wrote: "This report needs to be operationalized as soon as possible, since the current times require new, creative and well-thought ideas."

Unknown wrote: "Abdel Monem: My advice to you is to leave the Brotherhood."

Anwar wrote: "It is puzzling to me why other posters haven't discussed the details of the report."

Attia wrote: "The current Brotherhood generation has not learned any of the group's principles, except blind obedience to the leadership. The group is also not tolerant of former members who decided to leave the group and then wrote about it after they left."

Fahmy wrote: "I am a member in the Brotherhood and I am willing to be the first one to abide by the suggestions included in Dr. El-Erian's report. I am also proud that the group has members who care about its future and work for its success."

Awad wrote: "I am pleading to all the members of the Brotherhood's Guidance Bureau to resign from their current posts and pave the way for new, open elections on the Internet, and we will all respect the outcome of these elections."

The post mentioned above provides an analytical assessment and a glimpse into the Muslim Brotherhood's role and ideology through a report by one of the group's senior members that was presented by Abdel Monem Mahmoud, who is affiliated ideologically, rather than organizationally, with the group, as he likes to describe himself. The post also sheds light on the restrictions on freedom of expression and the many forms of repression that were practiced against the group by the Mubarak regime. It was unfortunate that the posters' comments did not reflect the form of proactive civic engagement that was previously witnessed in analyzing other threads. Despite the fact that there was almost a collective endorsement of the discussed report on the part of the posters, there was no call for action, except for the last poster, who called for holding new elections inside the Brotherhood, an issue that did not directly address any of the points or aspects that were highlighted in the report. El-Erian's report called for action, since it clearly delineated specific steps that ought to be taken by the group's leadership in order to aid reform and positive change. However, none of the posters attempted to seriously address or critique any of these steps.

One interesting and important aspect in El-Erian's report is acknowledging the role of the Brotherhood's bloggers and the need to nurture them within the group. For this to come from a senior Brotherhood member reflects a special interest on the part of the Brotherhood's leadership in the growing role of social media. In this context, Abdel Monem Mahmoud told the authors in a personal interview: "Some of the ideas that we post on our blogs are being discussed in the general Brotherhood forums offline. Also, thanks to the blogs, the youth's voice inside the Brotherhood movement has started to be heard and appreciated.... Having said that, there are still some senior leaders in the movement who oppose dealing with some issues openly online."

Mahmoud also expressed his disagreement with some of the Brotherhood's latest policies. He told the authors in a personal interview in Cairo in July 2011, six months after the January 25 revolution:

> I don't want to associate myself with the Brotherhood group now because the current leadership of the group has tainted the group's reputation. I will continue to be proud of my Islamist roots and my Brotherhood ideologies, but I have serious reservations about the current policies of the group. I believe the current Brotherhood leaders do not represent the true spirit of the group. This was the spirit that the group has been founded upon. After the revolution, the Brotherhood has committed the same sins that used to be committed by the toppled National Democratic Party by getting closer to the military regime,

> and attacking the people who disagree with them. That is why the younger generations of the group, like myself, have decided to stay away from it.

It is this position on the part of Mahmoud that provides some explanation as to why he defected from the Brotherhood organizationally, despite his ideological loyalty to the group's values and principles, as reflected in his blog's name *Ana ikhwan,* or "I am from the Brotherhood." It is worth mentioning that Mahmoud stopped this blog shortly after the 2011 revolution, as will be fully discussed in chapter 6.

This thread demonstrates a relatively different type of online deliberation, which is engaging in the ongoing process of self-reflection, criticism, and evaluation, as a corrective mechanism that allows for adjusting, improving, or reshaping the actions and activities of a certain group, in this case the Muslim Brotherhood, over an extended period of time and under different political leaderships.

What emerges here is an important focus on the "discourse" that is being created, shared, and deliberated in cyberspace. This compels us to look at cyberspace as "a culture in its own right, as well as a cultural artifact. As a cultural artifact, the [I]nternet is constructed by technology, policy, social practices, and its users, among other factors, but also through discourse" (Silver & Garland, 2004, p. 161). According to this perspective, "cyberspace is not only a site for communication and community but also a site of discourse, at once a real and imagined place where a variety of interests stake their claims" (Silver & Garland, 2004, p. 162). What makes this process of deliberation, discourse formation, and staking claims more vibrant, engaging, and rewarding is the nature of the Internet "as a space free of traditional cultural and geographic barriers, thereby erasing racial, ethnic, and gender prejudices" (Silver & Garland, 2004, p. 162).

These processes of using cyberspace effectively to challenge, negotiate, and reformulate various thoughts and ideas signify, according to Steven Jones (1995a), the creation of new forms of community brought about by computer-mediated communication (CMC) and the new social formations he termed "cybersociety" (p. 2). "This notion of community depends on CMC and on the ability to share thoughts and information instantaneously across vast distances" (Jones, 1995a, p. 2).

Here, it could be argued that members of an actual society in the real world, in this case the Muslim Brotherhood, have taken advantage of the deliberative opportunities provided to them by new media technologies and computer-mediated communication to form their own "cybersociety" in the virtual world. This was made possible through certain Internet-based discussion forums and platforms, as exemplified in political blogs.

The above group of threads reflected a clear focus on online deliberation or exercising electronic democracy through opening the platform for dialogue and exchange of ideas between the bloggers and their followers around issues of public concern, whether it is contemplating the positive sides and the valuable gains of the revolution; comparing and contrasting the example of mini-democracy that exemplified itself in Tahrir square to the overall changes and developments that unfolded in the country as a whole; or engaging in some form of self-reflection by members of a certain group, such as the Muslim Brotherhood, in an effort to reevaluate their role and reshape their mission.

The richness, depth, and breadth of the online deliberations that manifested themselves in these threads remind us that in cyberspace "the possibility of new social formations is certainly alluring...The systems of cultural significance and methods of social control...in on-line worlds in some instances parallel ones we are already accustomed to and in some instances do not. In all instances, though, they do form a new matrix of social relations. What impulses those formations are propelled by is an important matter that should not be overlooked" (Jones, 1995b, p. 15).

Moreover, these cyber-based discussions and deliberations also remind us that "computer-mediated communication is, in essence, socially produced space" (Jones, 1995b, p. 17) and that " the space of cyberspace is predicated on knowledge and information, on the common beliefs and practices of a society abstracted from physical space...the important element in cyberspatial social relations is the sharing of information. It is not sharing in the sense of the *transmission* of information that binds communities in cyberspace. It is the ritual sharing of information that pulls it together" (Jones, 1995b, pp. 19–20).

It is this process of "pulling together" through the constant exchange of thoughts, ideas, and discourses in cyberspace, that contributes to the formation of virtual online communities. "Such a formation is reoccurring in the discourse within CMC and without it, in the conversations its participants have on-line and off, and in the media coverage of electronic communication, electronic communities, and virtual reality" (Jones, 1995b, p. 20).

The deliberative potential that was demonstrated through the back-and-forth exchange of ideas and discourses in the previously discussed threads fits neatly with Sen's (2000) argument that political freedoms and civil rights "especially those related to the guaranteeing of open discussion, debate, criticism, and dissent, are central to the processes of generating informed and reflected choices" (p. 38), adding that these political discussions are "crucial to the formation of values and priorities" (p. 153). It is also in line with Crocker's (2009) remark that "democratic deliberation" enables groups to make "collective choices and contributes to individual agency and group empowerment" (p. 87).

In light of this last point, we can safely infer the connection and overlap between the three functions of mobilization, documentation, and deliberation, which clearly manifested themselves in the analyzed threads throughout this chapter. This is especially true since the engagement in vibrant and lively political discussions online, for the purpose of raising public awareness about pressing issues, such as the atrocities and crimes committed by a regime against its own people, by providing supporting evidence and proof, are necessary prerequisites for effective action on the ground.

Concluding Remarks

This chapter focused on how blogs, as a relatively new type of social media, played an effective role in paving the way for the 2011 revolution by raising public awareness about severe governmental violations of human rights and restrictions on various forms of freedom, as well as encouraging effective action and organization during the revolution itself to help rally public support and orchestrate the mass movement against the regime in power, in addition to providing platforms for vibrant debates and lively discussions around these important issues. In doing so, they provided multiple examples of how the process of political blogging can boost civic engagement and enhance citizen journalism.

This phenomenon reminds us that "as increasing numbers of young people seek to master the use of media tools to express themselves, explore their identities, and connect with peers—to be active creators as well as consumers of culture—educators have an opportunity to encourage young media makers to exercise active citizenship" (Rheingold, 2008, p. 97). This is especially important taking into account the heightened level of political activity exhibited by young people today, both online and offline simultaneously. As Rheingold (2008) rightly puts it, "Whatever else might be said of teenage bloggers, dorm-room video producers, or the millions who maintain pages on social network services like MySpace and Facebook, it cannot be said that they are passive media consumers. They seek, adopt, appropriate, and invent ways to participate in cultural production" (p. 97).

Although the threads that were analyzed in this chapter reflected an overarching concern for the issue of violations of human rights and limitations on freedom, the focus or the angle that the different bloggers adopted in tackling the issue at hand and figuring out what to do about it differed, based on whether their main focus was on public mobilization, documentation of governmental violations, or online deliberation and brainstorming.

The first approach that was adopted by political bloggers in some of the threads analyzed in this chapter was public mobilization. This approach encouraged taking some concrete action, such as figuring out the practical steps needed to start one's own blog or to help other bloggers; the best places to target or to avoid at the time of heightened political tensions; or the need to gather in certain locations at a certain time to support an important cause and make a statement about it. These examples show how the phenomenon of cyberactivism can aid the process of mobilization on the ground by helping political activists to organize themselves, escape from danger, coordinate their actions, and ensure that their voices are heard. This "call for action" approach goes beyond engaging the posters intellectually in online discussions to involving them practically in effective action in the real world.

Here, it is important to note that "the key to online civic engagement programs is the content that is offered online. If the goal is to have people become active offline, the public needs to see credible information that spurs them to action" (Mildner & Tate, 2004, p. 206). This is especially significant bearing in mind that "a democracy is based on a public engaged in all parts of government . . . [not] simply voting on Election Day" (Mildner &Tate, 2004, p. 206). Therefore, it could be said that the main purpose of these online mobilization initiatives is to broaden the spectrum of democratic practice by allowing the public to become fully and actively engaged in every aspect of government and politics, not just casting a ballot in an election.

In discussing this phenomenon, however, we should not overestimate the role of new media technologies and their potential to bring about actual change at the expense of the human efforts or agency behind it or the underlying contexts shaping it. This is in line with Peter Shane's (2004) comment that

> the evolution of any technology depends on its interaction with human agency in specific economic, social, political, and cultural circumstances. What [this technology] can accomplish for any particular

> political system will have very much to do with what members of particular communities, individually and collectively, determine to do with such technologies in particular contexts. Economic and cultural factors, public policy, democratic design, and grassroots initiative will all have a role in framing the future of electronic democracy (p. xii).

Along the same line of argumentation, Rheingold (2008) reminds us of the centrality and vitality of the publics' role in determining the success and effectiveness of various blogs by stating that "it isn't 'voice' if nobody seems to be listening. Finding the first publics who can respond to bloggers is as important as introducing people to blogs as vehicles of potential public influence. In the blogosphere, speaking your mind is necessary to be hearable, but doesn't guarantee that you will be heard" (p. 99).

Additionally, it is important to bear in mind that

> participants, like literate citizens, aren't automatically produced by computer ownership: access to the Internet and the capability of publishing a blog by a population is not sufficient to guarantee that blogging will have a significant positive impact on the political public sphere. The way in which that population *uses* the medium will matter.... Knowing how to take a tool into one's hand is no guarantee that anyone will do anything productive, but without such knowledge, productive use is less likely—and hegemonic control becomes more likely by those who do know exactly how to exercise the power of the new media" (Rheingold, 2008, pp. 103–104).

This approach compels us to look at political blogging as a two-way process, where the roles of both the senders and the receivers, or the bloggers and their publics, have to be equally considered, sufficiently acknowledged, and deeply investigated.

Another approach that was adopted by some of the bloggers in some of the analyzed threads in this chapter was the documentation of governmental violations of human rights and restrictions on freedom. This documentation was an attempt to expose the malpractices and atrocities of the ruling regime and its security apparatus and to raise the public's awareness about such crimes and abuses, which included torturing prisoners, plotting and executing the killing of a police general who refused to allow prisoners to escape from jail, and prohibiting a journalist from covering an important event due to his ideological affiliation.

This was accomplished through providing forums for enabling both the bloggers and ordinary citizens who were posting on their blogs to document governmental brutality and violations of human rights and to disseminate these recorded words and images not only to each other, but, most importantly, to the outside world by reaching out to a transnational, global audience. In doing so, they were, in fact, providing forums for the exercise of citizen journalism locally, regionally, and internationally.

A third important aspect of cyberactivism that revealed itself clearly in this chapter was the process of online deliberation, or the exercise of electronic debate and virtual democracy that was made possible through the cross-fertilization of ideas and the intellectual stimulation that took place when the bloggers and their posters exchanged useful ideas and engaged in fruitful discussions related to the issue of violations of human rights and the limitations imposed on different forms of freedom.

The purpose of such online discussions and deliberations was to provide a forum to evaluate the political changes taking place in the country; assess the transition toward democratization and political reform that was happening on the ground; highlight some of the positive gains of the revolution; and come up with an enlightening comparison between the model of activism taking place in Tahrir square and the transitional stage that was prevailing in Egypt as a whole. This shows how cyberactivism can provide a platform for a different form of civic engagement, which exemplifies itself through intellectual engagement, brainstorming, and exchange of ideas.

An important aspect that revealed itself through this process of online deliberation was the attempt at self-reflection and evaluation that was exemplified in the discussion of the changing role of the Muslim Brotherhood over time, its evolving mission, its shifting relationship with different regimes, as well as the challenges and difficulties that faced it. This was an attempt to reach a deeper and more comprehensive analysis of this group's role and, therefore, engage in a self-corrective mechanism that allows it to improve.

This process of online deliberative democracy "involves moving from individual opinion to group choices and plans of action. A threshold condition for deliberation is reciprocity—the back-and-forth in a conversation as people engage with what others have said. Public comment processes are low in reciprocity; deliberative processes—such as policy dialogues, negotiations, or mediations—are generally high in it" (Beierle, 2004, p. 162). There was certainly evidence of this back-and-forth exchange of ideas, or reciprocity, in the threads that exemplified this online deliberative function.

The importance of these online deliberations lies in the fact that "less visible forms of mobilization may occur, particularly of social movements comprising highly motivated people with nonmainstream political concerns[, and]...there may be subtle yet important effects...on political activity. For instance, political discussion online is often more public than in face-to-face settings, which may affect the motives and behavior of those involved" (Muhlberger, 2004, p. 226). This highlights how "the Internet affects one type of political activity—political discussion. Political discussion plays an important role in conveying political information, stimulating political participation, and helping people decide how to vote. Thus, political discussion promotes both political action and political knowledge" (Muhlgerger, 2004, p. 226).

In other words, we can reach the conclusion that even the threads that focused only on political discussions, deliberations, and debates, without direct calls for action on the ground, could be performing an indirect, yet important, role in terms of promoting civic engagement by providing the public with the needed information, necessary knowledge, and suitable platforms for expressing and exchanging views and opinions, which were then translated into effective action on the ground, as witnessed in the Egyptian revolution of January 2011.

This, again, highlights the significant intersection and interconnectedness between the three functions of public mobilization, documentation, and online deliberation, which augmented and complemented each other, as evidenced in the findings of this chapter, in paving the way for the transition to democratization in Egypt by providing platforms for strengthening civic engagement and exercising citizen journalism.

Overall, whether the main aim of the analyzed threads was public mobilization, documentation of governmental brutality and violations, or allowing democratic online deliberation, one important finding that is worth highlighting is that the target audience, which actively posted and participated in many of these threads, was not only a local, Egyptian audience, but also an international or global audience as well. This was clear in the comments by some of the posters from outside Egypt, whether they were Egyptians living abroad or foreigners, many of whom offered insightful comments and useful feedback on the issues under discussion or expressed their desire to take effective action and offer tangible help.

This last point highlights an interesting phenomenon, whereby Egyptian activists were supported by the flow of information coming to them from abroad, while simultaneously influencing international public opinion abroad, through their own coverage of the Egyptian uprising and the information they provided on it. This clearly signals the "indispensible role for the mobilization of communication networks across borders in an attempt to recruit political support and [the] resources required for public will to emerge and gain traction" (Salmon et al., 2010, p. 162).

This shows how political blogs empowered activists to associate and share ideas with others globally, enabling collaboration between activists inside and outside of Egypt, as well as between Egyptian activists and Arabs in the diaspora; democracy activists in other countries; and Internet activists, who assisted them in their struggles. Thus, new media not only energized political activism inside Egypt, they also created a "virtual global public sphere" (el-Nawawy & Khamis, 2009), where acts of political resistance could be proliferated and supported internationally.

It also provides an excellent example of the process of "exogenous mobilization," which takes place, according to Salmon, Fernandez, and Post (2010), when governments "actively suppress a group that is attempting to voice its will and express its grievance. In such a case, communication networks outside the social system mobilize support in a variety of forms" (p. 163). As the case of the Egyptian revolution reveals, "For these types of efforts, communication is particularly important because of the structural disconnect between the group impacted by the change and those groups mobilizing on their behalf" (Salmon et al., 2010, p. 163).

The following chapter, which deals with the notion of blogging against governmental corruption, provides other examples of both the overlaps and divergences between these bloggers, their respective blogs, and their target audiences, in the context of using cyberactivism to boost civic engagement and promote an active civil society.

CHAPTER 5

Blogging on Governmental Corruption

Introduction

Corruption was one of the main pitfalls that characterized the regime of ousted president Hosni Mubarak in Egypt. Nepotism, money laundering, bribery, cronyism, market monopolies, and the marriage between business and politics were defining features of Mubarak's era. It was a common practice for the government to allocate contracts for various economic projects to certain businessmen in return for monetary favors or illegal commissions. "In 2008 the Corruption Perceptions Index produced by Transparency International ranked Egypt at 115 out of 180 states, noting that its overall score had worsened in relation to the previous year.... In the Middle East, Egypt is ranked 13 out of 18 [most corrupted] states" (El-Naggar, 2009, pp. 46–47).

In 2006, a prominent civil society, grassroots movement called "The Egyptian Movement for Change," known as Kifaya (Arabic for "enough") issued a report titled "Corruption in Egypt," which shed light on the mismanagement of the country's resources and the misconduct in both the public and private sectors, as well as in various ministries, such as agriculture, health, antiquities, and finance (El-Naggar, 2009). One of Kifaya's senior members was quoted as saying: "Corruption in Egypt, neglected for years, is like a cancer that has now spread to every part of the body.... It is a way of life" (El-Mahdy & Marfleet, 2009b, p. 157). A political observer at Al-Ahram Center for Strategic Studies—a semi-independent think tank—argued that fighting corruption had been futile "with the result that corruption has become a system of law in Egypt organizing relations between citizens and public officials, and between workers and employers in the private sector" (El-Naggar, 2009, p. 47). Since the salaries of civil servants and police officers were generally low, it had become a common practice among Egyptians to bribe government employees so that they could issue official documents, such as birth certificates, drivers' licenses, and personal identification cards (Gelvin, 2012).

It was the system of "crony capitalism" that topped the corruption list in Egypt during the Mubarak ruling through the "nexus of [National Democratic Party] leadership, cabinet or parliamentary membership, and economic opportunity" (Gelvin, 2012, p. 41). This nexus or corruption allowed businessmen such as Ahmed Ezz to control more than 60 percent of the Egyptian steel industry. Ezz, who was a close friend to Mubarak's younger son, Gamal, was the ruling party's secretary for organizational affairs and chair of the parliamentary planning and budget committee. Through these legislative positions, he made sure to serve his own interests and to legislate bills that were tailored to his own company's needs. "One independent analysis of the Egyptian sector describ[ed] 'a very strong and excessively dominant monopoly power [that of Ezz]...seven times as strong as its next best challenger'" (El-Naggar, 2009, p. 40). Ezz utilized his connections with the ousted president's son to become "the emperor of steel" in Egypt (Gelvin, 2012, p. 41). These high levels of corruption led the protestors who went out to the streets on January 25, 2011, to call for increased social justice and an end to corruption. Ezz, as well as many other corrupt businessmen who turned into politicians, were indicted on corruption charges, cronyism, and embezzlement of public funds. According to estimates by the US Department of State, Mubarak's fortune had reached \$2–3 billion over the course of his 30-year presidency (Gelvin, 2012).

Corruption cases were too many and too widespread for the semi-independent and the private media outlets not to report on them. But it was the bloggers who played the biggest role in uncovering corruption and fraudulent conduct by members of the Mubarak regime. This chapter will analyze a number of threads selected from the five blogs under study that deal with corruption, and it will shed light on the degree to which they reflect effective civic engagement and citizen journalism, as well as serving the functions of a vibrant civil society.

Here again, the analyzed threads will be divided according to the main function they seem to focus on, whether it is mobilizing the public, documenting the regime's corruption, or deliberating and brainstorming on key issues.

First: Threads Urging Public Mobilization

Important Decree

This thread was taken from Nawara Negm's blog and was posted in Arabic on November 21, 2011. Negm proposed a decree—calling for an end to military rule, as exemplified by the Supreme Council of the Armed Forces (SCAF)—to be voted on and adopted by her followers on the blog.

Negm wrote: "We, the protestors at Tahrir Square, announce our opposition to the policy of violence and confrontation that the . . . [SCAF] has adopted in its dealings with the people's demands. We hereby propose the following decree which we hope will be supported by the political activists all around the country: 1) SCAF should leave power to a transitional council composed of judges to ensure the safe and smooth transition of power in the period of time between SCAF's departure from power and the coming of the new president and his cabinet; 2) Parliamentary elections should be held on time, followed by presidential elections; 3) The elected parliament should form a committee to write the new Constitution, which will have to be voted upon in a national referendum under the supervision of the newly elected president; [and] 4) Ending all military trials for civilians."

Negm's suggestion elicited several enthusiastic posts. Mahfouz wrote: "I wholeheartedly agree with you Nawara."

Sakr wrote: "I believe that it would be ideal if the head of the Supreme Constitutional Court runs the country, while calling to hold the presidential elections during the next 60 days. This goes along with the articles in the 1971 constitution, which were amended in a national referendum."

Taymour wrote: "This is the first decree that I agree on."

Zaid wrote: "I would add to your suggestions the firing of the current cabinet, which hasn't achieved much on the ground, and which was totally controlled by SCAF."

Hady wrote: "Please do not suggest that the chairman of the Supreme Constitutional Court acts as an interim president, and rule out any judge for that kind of position. You have to select someone who has a well-known political record."

Gameel wrote: "I suggest that we select the elected heads of all the professional syndicates to form a presidential council. This group would be the only one that has actually been elected by the people."

Naglaa responded: "I wouldn't trust the judges to be part of the presidential council or to be involved in anything that has to do with this interim period. Those judges have let us down on several occasions and have proven their corruption and their collaboration with the ousted regime."

Ashraf wrote: "The chairman of the Supreme Constitutional Court and the Supreme Judicial Council as a whole may be a front for SCAF. We all know by now that the judicial institution in Egypt had been corrupted by the Mubarak regime."

Sameh wrote: "If we have an elected parliament, it will be able to take over power from the unelected SCAF. Elections are the true solution to get us out of our current deadlock."

Mustapha wrote: "The true solution is that SCAF should promise to hand over power once we have a truly elected parliament that enjoys all the rights guaranteed to it under the constitution."

Khadija wrote: "I thought that you voted 'yes' in the latest referendum over the constitutional amendments. And today, here are the consequences of voting 'yes' over these amendments: The new Constitution will be written after a new president is elected, and this means that it will be tailored to fit the new president's wishes. The parliament will select the 100 members who will serve on the constitution committee, and so if the Muslim Brotherhood takes over in the parliamentary elections, they will monopolize the process of writing the constitution. The newly elected parliament will control the process of appointing a new cabinet, and in case the Muslim Brotherhood wins the parliamentary majority, they will run the country and form the government."

The thread mentioned above was a good example of encouraging civic engagement in Egypt's postrevolutionary phase. In her post, Negm proposed a decree to get the country out of its ongoing political and legal crisis since the ousting of Mubarak. In a way, Negm's suggestion coincided with two of Diamond's civil society functions, which are "developing techniques for conflict mediating and resolution," and "strengthen[ing] the social foundations of democracy" (Diamond, 1999, p. 248). Negm, who got the visitors to her blog involved in the democratic process by seeking their support for her proposed decree, tried to "build social capital by bringing citizens together to cooperate as peers for their common advancement" (Diamond, 1999, p. 249). Negm's initiative paved the way for citizen participation and self-governance, and that always has a positive impact on democracy (Booth & Richard, 1998, p. 780).

Negm's initiative was posted during a time of political transition in Egypt, which is the time frame that separates one regime from another. During that time, the role of political institutions is expected to grow. As Bratton (1994) states:

> From this moment onward, and especially following the announcement of competitive elections, the initiative in the democratization shifts back from civil society into a reconstituted political society.... [It is during that transitional time that] the institutions of civil society have a crucial role to play in the consolidation of democracy. At the deepest levels of political culture, civic institutions include the political norms and values that underpin the rules of democratic competition. (pp. 10–11)

Shedding more light on this thought and assessing the role of blogs in enhancing democracy, Dina Shehata, an analyst at Al-Ahram Center for Strategic Studies, argued that blogging cannot replace institutional democracy. Shehata told the authors in a personal interview in 2009: "Democracy is strongly associated with institutions: parties, elections, and the parliament. Blogs have expanded the platform of voices in the public debate in Egypt, but they cannot make up for the absence of democratic institutions. We don't have participatory democracy in Egypt, and blogging is a tool rather than an end for democracy."

A strong sense of collective engagement was reflected in the messages posted by most participants in this thread, who felt the urgency of the issue at hand and the need and value of their contributions to the ongoing discussion. Their high level of engagement and the concrete solutions that some of them proposed were a testament to the effectiveness of Negm's post in "mobilizing and conveying citizens' interests to government, constraining government behavior by stimulating citizen activism, and inculcating democratic values" (Booth & Richard, 1998, p. 780).

The action-oriented nature of this thread, as exemplified in proposing a decree for posters to vote on, is a good example of "cause-oriented engagements [that] provide [a] connection to a community of other interested persons and [it shows] that petition writing and signing can be a forum for learning how to express oneself in a collective context" (Earl & Schussman, 2008, p. 88). Here, it is particularly important to investigate

> how it is that participants come to take part in online petitions, or online protests more generally.... [B]eing asked to participate, for example, is a factor that seems important to offline political and protest

> engagement, and it is also likely to fit an online model of forwarded e-mail, blog entries soliciting comments, and petitions that encourage signers to add their e-mail address to the list.... One likely possibility is that people are often more likely to participate in protests, or politics more generally, when they think that their efforts may "matter". There are numerous anecdotes... of even small online petitions (a few hundred signers or less) resulting in changes. (Earl & Schussman, 2008, p. 89)

This last point draws our attention, as Earl and Shussman (2008) rightly point out, to the fact that "a personal sense of efficacy may be an important factor that prompts young people to engage in collective action. That sense of efficacy may be something young people are gaining from their cultural contestation that they do not get from interactions with government," and "if this efficacy is a motivator for participation, then online petitioning will translate into broader political engagement only where youth feel like their voices will matter remains to be seen whether... efficacy in cultural contestation will translate into... activity in the future" (p. 89).

Indeed, there is enough evidence in this thread to support this argument regarding the significance of efficacy as a key motivator for participation, taking into account the salience of the discussed issues in this thread, the decentralization, egalitarianism, and spontaneous nature of the exchanged discourse, and, most importantly, the autonomy that the posters exhibited in putting forward their ideas, voicing their criticisms, challenging other people's opinions, and proposing effective actions and concrete plans. This draws our attention to the fact that "young people are learning these things while they work on issues they care about—as opposed to issues that adults believe they should care about—and using tools that they appropriated—as opposed to tools that were assigned to them. The authenticity of these actions, then, might also be independently important to the experience of young people involved in cultural contestation" (Earl & Schussman, 2008, p. 88).

Another important point worth highlighting is the fact that Negm was practicing street activism in the real world and was camping out with the protestors at Tahrir Square that might have increased the degree of "social trust" between her and the visitors on her blog in a way that "facilitat[ed] coordination and cooperation for mutual benefit" (Booth & Richard, 1998, p. 780).

This is especially significant since trust is a key component for the success of social capital and civic engagement. As Lehning (1998) points out:

> Generally speaking, the more we connect with other people, the more we trust them, and vice versa. People who join are people who trust. In civic communities, individuals become citizens who will act with and trust others, even when they do not know them personally. Participation in voluntary associations creates social capital in the form of dense networks of civic engagement that foster sturdy norms of generalized reciprocity and encourage the emergence of social trust. (p. 237)

This raises the issue of whether bloggers like Negm—who have gained the public's trust, thanks to their offline activism—also have the ability to mobilize the Egyptian public. Addressing the issue of the bloggers' limitations when it comes to inspiring street mobilization, Negm told the authors in a personal interview in Cairo in 2009:

> I think that change has to come from the streets, not from the bloggers. And until now, I don't think that bloggers have been capable of moving the streets. And I don't think that it is the right thing for bloggers to mobilize the streets. I have great respect for the Egyptian people, and I believe that they are cautious and wise. Not all bloggers are sincere or honest. Even the bloggers who are sincere and honest may not be leaders. They need someone to lead them. So, in short it is not the bloggers' job to mobilize the streets. The Egyptian people are able to get their rights. We, bloggers, have a certain cause, and we express ourselves on our blogs. We are not mobilizing people, but we are sharing and rendering their voices to the world. People are independent and they will decide when and how to take action.

Ironically enough, Negm's blog has been one of the most highly inspirational blogs when it comes to encouraging people to take effective action on the ground and to "do" something—whether it is protesting, gathering in a certain location, endorsing a certain cause, raising awareness about the blocking of certain Internet websites, signing a petition, or voting on a decree, as witnessed in this thread—and yet she is fully aware of some of the limitations of the bloggers' role as instigators of public mobilization. Her statement mentioned above highlights the fact that she sees the bloggers' role as, at best, complementary or supplementary to real-world organization, activism, and leadership, rather than being a substitute or a replacement for it.

Another blogger and political activist, Ramy Raoof, echoed Negm's argument, saying, "Online platforms cannot initiate change, but they can increase people's awareness and draw their attention to particular issues. It is our hope that people themselves can take action and initiate change based on their awareness."

Ayman Nour, a prominent Egyptian political activist and founder of Al-Ghad political party, tended to agree with Negm and Raoof with regard to the blogs' role. Nour, who ran for presidency in the 2005 elections against ousted president Mubarak, told the authors in a personal interview in Cairo in 2010:

> The Internet is a virtual medium that has virtual audience. You can post an invitation for a demonstration where 100,000 people accept this invitation online, but then actually 100 people show up. So, you cannot build all your expectations through the Internet, but you can expect that social media can affect people's awareness and ability to mobilize and act. I think that blogs and social media can help rejuvenate and revitalize the Egyptian spirit, but they cannot be utilized as tools for actual change. They can create the awareness that can eventually lead to change. The Internet can create an environment that is conducive for change. It is a catalyst for change.

The above discussion regarding the limitations of digital media in fostering democratization and bringing about actual political change has been echoed by a number of writers on this topic. For example, Montgomery (2008) acknowledges that there is "abundant evidence of the ways in which many youth are seizing the new digital tools to participate more fully in democracy. The hundreds of civic Web sites created in the last decade are helping to provide young people with some of the essential skills for civic and political engagement. Interactive media make it much easier for them to learn about critical issues of the day, insert their own voices into the public discourse, and actively participate in a wide range of political causes" (p. 41). Yet, she equally acknowledges some of the limitations of the democratizing potential of digital media, stating that

> despite the numerous examples of young people's empowerment through digital media, serious questions remain about whether such forms of participation can be extended to a broader segment of the youth population, and sustained beyond the occasional bursts of activity surrounding extraordinary events, such as high-stakes national elections. There are also opposing tendencies in the new media that could serve both to enhance and to undermine its democratic potential in the lives of young people. For example, the capacity for collective action, community building, and mobilization are unprecedented. But the move toward increasingly personalized media and one-to-one marketing may encourage self-obsession, instant gratification, and impulsive behaviors. (Montgomery, 2008, p. 42)

Therefore, she concludes that "whether the Internet ultimately becomes a force for civic and political renewal among youth remains to be seen" (Montgomery, 2008, p. 42).

Likewise, Rheingold (2004) voiced his own concerns, indicating that "we definitely need to be skeptical of claims that online discourse can effectively substitute for or revitalize the public sphere that was enclosed and fragmented by mass-media technology and public relations techniques. Every symbolic communication medium distances people in some ways while it connects them in others" (p. 264). In explaining this last point, he states that "in many cases, the availability of online social interaction can exacerbate the isolation and dehumanization of people who live in the modern world" (Rheingold, 2004, p. 264).

Furthermore, he adds that "the most important critiques of virtual communities are those that attack the validity of claims that many-to-many communication media have the potential for being used as a democratizing tool in the political sphere. Now that every desktop is potentially a printing press, a broadcasting station, and a place of assembly, has an important decentralization of the power to inform, witness, influence, and persuade taken place?" (Rheingold, 2004, p. 264).

In attempting to find an answer to this last question, Rheingold (2004) comments on the role of digital media, indicating that "like all technologies, this medium has its shadow side, and there are ways to abuse it. Like all communication media, virtual communities enable people to misunderstand each other in new ways" (pp. 265–266).

Additionally, he also poses the question, "Can virtual communities help revitalize civil society, or are online debates nothing more than distracting simulations of authentic discourse?" (Rheingold, 2004, p. 274). In trying to answer this question, he contends that some young digital activists may have discovered that "talking to each other online seems to be at least marginally better than sitting stupefied in front of the tube, but we need to know how far, exactly, all that talk can carry us. Will worldwide Usenet discussions, up-to-the-minute legislative news listservs, World Wide Web pages, and e-mail chain-letter petitions add to civic life, or remove people from it?" (Rheingold, 2004, p. 275).

In summing up this discussion, he reaches the conclusion that

> electronic communications do not offer a utopia, but they do offer a unique channel for publishing and communicating, and the power to publish and communicate is fundamental to democracy. Communication media are necessary but not sufficient for self-governance and healthy societies. The important stuff still requires turning off the computer

> and braving the uncertainties of the offline world. When we are called to action through the virtual community, we need to keep in mind how much depends on whether we simply "feel involved" or whether we take the steps to actually participate in the lives of our neighbors, and in the civic life of our communities. (Rheingold, 2004, p. 276)

The case of the Egyptian revolution certainly proved this argument to be correct. If it was not for the willingness of Egyptian activists to become truly involved in confronting the many challenges facing their community, paying a big price for freedom, and even risking their own lives and facing the possibility of torture, injury, or imprisonment, nothing would have changed. In other words, it is the unique combination of online activism in the virtual world with offline activism in the real world that paved the way for actual political change.

"Why Are Those People Arrested and the Famous Three Are Not?"

This thread was also taken from Nawara Negm's blog and was posted in Arabic on March 25, 2011, two months after the revolution. In her post, Negm questioned the arrest on terrorism charges of some Egyptians returning from Afghanistan, Bosnia, and so on, in contrast to Mubarak, his family, and the "famous three" (Fathi Sorour, Zakaria Azmy, and Safwat El-Sherif)—all strong men in the Mubarak regime—who were not arrested, even though they were implicated in many crimes dating from the regime's time in power and the revolution. Negm also criticized the virginity testing that female Egyptian protesters were subjected to by the Egyptian army, and which was seen by her, as well as by the posters, as shameful, disgusting, and inappropriate.

Negm wrote:

> Several Egyptians who came back from countries such as Afghanistan, Bosnia and Albania were arrested and imprisoned on false charges having to do with terrorism. In fact, they were encouraged by the state media to travel to these countries and get involved in jihad, but when they finished and returned, they found themselves in big trouble. What about the crimes committed by Mubarak, his wife, his two sons and his strong men: Fathi Sorour, the former Egyptian parliament speaker; Zakaria Azmy, the former chief of presidential staff; and Safwat El-Sherif, the former secretary general of the now dissolved National Democratic Party? The office of the General Prosecutor announced that it has some preliminary evidence showing that all three men were

> involved in killing the protestors at Tahrir Square. If there was any act of terrorism before the revolution, it was committed by Mubarak, his son Gamal and the state police. But instead of arresting Mubarak and his people, I was appalled to see the Egyptian military, which is known for its ethical conduct, carry out virginity tests on some of our female protestors. This is not the appropriate way to deal with the protestors, who are risking their lives for a noble cause. You should have known that our female protestors are well behaved, and I know that the results of the virginity tests have proven what I just mentioned.
>
> To the military, I say if you are bothered by the continuation of the street protests, arrest Mubarak and his corrupt men, particularly the three whose names I mentioned before and put them on trial. They have to pay the price for the horrible acts that they committed against this nation and its people.

Most of the posters on this thread agreed with Negm's perspective, and some called for specific actions to get out of the political stalemate situation that the country suffered from after the revolution.

Shokry wrote: "Who is responsible for delaying the arrests and trials of Mubarak and his corrupt collaborators? Who is standing in the way of achieving the revolution's goals?"

Nazly wrote: "I agree with you Nawara. But what exactly do we need to do at this point to make sure that we put an end to this mess?"

Hakeem wrote: "Nawara: I think you hit the jackpot with your words, and I believe that protesting is the only way to achieve the revolution's goals. Let me know if there is anything that I can do from Canada, where I currently live."

Montasser wrote: "Nawara: I would like to create a Facebook page to invite people to vote for you as our next vice president or minister of foreign affairs."

Magda wrote: "I agree with everything you mentioned Nawara, and I propose that we do our best to disseminate your words through social media so that they can be read by as many people as possible. I also suggest that we organize campaigns to enhance the political awareness among the inhabitants of the countryside so that they don't become easy prey to the false publicity by the remnants of the Mubarak regime."

Gouda wrote: "All the political movements need to unite and sign a petition to arrest the three corrupt men whose names you mentioned in your post. They represent a great danger to everything that the revolution has called for."

Nassef wrote: "Dear all: Kindly circulate that there is need for signing a petition including these fair demands, written by an honorable lawyer working at a human rights center. We have to get rid of our fears, and stand for our beliefs, even by such a small contribution as signing this document. It is a civilized way of speaking out loud against corruption. We should set an example."

Shahin wrote: "Nawara: What you have been calling for in terms of putting the pillars of the ousted regime up for trial on treason charges makes perfect sense, and should be easy to understand for anyone with even half a brain. The military council's failure to go along with it is inexplicable, in light of its supposedly patriotic position (according to your hypothesis). A patriotic council shouldn't need to see a million signatures, or a million-man march to do the right thing. If it does, then we should reach one of three conclusions: either it's stupid (which it's not), or indifferent (meaning it doesn't care about the country, which is also inconceivable), or it serves other agendas (refer to my earlier posts)."

Omneya wrote: "Nawara: Good job. We are supporting you 100 percent and getting people's signatures and spreading the link that includes the petition to arrest those people. But that is not enough. We need to increase our numbers on the streets to make them realize that we are serious about our demands."

In the thread mentioned above, Negm's post, which called for the arrest of Mubarak and his corrupt entourage, was successful in getting many of her followers engaged and enticing them to post action-oriented messages. Negm also presented the latest, most up-to-date information as to what was taking place on the political scene so that her followers could act accordingly. In this context, Mahmoud Salem (aka Sandmonkey) told the authors in a personal interview from Tahrir Square where he was protesting in July 2011: "Before the revolution, the average Egyptians were not discussing or they did not know what they know today, and so our role as bloggers was to make them aware of what was going on. But after the revolution, people are discussing different kinds of political issues freely, and so our role as bloggers today is to inform people about the inside information regarding the revolution itself and the post-revolution developments that are not dealt with or covered by the mainstream media."

Through encouraging people to call for the arrest of Mubarak's corrupt men, Negm's post also contributed to "stimulating political participation" (Diamond, 1999, p. 241) through "mobiliz[ing]...new information and understanding" (Diamond, 1999, p. 247). Moreover, through her call for eradicating corruption and her criticism of the inexplicable virginity tests that were conducted on female protestors, Negm contributed to the mounting pressure on the rulers of postrevolutionary Egypt—namely, the SCAF—to engage in "accountable governance." Negm's post was an attempt to hold the SCAF "accountable to the ostensibly sovereign citizenry" (Fox, 2000, p. 3).

It is especially worth noting that the call for action in this particular thread did not just come from the blogger herself, but, most importantly, it also came from the posters, many of whom called for different action plans and posted a number of action-oriented messages. This "bottom-up," grassroots approach in civic engagement and public mobilization offers a clear indication that "political engagement and culture are subject to change as digital technology proliferates" and that "there are reasons to believe that [these] kinds of [online] engagements . . . could in fact lead to more standard forms of political and civic engagement later" (Earl & Schussman, 2008, p. 88).

Here, it is worth highlighting two criteria for activities "that are more likely to turn Internet use into online [and offline] political engagement: (1) whether the activity involves connection to others and (2) whether young people learn to express themselves" (Earl & Schussman, 2008, p. 88). In light of these two points, it is safe to conclude that this thread met the required criteria for turning the experience of Internet use into an effective process of online political engagement that could be conducive to practical forms of offline political engagement in the real world at a later stage.

The level of mobilization and activism witnessed in this thread provide clear evidence that "online communications can strengthen civil society" (Rheingold, 2004, p. 275), bearing in mind that civil society is "a web of informal relationships that exist independently of government institutions or business organizations, [and] is the social adhesive necessary to bind divergent communities of interest together into democratic societies" and that "around the world advocacy and action networks, community groups, and voluntary organizations are reemerging as a social force. Interestingly, many are beginning to utilize the Internet and other communication technologies to make their voices heard" (Rheingold, 2004, p. 274).

Both of the above threads bear witness to the "rights of citizens to communicate online" and to the fact that in exercising this right, "net activists are broadcasting action alerts, directing citizens' attention to the implications of proposed legislation, and furnishing contact information for key legislators on crucial votes" (Rheingold, 2004, p. 275), in addition to calling for supporting decrees and signing petitions online.

These threads lead us to believe "in the democratizing power of virtual communities" and the fact that "online social networks constitute an important technology-enabled practice that has the potential to shape society. As a means of critical inquiry into how this technology affects our lives[,]...it is more important to examine the nature of collective action in cyberspace....The point is to understand how many-to-many media enable people to act together to create public goods" (Rheingold, 2004, p. 276).

Overall, it can be concluded from these threads that "electronic space remains a crucial force for new forms of civic participation, especially in its public access portion" and that "civil society, whether in the form of individuals or nongovernmental organizations (NGOs), is an energetic presence in electronic space...the [I]nternet has emerged as a powerful medium for nonelites to communicate, support each other's struggles, and create the equivalent of insider groups on scales ranging from the local to the global" (Sassen, 2004, pp. 297–298).

In this context, it could be understood why the Internet "is perceived as a contributor to democracy and equality even though it is not accessible to nearly as many users as are other mass media" (Nakamura, 2004, p. 72). This is mainly because "the internet does still retain at least the potential for interactivity that television lacks. Because 'the people' are able to add content to the internet, this would seem to qualify it as a form that is popular...and thus as a possible site of resistance to the majority culture and the mass media that support and promulgate it" (Nakamura, 2004, p. 73).

It could be said that these elements of popular interactivity and resistance to those in power were clearly evident in the previous threads that called for effective action on the ground to combat governmental corruption and mobilize people against it.

Second: Threads Documenting Governmental Corruption

"Mubarak's Gold in the U.K."

This thread was taken from Wael Abbas' blog and was posted in Arabic on February 2, 2011, during the revolution. In the thread, Abbas posted English documents that "supposedly" exposed ousted president Mubarak's smuggled money and stolen fortune that were hidden in UK banks and elsewhere. Wael wrote: "I have received these documents from an unknown person, and I haven't had the opportunity to independently verify their authenticity. Some of these bank documents include information about Mubarak's fortune of pure gold. I hope that those working for British banks can help us authenticate these documents."

One of the documents—a safekeeping receipt allegedly issued by the Caledonian Banking Group on December 17, 2009—read as follows: "We, the undersigned, being duly authorized officers of the Caledonian Bank hereby confirm with full bank responsibility that we are holding in safekeeping under the above safekeeping number the following bond security with a nominal face value of USD 620,000,000,000."

The reactions from posters were diverse: Some of them asked Abbas to remove these "forged" documents in order to restore his blog's credibility, while others suggested concrete steps to return the money to Egypt and to put Mubarak, his family, and his top officials on trial. Smith wrote: "That's 620 BILLION US dollars, which is over three and a half trillion Egyptian pounds. That's roughly 1/6th of the U.S. Federal budget and about 16 months of Egypt's GDP. If frozen and returned to Egypt, it would be $7,500 for every man, woman and child in the country. It's also nine times any other figure I've seen mentioned for Mubarak. It might be real, but I have to be a little skeptical."

Atef wrote: "Stop disseminating these rumors. I don't think that the posted documents are authentic."

Afaf wrote: "Whether or not these documents are authentic, Mubarak has committed so many horrible crimes in this country, and he needs to be punished for his deeds which the whole world was witness to."

Emad wrote: "We are not the jury, judge or court to prosecute; hence we do not need verified documents. The truth is known and clear and whether it is 50 billion or infinity, it does not change the fact that the Egyptian gas was sold to Israel at a quarter of its market price (at a loss) while Israel has natural gas reserves. The Egyptian debt rose from 20 billion to 300 billion dollars!! Fifty percent of Egyptians live on a few dollars a month!! This, I believe, is the real chaos, not the peaceful demos."

Fayed wrote: "These are unfortunately just bad fakes done by someone who doesn't speak English properly. 'Caledonian Banking Group' is not a bank (I did an Internet search—Caledonian Bank was founded in 1832 and closed in 1907). And for the other posted documents, it should be 'Treasury Bond' not 'Treasure Bond,' 'Barclays Bank' not 'Bank of Barclays.' So, there are many incorrect things. And imagine if you had 620 billion dollars, would you deposit it all in one place, on one piece of paper? You should take these documents down, really."

Magdy wrote: "I have been living outside Egypt for 15 years since I couldn't find a job in my home country. I have spent most of my youth away from my country so that Mubarak and his family could enjoy the billions of dollars that they collected from the people. They sucked the blood out of this country, while many Egyptians were feeding on garbage and living under the poverty line."

Fareed wrote: "The richest guy on the planet has only $53.5 billion and you're suggesting that Mubarak is about 12 times richer?"

Kevin wrote: "I totally support the demands of the people at Tahrir Square and hope that Hosni Mubarak soon leaves office but this kind of misinformation can be deeply damaging to international opinion as it discredits the protestors. For the good of the uprising, I think you should take this material down and replace it with a note that you have now discovered they are not authentic."

Armando wrote: "Even if these documents are fake, it all makes sense, even if the real investments are in hotels, luxury resorts, yachts, etc. You name it. We know of the London palace Mubarak's younger son owns. If there is more, good for them. No envy on my end! But I would not want to be in his skin walking around in his city!"

A.M. wrote: "Mr Abbas: Even without any knowledge of U.K. banks, any native speaker of English can tell you the second and third documents posted are not authentic. The text is full of very strange mistakes that no competent English speaker would make. The language of the first and fourth documents appears to be correct, but if they are all from the same source, then their authenticity is also in question. And then the sum of money mentioned (US$ 620 billion??) is logically implausible. I suggest you take them down in order to protect the credibility of your site."

Gaby wrote: "Dear Wael: I am not sure if you read the comments, but the numbers showing in these documents are ridiculous. There is no such thing as 620 billion dollars that Mubarak would have been able to collect. If they sold Egypt as land, they would not have been able to collect such a number. My guess is these documents are forged."

Jamie wrote: "One of two things is going on here—and either one is very interesting: 1) Either these documents are legitimate and someone exposed themselves to massive personal risk by forwarding these documents to you; or 2) Someone went to a great deal of trouble to create forgeries for the purpose of discrediting you. Either way, they are important, and I hope you won't take them down. Full disclosure: I've been in touch with Wael since he posted these documents via Twitter, and I created a piece with a slideshow for Huffington Post (for which I am a blogger) and submitted it. That was days ago and NO ONE from the site has returned my emails or my phone calls about the piece. Not even to say that they think they're fake and not going to publish it—all of which is strange and a development I don't quite understand."

The thread mentioned above is a good example of citizen journalism where Abbas posted several bank documents that included certain figures about the alleged Mubarak fortune. Abbas did not try to influence the opinions of the posters on this thread one way or the other with regard to these documents. Moreover, he made sure to mention that there was no way for him to verify the authenticity of these documents, but made an open invitation to bankers to share their opinions about these documents' validity. So, in a sense, Abbas included the posters to this thread in the decision-making process (Haas, 2007).

Encouraging popular participation in the process of monitoring the government's abuses, as was the case in this thread, is an exemplification of "accountable governance," which refers to "power relations between the state and its citizens" (Fox, 2000, p. 1). More specifically, this is an example of "vertical accountability" through which civil society is organized to "drive the creation of certain institutional checks and balances . . . [in a way] that limits the use and sanctions the abuse of political power. Public exposure [of government abuses] is necessary but not sufficient to limit or sanction the abuse of power. Actors and institutions that promote accountability attempt to bind the exercise of power to specific benchmark standards. Political accountability can be promoted through both state and non-state institutions" (Fox, 2000, pp. 1–2).

Abbas, in the thread mentioned above, did, although in an indirect way, "play a role in checking, monitoring and restraining the exercise of power by the state and holding it accountable. This function can reduce political corruption, which is pervasive in emerging democracies [like post-revolutionary Egypt]. It can force the government to be more accountable, transparent, and responsive to the public, which strengthens its legitimacy" (Bunbongkarn, 2004, p. 141).

Addressing the issue of political accountability in postrevolutionary Egypt, Esraa Abdel Fattah, a prominent Egyptian political activist, told the authors in a personal interview in February 2011: "The best thing that came out of the January 25 revolution in Egypt is that we are starting to have a system of checks and balances that will hold everyone in power accountable for their actions. This will serve as a way to make future governments more afraid to get involved in corruption because they know that they will be held accountable for it."

According to Haas (2007), citizen journalists "should hold citizens themselves accountable for the outcomes of their deliberations. Thus, if the interventions endorsed by citizens fail to advance the overarching goal of reducing…[or ending corruption], journalists should see it as their right—indeed their responsibility to publicly say so, including by advocating their own alternative interventions and lobbying relevant government officials to enact those interventions in practice" (p. 45). In the thread mentioned above, Abbas, who is not a traditional journalist and does not work in mainstream media, shared some documents that allegedly showed the corruption of Mubarak and his family, but he did not propose a solution, a course of action, or a method of intervention to tackle the issue at hand. In other words, he focused on the function of documentation alone, but did not delve into the realm of mobilization or boosting civic engagement.

"Habib El Adly Is Imprisoned in the Same Cell Where He Imprisoned Us"

This thread was taken from the blog of Abdel Monem Mahmoud and was posted in Arabic on February 18, 2011, a week after President Mubarak was forced to step down. Mahmoud's post discussed the imprisonment of El Adly, the minister of interior during the Mubarak regime, who was known for his corruption and political abuses. Mahmoud reflected back on the horrors committed by El Adly and other members of the Mubarak regime.

Mahmoud wrote:

> I learned from my sources at a late hour last night that former Interior Minister, Habib El Adly has arrived in the Tora prison, where he has been placed in cell number 2. El Adly's imprisonment is for charges of alleged involvement in money laundry and corruption. Never in my life have I imagined that I would report on the imprisonment of an interior minister in the same cell where me and my colleagues were locked up in 2003 and 2006 for our political activism as members of the Muslim Brotherhood. I have never imagined that I would report on the imprisonment of the man who was the reason for my late father's death as a result of his sadness over my imprisonment. The fact that my late father went through a coma for almost a month did not play any

> role in making El Adly and his men release me for human purposes. My father's coma was not enough for justifying my release on bail to be able to take care of him or to be close to him before his death. I am not rejoicing at the misfortune of El Adly or gloating over his possible grief, but I hold the ousted President Mubarak and his loyal man El Adly responsible for the death of my father.

Mahmoud's message had four comments that were sympathetic to him.

Anonymous wrote: "This is God's will Abdel Monem. Don't be surprised by the turn of events. The toppling of the Mubarak regime has brought shame and disgrace to many of his men for the outrageous injustices that they have committed."

Fisherman: "I am from Alexandria and a good friend of your younger brother. I did witness most of the events that you have mentioned in your post, and all I can say is that human deeds never go unnoticed by God. The suppressed people always redeem their rights. We have really suffered enough from the acts of corrupt people like El Adly. May your father's soul rest in peace, along with the souls of all the Muslim martyrs. I hope to see Egypt the best country in the world."

Hassan wrote: "I hope God breaks all the other suppressors who have committed acts of aggression against the Egyptian people. You, Abdel Monem, are one of the people who did suffer a lot during the Mubarak regime, and I hope to see the revolution achieve all its noble goals so that people like you feel dignified and victorious."

Tamer wrote: "What happened to El Adly is the result of the pleas of all the people who were suppressed by him. I wish the best for Egypt and its people."

This thread, despite its brevity and the few posters who participated in it, is a good example of citizen journalism where Mahmoud reported on information regarding the punishment of one of the key members of the Mubarak regime whose name was associated with corruption and abuses of power. Through his post and the reactions it elicited, Mahmoud seemed "to be committed to a form of deliberative democracy in which government officials are held accountable to the citizenry and in which citizenry actively participate in local community affairs" (Haas, 2007, p. 3).

In his post, Mahmoud did not just report on the issue of El Adly's imprisonment, but he seemed personally involved in the issue at hand. It was a form of "political advocacy" rather than "political neutrality" on his end (Haas, 2007, p. 76). Political involvement in the journalistic report is what distinguishes citizen journalism from traditional or mainstream journalism. In this context, Mahmoud told the authors in an interview in 2011: "Bogging has liberated me from the restrictions included in the journalistic profession, such as the mixing of news and opinion. I don't believe there is objectivity when covering injustices in the world. The true objectivity is to side with the people in their cause. Even the newspaper that I work for, *Al-Dostor*, is a blog in the form of an online newspaper."

The above threads provide clear examples of the phenomenon of "youth-led citizen journalism" (Rheingold, 2008), as previously discussed in chapter 4. In order to better understand this process, we have to bear in mind Rheingold's (2008) definition: "Citizen journalism, still in its infancy, is a general term that covers different kinds of activities: Reporting news; investigative blogging; hyperlocal journalism; and digital storytelling" (p. 112).

The last activity, namely, digital storytelling, deserves special attention, due to its relevance to the threads mentioned above and the documentation function they seemed to perform. According to Rheingold (2008), "digital storytelling, when used to construct a narrative presentation of true historical events, personages, and geographical locations, is one way of introducing [people] to participatory media, to the communication basics of compelling narrative production, and to local civic affairs. Journalism doesn't have to be global. Hyperlocal journalism that delves more deeply into local events than mass media does can also serve as a springboard for civic engagement" (p. 112).

Furthermore, digital storytelling can provide a unique opportunity "in which the fun of putting interviews, found images, photographs, and artwork together into an entertaining narrative can be combined with serious discussion of public issues" (Rheingold, 2008, p. 113). Indeed, there is evidence in the threads mentioned above of the existence of this "digital storytelling" function of citizen journalism, with both its "hyperlocal" focus on domestic affairs and national concerns, which are of prime importance to Egyptian citizens, in particular, in addition to the unique combination of an entertaining narrative and simultaneous engagement in serious political discussions around key issues.

In analyzing this process of "digital storytelling," it is important to ask questions such as "in which part of the digital storytelling process does 'public voice' enter into it? In what way do the decisions about questions to ask, who to interview, and how to edit the interviews represent a deliberate point of view, a kind of public voice on an issue, represented perhaps in words other than those of the author, but representing the perspective the author intends to present?" (Rheingold, 2008, p. 113).

In answering these questions, we have to bear in mind Rheingold's (2008) assertion that "identifying and discussing the specific narration, captions, choice of subject matter, juxtaposition, and editing decisions that present the storyteller's point of view is a way of connecting media production practices with a public voice" (p. 113).

Looking at the content of the threads mentioned above, we can clearly see evidence of the coexistence of media production, as exemplified in the strategic selection of the images and words included, with expressing a "public voice," as exemplified in the vocalization of the bloggers' opinions around the discussed issues and the platforms they provided their posters to voice their concerns, express their ideas, and propose their own suggestions.

Additionally, the fact that the bloggers were able to use the digital capabilities provided by the Internet to document the issues at hand and raise awareness about them is indicative of the existence of a high level of "technological fluency," which could be defined as "the ability to use and apply technology in a fluent way, effortlessly and smoothly, as one does with language" (Bers, 2008, p. 156). This process "involves mastering not only technological skills and concepts but also the ability to learn new ways of using computers in a creative and personally meaningful way. During the process of using the technology in a creative way, people are also likely to develop new ways of thinking; therefore the computer's role goes far beyond being an instrumental machine. Thus, we need to understand what level of technological fluency [people] need to have in order to benefit from technology-based interventions to foster civic engagement?" (Bers, 2008, p. 156).

The significance of better understanding this process lies in the fact that new research in the area of using new media to increase political awareness and aid civic engagement revealed "how the Internet can provide a safe space to experiment with civic life, by forming on-line communities that extend and augment the possibilities of young people to engage in face-to-face civic conversations, attitudes, and behaviors" (Bers, 2008, p. 156). This last point is of special relevance to the Egyptian case, whereby virtual online communities, such as those that were formed around Facebook pages or blogs, played the role of catalysts, which paved the way to the process of political change and supplemented face-to-face efforts in the struggle to secure freedom and achieve democratization. There is no doubt that the citizen journalism function performed by some blogs, for the purpose of enabling documentation and raising awareness about serious problems, such as corruption, augmented the efforts of political activists on the ground and encouraged them to take effective actions to overcome such problems.

Third: Threads Encouraging Deliberation

"Lacrimosa."

This thread was taken from Sandmonkey's blog and was posted in English on July 5, 2011, six months after the January 25 revolution. In his post, Sandmonkey highlighted the problem of corruption in Egypt and its numerous implications on the country and on igniting the revolution. Sandmonkey wrote:

> They say that all revolutions follow the same cycle: They start in the winter, they heat up in the spring, they lag in the summer, and then you have the fall of the counter-revolution and the final battle for the future. If that cycle is to be believed, then again, the Egyptian revolution is ahead of its schedule, and we are still going through hyper-time. Events are accelerating ahead of schedule, and fatigue is getting to all of us. This is very evident in the national mood in Egypt now. We are all talking to each other, but we are not listening to one another. And yet no one really cares. The "non-revolutionary" population are sick and tired of the revolutionaries, whom they view as nothing more than hooligans without a plan, while the average revolutionary response to "regular" people's dismay or distrust is that they've always acted this way, ever since February. The "regular" people are always unhappy, but offer no realistic solutions or talk about the real problem objectively, so why bother? And this is why this revolution is the only revolution in history where the revolutionaries had to convince their people, time and time again, that they are on the same side. And even that has stopped.
>
> And beyond all this lies the truth that this revolution isn't a bunch of unemployed, unhappy spoiled kids and poor people in Tahrir Square; it's a violent reaction to a problem. And it's not just one problem; it's a set of problems that are detrimental to our country as a whole and that the majority chooses to ignore. Corruption has reached unprecedented levels in Egypt, accompanied by its cousin inefficiency, and the general consensus was this: every one cared, but no one did anything about it. They simply adapted, and thought only of today, until the day came when the country moved as one.
>
> But corruption isn't the problem that the revolution is the reaction to. The real problem is the relationship between the citizen and the state, on every level you can imagine: from the concept of legal justice and how the legal system should function, to the concept of

personal rights, to the concept of services provided (education, healthcare, etc..) and their quality, all the way to economic, social and urban planning, which are all missing or dysfunctional. And this isn't new and it shouldn't come as a surprise to anybody. It was all not addressed for the longest time, and when it was addressed it was done in the most reactionary way possible. There was no accountability; hence there was no advancement. More than anything, this revolution is about holding your government accountable, and unfortunately your only weapon, to ensure that some accountability is achieved and some progress is made, is pressure through demonstrations.

Sorry mom....Sorry dad....Sorry general population: we don't mean to upset you by confronting you with your problems. If it was for us, we can just wish them away.

You are forced into this game of Tahrir, where the general population just wants peace and quiet while change only happens through pressure applied there. So, you always end up going there because that's the pattern and you want this to stay peaceful, but you are always victim to organized attacks there by "thugs." And as time goes by, you find yourself getting accustomed to street battles, while your peaceful protests get you nowhere, so you start thinking that maybe, just maybe, peaceful protesting is no longer working. So you get dragged into one more violent confrontation after the other, while the media screams, "See, look, they are thugs. They can't be trusted," and some believe them while the others just watch in dismay as the illusion of the "peaceful revolution" starts dismantling before their eyes. All the while, the revolutionaries lose public support, are filled with fatigue, hysteria and in-fighting, like the protagonists of some psychotic Greek tragedy. They are continuing in their journey, as their compatriots keep falling left and right, half-way getting that the security apparatus is simply drawing out the battle to weaken them over time, so that when the time comes, they have their absolute victory, kill the revolution and we are back to business as usual.

If only it was that simple....

Here's the rub: this is not about the protestors. If we all die, or get sent to jail, it won't make an iota of difference, because, in reality, we are not the problem. The problem will continue existing regardless of us because people will no longer take mistreatment or abuse from the police or the army. The problem will continue existing because even the poorest, most uneducated Egyptian gets that something is wrong and needs to be changed. And with the eventual death of the concept of "peaceful protesting" as a means to achieve our demands, another type of not-so-peaceful protesting will become more popular. It's only, as always, a matter of time.

I have said it a million times: This revolution happened to prevent another revolution, one that will be much more violent and one that we all see coming. All of our demands were geared towards diffusing that powder keg, and as they don't get achieved, our ability to diffuse it becomes null. This is not fear-mongering. It's simply reality.

So please don't blame us when that happens. Everything we have ever done, and all that we are doing now is ringing the alarm, hoping to wake you up to help us resolve this before it's too late. We are pushing and fighting for police accountability, because we can't live in a country where the police can torture and kill its people and walk away. There is no pride in belonging to such a country. And we don't know what to do, but the police are rogue, and the courts are a sham, The...[SCAF] is either unable or unwilling to even remove the people that killed the January 25 protestors from their positions of power, and the system works for no one. We are stuck in this vicious cycle, and in the end something has got to give. They are counting on you hating us, on you reaching the inevitable conclusion that maybe, just maybe, we deserve what's coming to us. And maybe this is why we stopped talking to each other. We have taken different paths now, and we don't even insist on bringing each other along anymore.

One day, this will all be over, and this whole drama will be nothing but a distant memory of a time when the whole world was on fire, and the future seemed no longer as a promise, but a threat. Hopefully we will both be there, in a country that has finally healed, and has a future. And we will get there, not because the revolutionaries are right or smart, but because of one inescapable historical truth, that has been proven time and time again over the past 2000 years: You cannot oppress your people for long, for they are always too many for you to control forever. Eventually that coin flips. You can count on it.

Sandmonkey's post elicited many responses from his followers, inside and outside Egypt.

Samantha wrote:

Sandmonkey: It's a fight for democracy. I lived the Romanian revolution. It took 10 years to really get some freedom. You have to organize and fight. In Romania, the army and secret service removed Ceausescu when they saw the outraged masses/revolutionaries and then a socialistic regime was put in place. The army and secret service were smart enough to improve themselves. They retired secret service agents who were compromised. They gave them funds in some cases to start businesses and told the other ones to behave. And they totally changed the way they treated the public. Same thing as the attempted cleaning of Tahrir was planned and successfully implemented in Romania; however people believed in their liberties and human rights and continued to fight for their rights. It's a fragmentation and manipulation based on rumors that's happening in Egypt. As I told you before, democracy organizations will be willing to help you. Let me know if you come to Canada to visit—there are good organizations here also. You can always send me an e-mail or tweet questions. Good luck.

Yosry wrote: "Well said. You need to share your ideas with all those people who are not online. Egyptian people need to read what you write about this revolution. Your voice is one of reason amidst the building chaos, but it's not reaching those who really need to hear it. A thought: the new newspaper, *Tahrir*, might be one forum. Would they publish your blog posts? What about other major newspapers? There must be at least one that would run your posts, unedited. Yours is a voice that needs to be heard by more than just protestors and tweeters, if only to provide a balance to what is being broadcast by others. For what it's worth, we who are watching from the sidelines are still cheering for Egypt. Like you said, eventually all this struggle will be history, and when the dust settles, Egypt will be free."

Christy wrote: "Your revolution should begin with teaching the population to read and write and then teaching them about the foundations of a free society: individualism, human rights, separation of religion and state and so on. Also, isn't there an Arabic saying: 'Better a 100 years of tyranny than one day of chaos?' I bet you are hearing that a lot."

Peter wrote: "I agree, though it's hard not to sound Eurocentric. A 19th century Arab thinker, Gamal el-din al-Afghani, had some really interesting ideas about how to promote a fairer society in the Arab world, which, unfortunately, were largely ignored (and still are!) this article—http://thinkafricapress.com/egypt/marxism-and-nationalism-egypt—is quite good for some background. Fingers crossed for Egypt!!"

Miret wrote: "Dearest Monkey: It maybe more common than you suspect that revolutionaries must convince the change-fearing, stability-clinging, corruption-adapting, short-term-limited-vision masses that the cause of revolution is just and vital for all (see 'Easter Rising, Ireland' just one of many 20th c. examples). You are not alone. Please take solace from that, although it does not make your task any easier, to be sure. You are rightly clear-eyed, regardless, that the road grows murkier at the stage you've entered mid-revolution, but you, your comrades and the historic Egyptian (and Tunisian) revolution will prevail. Take heart, Monkey—you're a brave and courageous man, as are the men and women of Tahrir with you. All over the world we applaud you and send our heartfelt prayers for your steadfastness and perseverance as this most trying period of weariness and counter-revolution unfolds. Be strong and valiant and patient, you will succeed."

Kendra wrote:

> Mahmoud: I got an idea. In Egypt you have a large army and police. In large cities introduce rotations where policemen will switch jobs with military for six months for example. It is good job training and the other policemen can learn from the military persons assigned to the unit. Also human rights manuals for the police can be set up including examples of what is not acceptable and they should be evaluated for promotion based on how they respect human rights. Also, set a police ombudsman (complaint office) and whenever there are more than two complaints for a policeman, set a process where the policeman is transferred to the least desirable locations in the country. You first need a free press in which to publish important human rights breaches stories. You can set up your own newspaper (there are a few people who create newspapers on Twitter, two examples are @ToneyBrooks, @jeanpolochon). I am sure you will easily find donors to help you print the newspaper (could be two pages only and you can get advertising money).

Mervat wrote: "Dear Sandmonkey: Well this is a great interpretation to all the problems taking place in Egypt. You are analyzing the problems, but who are your audience? How many readers are you targeting? We are 87 million citizens; 45 million are illiterate and poor. Do you think they comprehend your message? Coming here today, do you have a hidden agenda? You are fighting for the youth's future. Are you one of them? Losing the future is not like losing an election or a few points at the stock market!! You are speaking for all generations to come. We teach kids in schools how to behave in the world, not to fight with others, to work things out, to respect others, not to hurt other creatures, to share and to have a VISION. We usually tell them, 'You are what you do, not what you say.' I challenge you. Please make your actions reflect your words."

Donna wrote, addressing her words to Mervat: "We usually say: 'You are what you do, not what you say.' Well. Mervat, if that is what you teach Egyptian children, they did not learn. The taxi drivers and people talk about corruption and how bad it is and at the same time they demand bribe-money themselves. There was talk about cleaning the stuff, but the streets are dirtier than before the revolution. A couple months ago, Sandmonkey was claiming that the religious party people (Salafis and Muslim Brotherhood) do not count for much in the new Egypt. But he changed his mind. I guess if he changed his mind about things, Egyptian people can change their mind about the revolution. They probably have more immediate needs, like the price of bread."

Tharwat wrote:

> The comparison between the Romanian revolution and the unrest in Egypt is completely irrelevant because Romania is part of the stable and prosperous Europe, while Egypt is part of the unstable Middle East. I will just shed light on some important facts about the Egyptian situation. The economy in Egypt has been under extensive reform for the past decade, and the Egyptian people were finally able to fill the huge gap between their developing nation and the technologically advanced Western nations. Let's not forget that Egypt has gone through 5 wars in 30 years, and the damage was tremendous and the need for stability in order to achieve the badly needed, long-term development programs was a priority. The stability by itself was viewed as a treasure because it paved the way for permanent development for a country with rapid growing population and limited resources. The sudden calls in Egypt, Syria, Tunisia, Bahrain, Yemen and Oman for the removal of their historical leaders seem suspicious to me. It's the new world order and the formation of a new Middle East in which there will be no place for a one united strong Egypt, but rather three or four little easy-to-control Egypts. It's obvious now that what seems to be a loud cry for freedom is actually a war on Islam. The enemy is indeed Islam, and the location is Tahrir Square and everywhere else in the Middle East from Casablanca to Baghdad. It's a new Christian crusade covered by the bright labels of freedom and democracy, but I have no doubt that Arabs and Islam will prevail. And the crusaders will go back to Europe defeated and sorry for their unlawful and dangerous game.

Glenn wrote, addressing his words to Tharwat:

> So you are saying that Romania had a big advantage over Egypt? Egypt has two huge drivers of economy; the Suez Canal and a tremendous tourism industry. And the Nile is a great source of economic activity in its own right. And most importantly, Egypt has a proud people with a long tradition of culture and a history of successful world leadership. What did Romania have? They were a bankrupt country, raped and pillaged by its Soviet overlords for nearly a century. And like Egypt, it also had a very corrupt governing system and a ruthless dictator. And they were never a world power or had a strong cultural base. The one advantage they had was the power structure that was imposed from afar collapsed, allowing them a shot at freedom. Egypt, with all its advantages, can be a world leader again. Their location at the center of the Arab world can make them an economic dynamo as a center of culture and trade. Throw off your shackles and grab this chance. Or live under those constraints that have left your region destitute.

Gullnar wrote: "I read your note from Tehran and I'm surprised as to how much our concerns are the same. It seems Iran and Egypt share a great deal of similarities. Convincing a passive portion of the society is indeed what the active one is doing now in Iran. We're being increasingly faced by the question of 'Is it worth it?' 'Is your youth worth the oppression, jail and deprivation of slavery?' And our fight has been increasingly turned into a warning not to be deceived by this fake peace and silence. In fact, some people capitulate to the current situation because of their fear of turbulence."

Sandmonkey's post in the thread mentioned above addressed several civil society functions, such as enhancing "education for democracy" (Diamond, 1999, p. 243), "developing techniques for conflict mediating and resolution," and "strengthen[ing] the social foundations of democracy" (Diamond, 1999, p. 249). In his post, Sandmonkey addressed the problem of the loss of trust between the revolutionaries and members of the general public who, according to him, had gotten tired of the dragging protests without seeing concrete results on the ground. According to Sandmonkey, the problem was not in the revolution, but in the corrupt system that had no accountability. Sandmonkey urged the people to become better listeners to one another and to be more involved in trying to confront and solve the country's problems and overcome their apathy. In a way, Sandmonkey alluded in his post to the negative attitudes on the part of what he referred to as the "average" or "regular" people. It might have been the negative, uncooperative attitude on the part of the people that has worsened the political environment and not vice versa. In this context, Sandmonkey, told the authors in a personal interview in June 2010, a year and a half before the revolution: "Our approach to dealing with issues can sometimes be stupid and misguided because our problems aren't all political. Our problems are philosophical and social in nature. For example, we have an election law in Egypt, but it is completely useless because people do not respect their rights. Egypt has a margin of freedom, not because the regime wants it to be that way, but because it is too lazy to censor everything."

It can be argued that Sandmonkey tried to address the negative aspects of civil society in postrevolutionary Egypt, such as the "the proclivities of a divided society" (Tusalem, 2007, p. 367), and the inability to formulate a majority opinion, the insufficiency of social capital needed to unite around one goal, and "the tendency toward 'pork-barrel solutions whereby each ... movement satisfies its interests/passions at the expense of the unit as a whole" (Fioramonti & Fiori, 2010, p. 87).

Despite his alluding to several troubles and raising some problems with regard to postrevolutionary Egyptian civil society, Sandmonkey started and ended his long post on a good, positive, and upbeat note, confirming that the revolution would succeed and that the counterrevolutionary forces would be disappointed. It might have been this optimistic and reassuring note that led Sandmonkey's followers to post several hopeful, encouraging, and generally problem-solving notes. Several of the posters suggested long-term solutions to Egypt's troubles, such as overcoming illiteracy, increasing public awareness about human rights, and setting the foundations for a free society. Other posters proposed short-term solutions, such as issuing human rights manuals for Egyptian police officers, setting up a newspaper on Twitter, and connecting Sandmonkey to democracy organizations to help get his message across to as wide an audience as possible.

But what made this thread stand out, compared to the other threads that were previously discussed in this chapter, was the posters' engagement in a truly deliberative, rational-critical dialogue that was inspired by Sandmonkey's insightful ideas. For example, Donna responded to Mervat's post regarding her suspicions about Sandmonkey's intentions, and Glenn responded to Tharwat's post with regard to the comparison between postrevolutionary Egypt and Romania. What further enriched the diversity of these deliberations was the fact that they were initiated by Egyptians as well as non-Egyptians. In this context, it can be argued that Sandmonkey's post led to "the possibility of new political spaces and the development of political as well as civil society at a global level" (Skelly, 2008, p. 141). The posters in this thread "act[ed] towards the universal... to reach beyond selfishness, sectionalism, and sectarianism... [and] to become global citizens therefore, within a global civil society" (Skelly, 2008, p. 141).

The globalized nature of the exchanged discourse in this thread and the diversity of those who participated in it support the existence of the process of "exogenous mobilization" (Salmon et al., 2010), as well as the existence of a "virtual global public sphere" (el-Nawawy & Khamis, 2009), as previously discussed in chapter 4.

In light of this last point, it could be said that a public sphere is characterized by three main features, according to Schuler and Day (2004),

> First, it presents communication opportunities in a broad sense.... Second, public spheres are "public" in two ways: people can enter the "spaces" without undue hindrances, regardless of their ethnicity, religion, sexual preference, gender, or economic status and the spaces themselves are visible; the discussions and decisions do not take

> place behind closed doors, gated neighborhoods, or private intranets. Third and finally, a public sphere mediates between people and institutions, between those that may be powerless and those that may be extremely powerful. Without this linkage or engagement, conversations would take place in walled-off zones and be ineffectual; the conversations may be full of "sound and fury" but if they are unheard and unheeded, they ultimately signify nothing (p. 4).

A close look at the discussions and deliberations that took place in the above thread clearly reveals that it meets all three criteria for the existence of a virtual public sphere, which can serve as a "mediating structure." According to Schuler and Day (2004), "A mediating structure is a *linking* mechanism; it is intended to connect disparate viewpoints, to give voice to all, to prevent the escalation of grievances into desperation or lethal conflict" (p. 4).

It is also useful to think about such deliberative discussions in cyberspace as forming "alternative public spheres whose *raison d'etre* is to challenge the assumptions and specifics of the more orthodox public spheres" (Schuler and Day, 2004, p. 5), and to ask ourselves questions such as how can the existence of such alternative public spheres "help us think about the Internet and its ongoing evolution. Can it be used to spur activism on a large scale? A global scale?" (Schuler and Day, 2004, p. 5).

In answering such questions, we have to bear in mind that a public sphere must be inclusive in several important ways:

> First, everyone should be able to participate on an equal basis: those with more money than others should not be able to purchase more influence with their money, either directly or indirectly.... This means that society needs to closely examine the ways people participate in public decision making... and help ensure that those mechanisms do not favor the privileged. Second, there must be ways citizens can place their concerns on the public agenda. If the public agenda is monopolized and manipulated by corporations, politicians, or the media, the public sphere is seriously imperiled. Third, the public sphere requires a deliberative public process in which all voices are equal—at least at decision points. This point entails the following critical ideas: *Deliberative*: Adequate time must be allotted for hearing and considering multiple points of view; *Public*: The discussion should take place openly, where it can be observed by all; *Process*: The procedures through which concerns are brought up, discussed, and acted on should be clear and widely known (Schuler and Day, 2004, p. 5).

It is safe to conclude that the above thread met all three requirements for an inclusive public sphere. Most importantly, it demonstrated the presence of a "deliberative public process," by providing an egalitarian, open, and accessible forum for differing, or even contrasting, ideas and opinions to be safely and freely exchanged and debated.

"Seven Economic Ideas for a New Egypt"

This thread was also taken from Sandmonkey's blog and was posted in English on June 8, 2011, five months after the January 25 revolution. In it, Sandmonkey offered some useful suggestions to improve the economic situation in Egypt. Since Sandmonkey's post was too long, the authors have included sections from it that would provide the gist of what he wanted to share with his blog followers.

Sandmonkey wrote:

> A lot of people complain that the government has no vision in regards to how to bounce back our economy, and is instead acting as if the revolution never happened and everything is business as usual. For four months now, I have been awaiting a single decent economic plan, or even emergency economic measures (like temporary welfare packages to the lower classes to be able to feed itself until "stability" takes place, or a stimulus package to the small and medium size businesses to keep them afloat for a few months and not have to fire any people). However, that's as likely as them inspecting the old budget or trying to find where the public waste or corruption is in it, and cut those costs. In case you didn't know, the new budget is like the old budget exactly, except that they are spending more money, and borrowing to cover it up, and not reducing the costs on anything. God knows that after reviewing our budget, I realized that if I was running a business the way the Egyptian government was running its finances, I would've been out of businesses years ago. That being said, expecting the government to come up with good plans is as likely as the police starting to act like respectable responsible humans and go to work without abusing anyone: It's not going to happen. So, instead of pointing out their flaws, I will offer here some ideas of things we can do.
>
> Idea # 1: Let's pay the people for their trash!
>
> Here is the concept in a nutshell: We live in a country of 85 million consumers. They consume lots of goods and produce a huge amount of trash, many of which never gets recycled or used correctly. Instead of people paying to have their trash collected, we will pay them money for their trash. We will provide trash bins everywhere that will divide the trash into organic and non-organic (with all of its variations) all over Egypt, and teach people how to separate their trash effectively. Then, once a week, the trash cars will come and start paying people by the kilo for their trash, provided that they have separated it first. The trucks will then head to one of many huge factories that will be

built all over Egypt, where the non-organic trash will be divided and recycled again into plastics, aluminum, papers, etc. to be sold in the market to factories again, and the organic trash will be taken and processed to produce methane gas that will be turned into electricity that will power up the different production lines in the factory, which would reduce the energy needs of the factory dramatically or possibly eliminate it all together. Zero Waste! This idea will do the following: 1) Put money in the hands of all Egyptians for their trash, and actually give them incentive to pick up any litter anywhere in their neighborhoods, because there will be money to be made off of it now, 2) Hire thousands of workers—because this will be nationwide—who will drive the collection trucks, collect the trash and pay the people, re-separate the trash at the factory, man the recycling production lines, and sell the recycled resources to the other factories or the people and 3) Make Egypt cleaner, reduce the horrible pollution from trash burning and increase efficiency in the usage of our resources.

Idea #2: Let's get out of Cairo now!

I love Cairo. Well, I love Cairo at night. Like maybe from 10 p.m. till 4 a.m. The rest of the time, I am starting to hate Cairo: It's a city overloaded with cars and people (25 million residents, almost one third of Egypt's population). The Cairo people are unhappy with how overpopulated and polluted their city is, and complain daily about the hellish traffic, and the rest of the country believes Cairo takes up all the economic development to itself. And the thing is, even when the Cairenes try to leave Cairo, they just go to 6 October or New Cairo, which are Cairo suburbs, and thus Cairo-centric as well, which now means that the traffic isn't just in Cairo, it's also facing anyone leaving Cairo, making Cairo a black hole of soul-sucking and misery. Let's change that dramatically by moving entire industries to other areas of the country, and thus creating new cities and new pockets of development. For example, let's move the entire IT and technology industry to the North Coast and build a huge technology-focused city—our very own Silicon Valley—right behind all of those touristic villages that we only use 3 months a year. That whole area already has paved roads, communication lines and utilities connected to it for those touristic villages; so we will simply need to scale up the existing infrastructure instead of building it from scratch. Moreover, it will provide the restaurants, shops and clubs in the area of year-round customers. The IT people will love it because it will take them out of the city; the shop owners will love it because it will provide more sources of income for them; and the population there will love it because it will mean more jobs whether in construction, factories or companies that will be erected. Another industry we could move elsewhere could be the movie industry, which we could move to Sinai, where huge studios can be built to cater for the Egyptian cinema industry and international cinema companies who will want to film in Egypt instead of Morocco, and thus also hire thousands of people. All the artists, directors, music composers and production people will be moved there, and thus creating the Egyptian Hollywood. And it won't just be for cinema; it can host the entire media industry, including TV stations, music companies, and production houses.

Idea #3: Let's give the Egyptian government a corruption colonic!

The biggest hurdle facing new businesses is the amount of corruption that exists in all levels of government, which means that if you want to start a new business, you have to pay a lot of bribes on many levels. A friend of mine once told me that Egypt is unique in the sense that while in most countries you pay bribes to get more than what's rightfully yours, in Egypt you pay bribes to get what's rightfully yours, and it's true. If we hope to live in a better country, we need to remove all the bribe-taking individuals from our entire government. I want the businessmen to unify and call for a truth and reconciliation initiative, where they will report every single bribe they paid to a government official in exchange for amnesty, and call on the rest of the population to do the same. This will help flush out every single corrupt government official out of the government once and for all, and highlight the weak points in Egyptian bureaucracy that allow such corruption to take place. This will also allow the government to get rid of many of its corrupt employees, which means that more openings in government jobs will become available, and the government can reduce its really high salary costs without bothering with early-retirement plans for people who are criminal parasites and who have held the economic development of the country hostage for years. And if the businessmen, or anyone for that matter, benefitted from that corrupt system, they should pay back the money they made off such corruption to the government or society through funding social projects that benefit the country. Everybody wins!

Idea #4: Let's have a real sports industry!

The sports industry in Egypt is a paradox that I can't figure out, especially the football industry. Here is what happens: The sporting clubs, with their football teams, are technically owned by the government, and the government funds them with half a billion pounds a year. This money never goes back to the government, but it goes to the Football Union. The money from the games of the Egyptian leagues, the sponsorships and the TV broadcasting rights never goes to the corrupt Football Union, whose budget is spent without any oversight. That is not to mention the football teams that are affiliated with government institutions. Has anybody ever wondered why a government-owned oil company would have a football team? Isn't that a waste of public resources and money?

Instead of that ineffective structure, let's do the only thing that makes sense: The government must stop wasting money on the sporting teams of the government institutions and offer the rest of the actual sporting clubs up for privatization, selling 80 percent of their shares for example, and keeping 20 percent as a silent partner, or giving it to the members. Can you imagine how much money the government can make from selling a big team to investors? Billions. That is money that they can use to fund the under-funded sport-centers and our Olympic teams. And those investors who will buy the clubs will start running the football teams correctly: We are talking real broadcasting rights negotiations, factories creating sports merchandising, and team and club development. We could then afford to buy expensive international players and have them play in the Egyptian league. We would elevate the game, start industries, and maybe even fund other sports. As for the Football Union, it would be comprised of the representatives of club owners who will make sure that no club gets favorite treatment over another and that the resources are not wasted because it will be THEIR MONEY. We could change the game, forever!

Idea #5: Let's fund our country!

Let's create "Patriotic Funds,"—a huge fund per governorate that everyone can buy shares in, and that will take the money and invest them in two things: investment projects that the governorate needs, and development projects like schools or hospitals. The income generated from these investment projects will fund the development projects and provide a modest return of maybe 5 percent for their investors. Or, we can have a law that states that every business should donate a tax-deductible 2 or 3 percent of its revenue to fund an actual social project; e.g. a school, a hospital or the infrastructure of an underdeveloped area.

Idea# 6: Let's bring those Egyptian expatriates back for a visit!

Why not create a special event, where we call on all Egyptians who live abroad to come down to Egypt and have their own Tahrir experience? And what better time to do this other than next September for the elections? Instead of worrying whether or not they will be able to vote, we should invite those Egyptians abroad to come back to Egypt for a week to vote and enjoy the country's beaches or touristic sights. By doing that, they will 1) ensure that their votes will count and 2) provide a much needed boost to our tourism industry. If you have 2 million out of the 12 million Egyptians who live abroad come back, and each spends U.S. $3,000 on the trip, that's 6 billion dollars entering the country right there. And we will host festivals and concerts to celebrate their homecoming and their participation. The world will see that Egypt is now safe to come back to, and if the tourism companies provide good packages to entice the tourists, our tourism will come back full force!

Idea # 7: Let's provide our people with food security!

We have a food shortage in Egypt due to three factors: 1) We have a population that refuses to stop increasing, 2) We don't have enough farmland to feed this population[,] and 3) we don't have enough water

> to create new farmland. Nothing can be done regarding the population increase, and so we have to create new farmland in order to provide food security, which we can't do without more water. So, it all comes down to water. But the question is: do we really not have enough water? Or are we simply wasting what we have? Well, anyone who works in agriculture will tell you that we waste our water ridiculously, because many farmers insist on just flooding their farmland with water, instead of using irrigation systems that will efficiently water their crops without wasting our most valuable resource. Actually, if we make it a law that all farmlands need to have irrigation systems, not only could we cut down our waste, we could have enough water to at least double our farmland with ease! And farmers shouldn't pay for it, but the government should... make it available, especially for the poor farmers. And while we are at it, here is a question: how come no one has ever used the lands surrounding Lake-Nasser as farmland? We are talking hundreds of thousands of acres, with water access right there. The movement of water in Lake Nasser to farm that land will ensure that we don't lose seven percent of our water reserves to vaporization, like we do right now, because it won't be sitting still. This water from Lake Nasser can be used to increase our farmland and provide us with more produce, which will be sent to factories for packaging and ensure our food security. And since we are talking about Lake Nasser and food security, why not take advantage of the huge amount of fish that lives in this lake's water? We could create an entire fishing industry, build a factory that will put the fish in cartons and ship it in frozen trucks or trains to be sold all over Egypt, feeding everyone cheaply. New Farmland, new factories, more jobs and food security, and it won't cost much. Why don't we do it? Just think about it!

Sandmonkey's somewhat long post elicited enthusiastic responses from various posters.

Tawfik wrote: "Egyptians will not even think about any of the ideas you mentioned for the time being simply because those in charge of the country are stuck in the traditional schools of thinking. They need to utilize young people's effort, spirit and creative thinking to move ahead, and they are not doing that. Still, I am very optimistic that change will happen. Those people will retire soon and will be replaced by creative thinkers. Also why aren't you writing your articles in Arabic or at least have them translated and published[?] Your words are very powerful. You can have a positive influence on a lot of people. Keep up the good work."

Ashry wrote: "I totally agree with all your suggestions. I just want to mention that, for the last point, it is NOT only about water. There are many other issues, land-quality-wise, policy-wise, that are of high importance (positively or negatively) in reforming our agricultural infrastructure."

Selim wrote: "If Egypt can become food independent, it can default on the IMF loans and use its money to develop its economy, and some of those ways were outlined in your article. That is the real issue which Egypt faces, not being capable of feeding its people and[,] therefore, held hostage to the-powers-that-be at the IMF. There is no country that I know of in the world where the people are less capable of accepting austerity measures."

Armando wrote: "We are going to Egypt in July/August—my wife (originally from Luxor), our two girls and myself. Yes, we would like to contribute as well—and MANY I know would love to give some hours or days to what's happening in Egypt now. Not only Nile Valley tourism, Red Sea tourism or desert tourism—but 'Tahrir tourism' where visitors from any country combine a holiday with our smaller or larger help. You guys and gals of the Tahrir-revolution have done the change. Let's help in whatever way you find it right."

Kent wrote: "I never understood how Egypt can lack water—doesn't your country have an enormous coastline, north and east? How about desalinization plants on this vast shoreline? In any case, I love that you can dream so vividly and hope for your success, although between 40 percent illiteracy, the IMF and the military junta, you really are climbing one steep hill."

Gasser wrote: "Sandmonkey for president!"

Maged wrote: "Your idea about Egyptian expats is a good one. Not sure if it will sell. Expats choose to be Egyptians despite having other alternatives (arguably better). In return, they are considered unpatriotic, not worthy of special arrangements for voting and confined to money-grabbing schemes. Check my blog for the opinion of some expats regarding the current fiasco in Egypt."

Gad wrote: "All great ideas—thank you for thinking out of the box. But the devil is in the HOW? I don't think we have a dearth of ideas....We just don't know how to implement. I don't like to think of obstacles but really HOW can we get the ball rolling on ANY of these? Now if you can come up with THAT...you won't be a Sandmonkey; you'll be a SandGod!"

Abdel-Rahman wrote:

> All good ideas—I'd also like to hear about your longer-term rantings! I truly believe that education is one of them? By education I mean

> enhancing social reasoning. This will encourage ongoing self (group) development through logic. After all, it's very hard to reason with a group that does not understand logic and has no knowledge. I'm sure you agree. Getting the remaining 40 percent of the Egyptian population to start reading would be a good start. But teaching principles and ethics from childhood is really the way forward. See, I believe that we (us Egyptians) have lost some touch along the way, and of course you can blame it all on the system, but seriously, ask an old wise man who is at least 70 years old. To make a point, Cairo used to be the most beautiful city in the world. Look it up! We have lost the touch of taste, and if not, then it's responsibility.... It is a long and bumpy road but it will pay back! I'd consider it as the long-term economic idea for a New Egypt! Keep up the good work! I am a new visitor to your blog, but one who will surely come back.

Noha: "Brilliant. Can you tell me why the cabinet is not listening? Why not post it on their webpage?"

Natalie wrote: "Excellent ideas! I especially loved idea #1 because we should be doing this globally—we are such a wasteful species; idea #2 because turning Sinai into an Egyptian Hollywood so appeals to me as an artist—I'd be there with bells on; idea #7 because I live in a farming community in Canada and have for some time wanted to connect with Egyptian farmers and have them connect with our local farmers who adore sharing farming ideas with people outside the area. Farmers are the backbone of our societies and they work hard in often thankless jobs. Sharing ideas can be rejuvenating. Also, farming tourism might help boost a farmer's income. So many ideas we could be sharing. With regard to the comment someone made about 'Tahrir Tourism'...excellent! Capitalize on that to bring a whole new kind of tourists[sic] to Egypt! Will pass the link to this list on to others. It is full of ideas that would work. Hopefully people will take it on board and run with it."

Jeremy wrote: "Fantastic post with great ideas Sandmonkey. Have you sent this to the Prime Minister?"

Calhoun wrote: "Hi Monkey: Just an idea from India for the corruption problem: http://www.ipaidabribe.com/ Helps people monitor, control and influence the amount they pay and what they get for it."

In the thread mentioned above, Sandmonkey adopted a pragmatic approach by sharing several concrete steps to help improve the Egyptian economy, put an end to corruption, reduce the national waste, and generate more income for the country. In his post, he addressed the interests of various social groups, such as investors, tourists, expatriates, and farmers. By doing so, he served a civil society function, which is to create a channel "for articulating, aggregating, and representing interests" (Diamond, 1999, p. 243).

In addition, Sandmonkey's creative ideas seemed to have encouraged and energized "citizens in the collective pursuit and defense of their interests and values" (Diamond, 1999, p. 247). This sense of collectivity was reflected in the remarks of the posters to this thread, most of whom agreed with Sandmonkey's ideas, and they encouraged him to post his note on the Egyptian cabinet's website, send it to the Egyptian prime minister, and translate it to Arabic so that more people can read it. One could sense that each poster on this thread felt an urgent need to support creative ideas and to even come up with their own suggestions to overcome Egypt's economic problems. The posters' collective support of Sandmonkey's ideas went against an Egyptian "cultural tradition, perpetuated by political laws that constrain freedom of expression and organization, that does not support collective action or concerted behavior, hence the inability of civil society to recruit people with pre-knowledge of the necessary skills for participation. It is a pervasive tendency to go for individualistic solutions, not for collective ones" (El-Mikawy & Mohsen, 2005, p. 11). In a way, Sandmonkey's success in generating collective encouragement for his suggestions could serve as an indicator for his ability to engage and mobilize new civil society leaders whose talents, skills, energy, and enthusiasm would be needed for the success of any plans for economic reform.

It can be argued in this context that Sandmonkey's articulation of his economic ideas could make him meet several of Diamond's criteria for efficient civil society leaders and activists:

> They learn how to organize and motivate people, debate issues, raise and account for funds, craft budgets, publicize programs, administer staffs, canvass for support, negotiate agreements, and build coalitions. At the same time, their work on behalf of their constituency, or of what they see to be the public interest, and their articulation of clear and compelling police alternatives may gain for them a wider political following. (Diamond, 1999, p. 246)

It might have been Sandmonkey's ability to mobilize the public and strengthen civic engagement that led one of the posters in this thread to encourage him to run for president.

Sandmonkey, like several other prominent bloggers in Egypt, has had a great impact on mobilizing the young Egyptian public.

Addressing this issue, Amina Khairy, an Egyptian journalist for *Al-Hayat* newspaper who has done extensive coverage on blogging, told the authors in 2009: "Despite the fact that it is only a minority of Egyptians who have access to the Internet, the young social media users have respect for the bloggers, who are sometimes regarded as courageous role models."

Echoing Khairy's thought, Fatima Abed, another Egyptian blogger and volunteer at a human rights law center told the authors in an interview in 2010:

> I think the Egyptian bloggers play a very vital role in affecting Internet users. The people who are involved in the Internet in general are well-educated, and usually it is the educated people who lead a society, not the illiterate people. Blogs and new media in general have been paving the way for change in Egypt. So far, we can say that the change is mainly taking place inside people rather than just out on the streets. And it is very important to change people from the inside so that they can take action and improve their societies. Today, people are not just participating in the political process, but they are also taking the initiative, thanks to the bloggers' impact.

Most importantly, the above thread provided another example of the "deliberative public process" (Schuler and Day, 2004) that has been discussed earlier by providing a platform for diverse voices to be heard from different participants representing various demographic and psychographic profiles and coming from places as far away as Canada and India, which also supports the presence of a "virtual global public sphere" (el-Nawawy & Khamis, 2009), as previously mentioned. This is line with Rheingold's (2004) remark that

> the democratic twist is that more people today have more to say about how their world is steered than at any other time in history. Structurally, the Internet has inverted the few-to-many architecture of the broadcast age, in which a small number of people were able to influence and shape the perceptions and beliefs of entire nations. In the many-to-many environment of the Net...mass media will continue to exist and so will journalism, but these institutions will no longer monopolize attention and access to the attention of others. (p. 272)

However, despite the acknowledgement of this "democratic twist," which is made possible by new media, such as the Internet, we agree with Rheingold (2004) that "it is not yet clear how this democratization of publishing power will translate into political change" (p. 272).

This is especially true since the following important questions remain largely unanswered: "First, how will new media affect the free and open discourse that forms the bedrock of democracy? Second, can professionally gathered news stories and civil-citizen discourse be blended in a way that enhances democracy? [And third,] What is the role for traditional journalism in a world where the power to publish and communicate is radically diffused and disintermediated?" (Rheingold, 2004, p. 272).

Moreover, the discussions and deliberations in this thread remind us that "the public sphere is where people, through their communications, become citizens... [and that] the Internet will affect democratic discourse in an evolving public sphere. However... we simply do not yet know what form the public sphere will take in cyberspace.... Will the Internet strengthen civic life, community, and democracy, or will it weaken them?" (Rheingold, 2004, p. 273).

Despite these uncertainties, however, one thing remains certain: "Because the public sphere depends on free communication and discussion of ideas, clearly this vital marketplace for political ideas can be powerfully influenced by changes in communications technology" (Rheingold, 2004, p. 273). Indeed, there is sufficient evidence in the analyzed threads so far that the nature of the process of communication is rapidly and drastically changing in the age of cyberspace, through the availability of more egalitarian, diverse, and open platforms for civic engagement, citizen journalism, and public deliberation, which are equally accessible to anyone who can join these digital conversations in cyberspace.

"The Army and the People Were Never One Hand"

This thread was taken from the blog of Maikel Nabil, and was posted in Arabic on March 7, 2011—two months after the launch of the January 25 revolution. In his post, Nabil expressed harsh criticism against the Egyptian army by posting many videos and pictures of soldiers torturing, hitting, or attacking civilians and showing graphic images of citizens injured as a result of their clashes with the military. Since Nabil's post was too long, the authors included sections from it that would provide the gist of what he wanted to communicate.

Nabil wrote:

> The revolution has succeeded in getting rid of the dictator Mubarak, but so far, dictatorship still exists in other forms. Many Egyptian revolutionaries share my opinion. For example, Mohamed El-Baradei

[the former director of the International Atomic Energy Agency and a political activist]...wrote in an article describing the current situation in Egypt that the military has been leading the transitional period in Egypt in a very mysterious and even monopolizing manner. I, among others, have been calling for a civilian council to lead the country, instead of the... [SCAF]. Given my position as someone who has participated in this revolution since day one, I have had the opportunity to live the whole experience with all its events. In the following report, I will provide evidence showing that the military has never taken the people's side in this revolution, and that it has been acting all along to serve its own interests, not the people's interests. With regard to the military's role, we can divide the Egyptian revolution into three stages:

Stage one: Before the military control over the situation on January 29, 2011: During this stage, hundreds of thousands of protestors took to the streets, and they were attacked fiercely by the police forces. During that time, Lieutenant General Samy Anan, the Chief of Staff for the Egyptian military, informed the U.S. administration that the Egyptian military was supportive of Mubarak and will not let him down. According to a news item posted on the American military news site, Start 4, on January 25, 2011: "It was not a coincidence that the Egyptian military Chief of Staff was in Washington, D.C. to assure the United States of the Egyptian military's backing of Mubarak." On January 28, 2011, massive numbers of protestors started heading toward Tahrir Square after the Friday prayers, and they were resisted by the police forces which used tear gas bombs, rubber bullets and live ammunition. On that day, the battle between the police and the protestors lasted for 10 hours until the police ran out of ammunition. At that point, the protestors saw several cars that belonged to the military making their way through the crowds and trying to reach the police forces. After these military cars left, the police resumed shooting at the protestors. That was when the protestors realized that the military was helping the police, and that it was not on their side. As a result of that recognition, the protestors burned down two military cars and they took over four tanks.

Stage two: Between January 29 and February 11, 2011 the day of Mubarak's stepping down: During that stage, the military realized that it could not face the increasing number of protestors in a direct confrontation, and so it changed its tactics by trying to suffocate the protestors through surrounding them and preventing them from reaching target places such as the Ministry of Interior and the Parliament building. During that stage, the military adopted a form of passive neutrality. While it announced on several occasions that it would protect the protestors, it did not prevent a group of thugs, supportive of Mubarak, from attacking the protestors by using camels and horses on February 2 and 3 at Tahrir Square. This incident results in 10 deaths and more than 1,500 injuries from among the protestors. All of this was going on under the watch of the military forces that did not even try to prevent the thugs from climbing up to the rooftops of the buildings surrounding Tahrir Square and throwing Molotov bombs at the protestors. It can be said that the military took the thugs' side because of its passivity and its intentional negligence in protecting the protestors.

After the protestors managed to enter the headquarters of the state security building, they came across a document showing the role of the military intelligence in asking some political figures to encourage the protestors to leave Tahrir Square and go home. According to this document, a senior military officer approached the Secretary General of the Arab League to ask him to make a plea to the protestors to leave the square. This was what actually took place, proving that the military was not siding with the protestors as it claimed. Then, on February 3, 2011, the military forces ambushed several buildings that housed NGOs specialized in civil service and arrested the leaders of these organizations.

The military forces, in collaboration with the state security forces, arrested several bloggers and political activists, including myself. According to credible estimates, the military and police forces arrested more than 10,000, and distributed them among several military prisons where they were tortured and mistreated. I can attest to that myself given that I was arrested on February 4, 2011 while I was on my way to Tahrir Square. Then, I was taken to the Military Intelligence headquarters, where I was beaten, tortured and sexually molested. Then, after my release, I learned that my father was transferred from his job. The British newspaper, *The Guardian*, also included testimonies by several protestors that they were locked up near the Egyptian museum building at Tahrir Square and tortured by the military. A report by Amnesty International also alluded to the arrest and torture cases of several protestors on the hands of the Egyptian military police.

Stage three: From February 12, 2011 until the present:

During that stage, the Egyptian military tried to convince the people that it was officially part of the revolution, but in reality it did everything possible to make the revolution fail by taking the following steps: 1) Trying to co-opt and control the media through appointing one of its members as the chief controller of the Egyptian Radio and Television Union; 2) using force to end the protests at Tahrir Square and preventing reporters from filming of taking photos at the square; 3) continuing the imprisonment and torture of the political activists and protestors who participated in the revolution; 4) not lifting the Emergency Law and taking up the same policies of political suppression that were adopted by the Mubarak regime.

> The most important question that I am posing in this context is: Why didn't the Egyptian military lead a full-fledged war against the protestors by using its heavy artillery and advanced weapons despite the fact that it was not supportive of the revolution? I can think of several logical answers to my question: 1) The military would never have been able to completely suppress the protests; in fact, some military officers would have taken the people's side if they saw a high number of casualties on the hands of the military; 2) The Egyptian military has received instructions from the U.S. administration not to use any U.S.-made weapons to suppress the protestors out of fear that this would destroy the U.S. image in the international world. It is known that the Egyptian military receives $1.3 billion as an annual aid from the United States, and there are strong ties between the Egyptian and U.S. military. So, if the Egyptian military were to kill massive number of civilians, that would have tainted the U.S. military as well; 3) The senior members of the Egyptian military were afraid of the legal repercussions if they were to use heavy artillery against the unarmed civilians.

Nabil's post elicited strong and varied responses from the posters. Anonymous1 wrote: "We all know that the military has some bad elements, but it doesn't make any sense for you to have such an inflammatory post now while the country is going through these highly sensitive circumstances. Your post is an open declaration of coup against the Egyptian military and a clear invitation for the destruction of Egypt."

Idris wrote: "We all regret that these abuses took place, and we look forward to a new era of political integrity."

Anonymous2 wrote: "The military has not been trained in tackling political issues or dealing with the protestors. This has made the military pressure Mubarak to resign with the promises that it will not haunt him or his family. I highly advise you against sharing some of the details that you showcased, since this is not the right time to do so."

Anonymous3 wrote: "Most of your post is nonsense, and your goal is to divide the Egyptian society. The military should stand firm against people like you."

Anonymous4 wrote: "Whoever posted this message should be arrested and indicted on charges of national treason."

Safwat wrote: "I personally testify to the nobility of the Egyptian military, which refused to listen to Mubarak's orders of surrounding the protestors. I was at Tahrir Square, and I heard a military officer tell the protestors to sleep underneath the military tanks since the military received orders to besiege the protestors and they will not execute these orders."

Anonymous5 wrote: "Maikel: Most of your information is not accurate. I was at Tahrir Square and I can confidently prove you wrong."

Anonymous6 wrote: "The military is the last resort for the security of this country, and that is why I totally refuse your words and I will not allow you to destroy the military which is our last bastion in this country."

Anonymous7 wrote: "Maikel: I used to respect and support you, but after reading your post, I changed my position. If you want to live peacefully in this country, don't try to create a division between the people and their military."

Hussein wrote: "Maikel: You hardly provided any evidence for what you mentioned. The photos that you included could have been fabricated or used in any other context. If the people lose confidence in their military, it will be a crisis. Who will secure this country against its enemies?"

Reem wrote: "Maikel: Your words are true; yet some people are still in denial when it comes to the military abuses against the protestors. People forgot that the military tortured political activists and conducted virginity tests on the female protestors at Tahrir Square. What do you expect from a military institution that was part of a highly corrupted Mubarak regime for 30 years?"

Anonymous8 wrote: "To all those who attacked the writer of this post: I would like to tell them that addressing any criticism to the military is not a crime; to the contrary, this criticism can be for the sake of having a better country. Nabil's suggestion that the military give up ruling the country to a civilian council does not necessarily mean a call for dissolving the military establishment. The military's main job is to protect the country and secure it against any enemies, rather than to rule it. It is our right as people to criticize the military and any other establishment in the country when we see they are doing something wrong."

Anonymous9 wrote: "The military leaders are not angels. They have committed some abuses, suppressed the political activists and proceeded with unjustifiable military trials against civilians."

Anonymous10 wrote: "I was one of the protestors at Tahrir Square, and I even got shot. I would like to clarify several points: The military has never provided any ammunition to the police forces during the revolution. I am totally opposed to doing away with the Emergency

Law now, given that the country is still unstable and there are many thugs that are threatening the internal security."

Mohsen wrote: "What a lovely invitation to tear Egypt up. Of course, there are violations from the army, but what do you expect from a dictatorship that lasted more than 60 years. The military is just another organization in the system that's doing what it can with what it has. The people are the ones who are demanding, and as we know Egyptians and what they have become, they won't do a thing unless it is demanded. The people demand, and the army tries to deliver with what it has. The French revolution lasted four years till they cleaned the scene completely. It will take time, but we have to remember that the army is the last line of defense we have. Have a look at Libya."

The thread mentioned above was the reason for Nabil's arrest in Cairo on March 28, 2011, a few days after he posted his article. He was set on trial before a military court and sentenced to three years in prison for "insulting the military." During his imprisonment, Nabil went on a hunger strike, and he was pardoned by the SCAF on January 23, 2012. In a personal interview with the authors in 2010, Nabil said: "My blog has been the only venue in Egypt that opposes the Egyptian military and that is critical of it. All of the articles that were published about the military in the Egyptian media were released and approved by the Egyptian military intelligence. That is why my blog is a breakthrough that has broken the 'military taboo' in Egypt."

In another interview with Nabil from inside his prison cell in Cairo in July 2011, he told the authors: "Through my blog, I uncovered several violations conducted by the military during and after the revolution, such as supporting political corruption, protecting the ousted President Mubarak, and delaying the trial of several members of the Mubarak regime, thus giving them the chance to flee the country. After the revolution, many people have started to realize that my blogs about the military corruption were right on the mark. And this has encouraged other bloggers to criticize the military." Nabil added, "The post that I put on my blog under the title: 'The military and the people were never united,' I included evidence, videos and photos about the military violations of human rights. This was one of the most effective articles that dealt with the military violations before and after the revolution."

The thread mentioned above was a good example of both active civic engagement and citizen journalism. Most importantly, however, it provided a vibrant platform for dialogue and deliberation, since Nabil posted several photos that he shot at Tahrir Square during the Egyptian revolution, and he tried to engage the people who follow his blog in a discussion about a highly sensitive issue, which was the alleged violations that were committed during and after the revolution and the extent of the military's involvement in these violations. It might have been the sensitivity of the issue that led most participants in this thread to use "anonymous" in their posts rather than their real or even fake names. The posters' feedback was highly emotional, either in their defense of the military or their taking Nabil's side and accusing the military of corruption.

While some posts were geared toward problem solving and a call for action to demand the military hand over power to a civilian council, there were no guarantees that these suggestions were going to be implemented. In this context, Haas (2007) argued that "while journalists can promote political change by sponsoring and reporting back on citizen deliberations, encouraging citizens to continue their deliberations and act upon their outcomes within civic and political organizations[,]...and applying pressure on relevant government officials, they cannot on their own ensure...that given citizen solutions are enacted, or that government officials implement given policy recommendations in practice" (p. 77).

In the thread mentioned above, Nabil adopted a civil society function, which is "checking and limiting the state influence" (Diamond, 1999, p. 242). The state here was represented in the military establishment that was running the country. Moreover, at least in theory, he "generated a wide range of interests that may...mitigate the principal polarities of political conflict" (Diamond, 1999, p. 245). However, in reality, Nabil's post hardened, rather than softened, political polarities, as was exemplified through the posts on this thread, which reflected a significant attitudinal division over how the military was perceived. A major reason for this polarization among the posters on this thread was because the political transition and the tremendous developments in Egyptian society during the months immediately following the January 25 revolution had bred a highly galvanized public opinion.

The high level of polarization and galvanization that was exhibited in this thread reminds us of some of the limitations of new media in fostering genuine political deliberation. As Howard (2004) states, "Although many pundits have lauded new media technologies for their potential roles in democratic deliberation, there is quite a difference between imagining how a technology might play such a role, building such applications, and getting the public to use them as desired" (p. 6). This, according to Howard (2004), signals "the complexities of the transition between technological dreams and political applications...[and the difference] between being technologically overdetermined and being sociologically overdetermined" (p. 6).

It can be safely concluded that although new media can provide platforms for online deliberation around political issues, this does not automatically translate into effective political participation, since "familiarity with a technology bears little relationship to a person's sense of duty or interest in politics" and "a growing number of people use the internet to enrich their political lives—participating in online discussion groups, researching candidates and policy options, and following political news[, yet]...the internet may have only a limited role in making people smarter citizens" (Howard, 2004, pp. 6–7).

Likewise, in "investigating whether better deliberative practice can produce better publics" Rheingold (2008) reminds us that "deliberation...is only part of public discourse. Investigation, advocacy, criticism, debate, persuasion, and politicking are all part of the process" (p. 101).

Overall, we can infer from the above threads, which exhibited a high level of deliberation and discussion, that

> "voice", the unique style of personal expression that distinguishes one's communications from those of others, can be called upon to help connect young people's energetic involvement in identity-formation with their potential engagement with society as citizens. Moving from a private to a public voice can help...turn their self-expression into a form of public participation. Public voice is learnable, a matter of consciously engaging with an active public rather than broadcasting to a passive audience (Rheingold, 2008, p. 101).

Moreover, we can conclude that "the public voice of individuals, aggregated and in dialogue with the voices of other individuals, is the fundamental particle of 'public opinion.' When public opinion has the power and freedom to influence policy and grows from the open, rational, critical debate among peers posited by Jurgen Habermas and others, it can be an essential instrument of democratic self-governance" (Rheingold, 2008, p. 101).

Additionally, in this context, we can contend that

> it is not clear whether the blogosphere or any aggregation of online arguments constitute the ideal of constructive debate that public sphere theorists posit, [yet if] many-to-many media afford a window of opportunity for populations to exercise democratic power over would-be rulers, it seems possible that education could play a pivotal role by equipping today's digital natives with historical knowledge, personal experience, rhetorical skills, and a theoretical framework for

> understanding the connection between their power to publish online, their power to influence the circumstances of their own lives, and the health of democracy. (Rheingold, 2008, p. 104)

This window of opportunity to exercise democratic power using many-to-many new media technologies was certainly evident in the case of the Egyptian revolution, which witnessed an active, dynamic, and participatory role for young political activists, many of whom engaged in deep political conversations, debates, and discussions online in an effort to redefine and reshape their country's political future.

Most importantly, the above discussions reveal that participants in computer-mediated communication "develop forms of expression which enable them to communicate social information and to create and codify group-specific meanings, socially negotiate group-specific identities, form relationships . . . which move between the network and face-to-face interaction, and create norms which serve to organize interaction and to maintain desirable social climates" (Baym, 1995, pp. 160–161). In doing so, it could be said that

> together they appropriate the possibilities offered by commonality and individuality in ways that weave them into distinct communities. These communities . . . create shared social realities through interactive negotiation[;] . . . the creation of forms of expressive communication, identity, relationships, and norms through communicative practice in computer-mediated groups is pivotal to this process of creating community. Social realities are created through interaction as participants draw on language and the resources available to make messages that serve their purposes. (Baym, 1995, p. 161)

In studying this process, we have to bear in mind that "all interaction . . . conveys social meaning and thus creates social context" and that "rather than being constrained by the computer, the members of these groups creatively exploit the systems' features so as to play with new forms of expressive communication, to explore possible public identities, to create otherwise unlikely relationships, and to create behavioral norms. In so doing, they invent new communities" (Baym, 1995, p. 151).

Concluding Remarks

This chapter discussed some of the most significant strengths and capacities of political blogs, as a new form of digital media, in aiding the process of political change by increasing awareness about key problems, such as governmental corruption, as well as some of their limitations in this regard. Our discussion of all these factors took into account the fact that

> as we consider the policy issues for the next phase of the digital age, the goal of fostering a healthy, democratic media culture for young people must be a top priority. These policies need to be understood as the building blocks for a framework that will support democratic communications in the future. The exact shape of the policy framework is less important than the key set of principles that must guide it. These include equitable access to technology, open architecture and nondiscrimination for both consumers and producers of digital content, flexible and fair copyright rules that allow for creativity and sharing of cultural content, and open-source applications that will encourage collaboration and innovation. (Montgomery, 2008, p. 42)

We agree with Montgomery (2008) that it is only through applying this framework, with all of its guiding principles mentioned above, that "the democratic potential of the Internet [can be] fulfilled and sustained over the long run, benefiting successive generations of young people" (p. 42).

Similarly, Rheingold (2004) reminds us, "We should not close the books on the debate about the mental or social health of virtual communities and their relationship to the nonvirtual world. And neither should we stop at a shallow level of analysis" (p. 265). He believes that this is especially important because "in coming years...the far more important questions will have to do with the nature of collective action in social cyberspaces" (Rheingold, 2004, p. 266).

Therefore, this compels us to consider both the strengths and weaknesses, as well as the potentials and limitations, of digital media platforms, such as political blogs, in promoting civic engagement, boosting democratization, and aiding political change. For example, we have to be aware of "the need to be cautious about assuming that simply adding new media to old electoral politics will entice new and younger voters to greater participation" (Xenos & Foot, 2008, p. 65). We also have to bear in mind that "understanding the generation gap in online politics as a clash between differing notions of interactivity clearly identifies the ways in which these differences must be negotiated, if the true potential of the Internet as a medium capable of facilitating significant changes in political participation among...youth is to be realized" (Xenos & Foot, 2008, p. 65).

In weighing the pros and cons of these new media technologies and their potential impact on reshaping the process of communication and democratization in the age of cyberspace, we believe that there is enough reason to be "hopeful that informed and committed people can influence the shape of tomorrow's cybersociety in a positive manner, although it has become increasingly clear that democratic outcomes will not emerge automatically. A humane and sustainable cybersociety will only come about if it is deliberately understood, discussed, and planned now—by a larger proportion of the population and not just the big business, media, or policy elites" (Rheingold, 2004, p. 273).

We agree with Rheingold (2004) that in order for these positive outcomes to be reached, "intelligent and democratic leadership is desperately needed at this historical moment" (p. 273). Indeed, we can argue that young political activists in Egypt, including bloggers, played a vital role in securing this needed leadership by engaging in myriad activities to boost civic participation and engagement, both online and offline.

In light of this last point, Rheingold (2008) reminds us that

> many bloggers serve as "intelligent filters" for their publics by selecting, contextualizing, and presenting links of particular interest for that public. In this context, a "public" differs from an "audience" because you, in your role as blogger, have in mind when you write a community of peers who not only read but actively respond to what you write, who might act upon your advice, and who might join you in discussion and collective action. The public you choose to address could be a public in the sense of a political public sphere that undergirds democracy—the communications you engage in with your fellow citizens, with whom you share responsibility for self-governance. (pp. 107–108)

Therefore, Rheingold (2008) suggests that every blogger should ask himself/herself the following set of questions: "What interests you, the blogger? What issue or idea strongly, even passionately, draws your attention and provokes your opinion? Is there a community that shares your interest? Could you and the others constitute a public? Clearly defining and understanding your public is the necessary first step to developing a public voice—the voice you use when you keep that public, and your potential to act together, clearly in mind as you blog" (p. 108).

Moreover, we also have to bear in mind that the effectiveness of blogs in terms of increasing civic engagement and involvement on the part of their followers does not depend only on the blogger, but also on the characteristics of the blog itself. For example, Raynes-Goldie &Walker (2008) remind us that "a site has to be relatively usable and have appealing technology so that people can easily accomplish their goals, just as it has to have a critical mass of the right kind of users. If the tools are frustrating, or there are very few members, a site is not likely to be used[, and]...successful online communities do not necessarily have to be the best designed, but at least have the right people" (p. 176). They also draw our attention to the fact that when it comes to engaging youth in particular, "the functionality and type of tools on [the] site matter for two reasons. First, the site has to have tools that are appealing, familiar, and useful enough so that youth will use them. Second, the site has to facilitate activities that help youth reach their civic engagement goals. These activities...are finding the right information, organizing, networking, and collaborating" (p. 176).

This last point is especially important, taking into account "that active use of networked media, collaboration in social cyberspaces, and peer production of digital cultural products has changed the way young people learn and that their natural attraction to participatory media could be used to draw youth into civic engagement" (Rheingold, 2008, pp. 114–115). The significance of this process lies in the fact that "young people who are interested in civic, community, or activist issues are looking to the Internet for information about causes important to them, connections to like-minded peers and organizations, and for ways to organize and mobilize. When these needs are met, youth report...that they are able to make positive change in their lives and in their communities, demonstrating that the action or result of online engagement is occurring offline" (Raynes-Goldie & Walker, 2008, p. 170). This is certainly applicable in the context of the Egyptian revolution that witnessed the translation of online youth activism and mobilization into effective civic engagement and action offline.

The threads which were analyzed in this chapter offered clear "examples and possibilities of a growing movement of youth who inform and organize themselves online, and then proceed to take action in their communities...[as well as] a growing movement of interactive online civic engagement sites based around social tools...aimed at facilitating youth engagement by providing access to peers, information and tools to mobilize and organize" (Raynes-Goldie & Walker, 2008, p. 186). In this context, we agree with Raynes-Goldie and Walker (2008) that "the most burning research question revolves around the development of an evaluation methodology that assesses the efficacy of online civic engagement sites, specifically the connection between online and offline preparation and action[, which requires]...more detailed investigations into the use and potential improvements to online civic engagement sites for networking with peers, finding information, and organizing" (p. 186).

Furthermore, the powerful role that the Internet, in general, and online platforms such as political blogs, in particular, could play in liberating people from political oppression, according to Bainbridge (2004), could be attributed to the fact that "no government will be able to regulate the internet. Electronic media will be disseminating information through many of the current physical barriers placed by governments.... Politically biased media will no longer be able to control populations since multiple opinions and potentially conflicting facts can be accessed over [the Internet]" (p. 321).

One of the key factors that can aid and facilitate this process is that "cybercommunities will grow in importance...[as] people will belong to virtual towns made up of their friends and family members far and wide. People will have moved away from physical communities, toward online communities" (Bainbridge, 2004, p. 321). The existence of these "on-line communities," according to McLaughlin, Osborne, and Smith (1995), is indicative of the fact that "the net is well suited for organizing distributed communities of persons with specialized common interests" and that "the effective use of a medium requires a good fit between its inherent characteristics and the communication activities it will be used to accomplish" (p. 101). According to Baym (1995), "The factors of temporal structure, external contexts, system infrastructure, group purposes, and participant and group characteristics have been put forward as the most salient preexisting forces on the development of computer-mediated community" (p. 161).

The high level of engagement and involvement that was witnessed in this chapter among both political bloggers and their followers in combating governmental corruption and calling for positive change, through active mobilization, thorough documentation, and meaningful deliberation, give us enough reason to be "excited about the potential of well-executed online civic engagement sites" and to believe that "when youth are engaged on their own terms...the future of young people and positive change in the world will be bright" (Raynes-Goldie & Walker, 2008, p. 186). We believe that the Egyptian revolution, and the myriad of youth-led activities that paved the way for it and helped to execute it, both in the online sphere and the offline domain, is a clear example of this positive change.

The next chapter sums up the most important findings and results of these two analytical chapters, offers concluding remarks, and highlights directions for future research in this area of study.

CHAPTER 6

The Future of Political Blogging in Egypt: Looking Ahead

The five bloggers whose blogs were analyzed in this book were part of a pioneering wave of online activists who planted the seeds for the popular revolution that took place on January 25, 2011, and toppled the corrupt regime of President Hosni Mubarak. Each of these bloggers contributed, in his or her own way, to mobilizing the Egyptian public and revitalizing Egyptian civil society. All five of them were part of the spark that was ignited in the blogs, discussion forums, and chat rooms in the virtual world and spilled over later to the streets, alleys, and squares in the real world, where it turned into a raging fire.

The study of these five blogs and the analysis of their content enable us to better understand the phenomenon of "electronic democracy," which according to Peter Shane (2004), can have two distinct meanings: "The first is the design and deployment of digital information and communication technologies (ICTs) to enhance democratic political practice. The second is a new stage of democracy, a stage during which the proliferation of digital ICTs will have deepened democracy's vitality and legitimacy, whether on a local, national, or even global basis" (p. xi). The exploration of this new phenomenon of "electronic democracy," as Shane (2004) points out, should help us answer a number of important questions, such as

> in terms of enhanced democratic practice, what is the world likely to see in terms of the evolution of new online forms of democratic initiative? What are the opportunities and challenges most likely to arise?...How will the future of ICT-enabled democratic practice be shaped by the social, psychological, and political contexts in which new technologies are deployed? In terms of deepening democracy's vitality and legitimacy, what can and should the world hope for? What should

> be the ambitions of "electronic democrats" if genuine revitalization is to occur, and how likely is the realization of these ambitions? (p. xi)

While each of the five blogs reflected different ideological positions and perspectives, writing styles, and analytical approaches, all of them exhibited varying degrees of the following multifolded functions: (1) Calling for action, mobilization, and organization by the blogger and/or by one or more of the posters; (2) spreading knowledge, providing information, and increasing awareness about one or more key issues; (3) engaging in interactivity, deliberation, and brainstorming between the blogger and the posters, as evidenced by the posted comments, disagreements, debates, and exchanged ideas; and (4) documenting governmental violations of human rights, limitations on freedom, and corruption, through citizen journalism, as evidenced by the posting of videos, photos, documents, and so on by the blogger and/or the posters.

The above multiple functions, which were accomplished by the blogs analyzed here, remind us that computer mediated communication (CMC) can "create opportunities for education . . . learning; [and] . . . participatory democracy; establish countercultures on an unprecedented scale; ensnarl already difficult legal matters concerning privacy, copyright, and ethics; [and] restructure man/machine interaction" (Jones, 1995b, p. 26).

These functions are also in line with the seven online actions highlighted by Schneider and Foot (2004), namely, "(a) getting information, (b) providing information, (c) getting assistance/support, (d) providing assistance/support, (e) allowing for personal expression, (f) accessing others' expression, and (g) engaging in political advocacy" (p. 143). Therefore, the findings of this study "illustrate the importance of the Internet, and particularly the Web, as a significant component of the public sphere, enabling coordination, information sharing, assistance, expression, and advocacy" (Schneider & Foot, 2004, p. 151). Moreover, these multiple functions highlight the potential of online modes of communication to boost the creation of a virtual, global public sphere by connecting people from across the world on a transnational scale (el-Nawawy & Khamis, 2009).

However, there were also some differences between these five blogs, in terms of the centrality of the blogger's role and ideas vis-à-vis his/her posters, that is, whether the blog centered around the expression of the blogger's own views and declared positions on various issues, or whether there was room for genuine dialogue and high level of interactivity between the blogger and the posters, through the exchange of free-floating ideas and two-way communication.

In this respect, it could be said that the highest level of blogger-centrality was found in the blogs of Maikel Nabil and Abdel Monem Mahmoud, both of whom used their blogs as platforms for expressing their personal opinions and perspectives on a wide range of controversial issues, rather than effectively engaging their posters, who were mostly limited in number, in either online dialogue or offline action. The role of the posters was also not as central or crucial in these two blogs, in particular, compared to the other blogs, since many of them simply posted comments or feedback that expressed mostly support, approval, or encouragement to the bloggers, and in some cases voiced criticisms against them, but without necessarily shaping the ongoing discussion in a certain direction, offering concrete suggestions, or calling for taking action on the issues at hand.

This is different from the three other bloggers, namely, Nawara Negm, Wael Abbas, and Sandmonkey, who mainly used their blogs as platforms for engaging their posters in lively debates, enabling them to express their views and exchange their opinions, and encouraging them to take effective action on various issues, when needed, thus exhibiting a lesser degree of blogger-centrality and a greater degree of posters' interactivity and involvement.

Also, the five blogs differed in terms of the basic functions they were attempting to perform, whether it was mobilization of the masses, documentation of governmental violations of human rights and corruption, or boosting deliberation and dialogue among the posters. While all five blogs exhibited some form of documentation, with varying degrees and in different forms, in line with the role of bloggers as citizen journalists, it could be said that Nawara Negm and Wael Abbas, in particular, mostly used their blogs to boost civic engagement and mobilization at the grassroots level, through direct calls for action on the ground, as evidenced by their encouraging their posters to sign petitions online, support certain causes, join certain protests, or gather in specific places. It is for this reason that these two blogs were characterized by a high level of audience interactivity, since the bloggers effectively engaged their posters in both online and offline activism, which included both active and vibrant discussions online via the blogs around key issues of importance and concern, in addition to calls for action and mobilization offline in the real world.

Sandmonkey's blog, in particular, which was the only one in English analyzed in this book, was characterized by a high level of intellectual discourse, deliberation, and sophisticated arguments. This was evident in the postings of Mahmoud Salem (a.k.a. Sandmonkey) himself, as well as the insightful comments and useful feedback from the posters on his blog, many of whom were either Western-educated Egyptian youth, as reflected in their high level of fluency in English; Egyptians living in the diaspora; or foreigners. This demographic profile, which is different from that of the posters on the other four blogs, most of whom were average Egyptians living inside Egypt, could be said to be directly related to the use of the English language in this blog, which enabled the inclusion of a more diverse, transnational, global audience, rather than only a local audience.

This different demographic profile could explain why Sandmonkey's blog, in particular, compared to the four others under study, had a more refined level of argumentation and more concrete and practical suggestions as to how to rebuild the country, both politically and economically, since it was generally noticed that the Egyptians living in the diaspora, who mostly posted in English, and the non-Egyptian posters, were less emotional, used less abstract rhetoric and less inflammatory language, and had more concrete ideas and specific calls for action, compared to the Egyptians living inside Egypt, who mostly posted in Arabic.

Therefore, it could be said that Sandmonkey's blog had greater value than the other four blogs in terms of educating his posters and engaging them in deep intellectual discussions and debates related to the ongoing issues, struggles, and controversies. Here, it could also be argued that the blogger's role was as central to the intellectual process as the role of the posters on his blog, who also shaped the online discussions and deliberations intellectually, despite the fact that these deliberations did not always lead to taking effective action in the real world.

The value of this form of online deliberation lies in the fact that "moving participation to the Internet can increase the number of participants by breaking down barriers created by geography, daily commitments of work and family, social and psychological insecurities, and lack of information. Dialogues can also support dynamic communication in which participants don't just make statements for others to hear; they listen to, respond to, and question statements made by others, all with adequate time to formulate ideas and responses" (Beierle, 2004, pp. 155–156).

Additionally, just as there were differences between the various bloggers and their roles, the reactions of the posters and the various roles they performed on these blogs also varied. Some of them simply cheered or supported the blogger, while others were solely criticizing whatever he/she had to say, or even fiercely attacking the blogger and/or the other posters. Between these two bipolar extremes, some posters represented the middle ground of enlightened deliberation and informed discussion by weighing the pros and cons of the various issues at hand and offering concrete suggestions and practical ideas to resolve problems and overcome challenges.

The use of "inflammatory language" by some posters on these blogs deserves special attention, because "flaming has a peculiarly contagious quality in network newsgroups; one flame often generates a host of bandwagon insults, again, because it is easy to 'follow on'...[and] the degree of hostility expressed in the messages can escalate to the point that someone calls for someone else's expulsion from the community via an electronic cold shoulder or 'kill file' (electronically blocking her or his messages) or by suggesting that someone's system administrator should deprive him or her of net access" (McLaughlin et al., 1995, p. 105). Indeed, evidence of such online "flaming," with its various forms, implications, and potentially contagious effect, was witnessed in the analyzed blogs, through the exchange of crossfire between angry posters and/or their fierce attacks on the bloggers, in some instances.

One of the main factors that contributed to this process of "flaming" is anonymity. According to Baym (1995), "the computer creates anonymity, which leads to a decrease in social inhibition and an increase in flaming. In this way, anonymity is conceptualized as something both inevitable and problematic...[since] people are more insulting when using anonymous CMC" (p. 153). The exacerbation of this "flaming" effect due to the presence of anonymity, which allows participants to conceal their real identities from each other and to therefore attack each other fiercely and vigorously, was also found in another study by this book's authors, which analyzed the exchanged discourses on mainstream Islamic websites (el-Nawawy & Khamis, 2009).

Yet, on the positive side, it could also be argued that "rather than being seen as a negative influence by CMC participants, anonymity is often valued because it creates opportunities to invent alternative versions of one's self and to engage in untried forms of interaction....Given time, anonymous CMC users do build identities for themselves. However, even in systems that are not anonymous, identities are actively and collaboratively created by participants through processes of naming, signing signatures, role creation, and self-disclosure" (Baym, 1995, p. 153). Indeed, there was ample evidence of all of these forms of identity creation by the posters on the various blogs, whether they were anonymous or not.

Along the same line, Rheingold (2004) also draws our attention to the dual effect of anonymity in cyberspace and its two-sided implications on online communication:

> The relative anonymity of the medium, where nobody can see your face or hear your voice, has a disinhibiting function that cuts both ways—people who might not ordinarily be heard in oral discourse can contribute meaningfully, and people who might not ordinarily be rude to one's face can become frighteningly abusive online.... Maintaining civility in the midst of the very conflicts we must solve together as citizens is not easy. The Net is the world's greatest source of information—misinformation and disinformation, community and character assassination—and we have very little but our own wits to sort out the valid from the bogus. (p. 270)

To help us achieve this last goal, Rheingold (2004) suggests that it is necessary to have "a clearly stated policy regarding online behavior that all participants must agree to. Having such a policy will not guarantee success, but not having such a policy probably guarantees failure" (p. 270). He reminds us that "some communities will have very loose rules, some will be far more formal and controlled, the most important point of the exercise is that every participant agrees to a clear written statement of the rules before joining" (Rheingold. 2004, p. 270), and he also emphasizes that "without a cadre of experienced users to help point out the pitfalls and the preferred paths, online populations are doomed to fall into the same cycles of flame, thrash, mindless chatter, and eventual dissolution" (Rheingold, 2004, p. 271). Here, it is worth noting that although all the blogs posted rules and guidelines outlining the expected conduct on the part of the posters, not all posters followed these rules or abided by these guidelines, as evidenced in the use of inflammatory language and attacks on others, in addition to insulting and cursing.

However, just like there was evidence of "flaming" in some of the exchanged discourses on these blogs, there was also equal evidence of voices of reason and moderation, who tried to absorb the anger of some of the agitated posters and to call for self-control and rational dialogue. As McLaughlin, Osborne, and Smith (1995) rightly point out, "It is not uncommon during such episodes to see voices of calm emerge as well as sharper reproaches to flame throwers. Just as the technology encourages flaming, so too does it encourage calls for restraint" (p. 105).

Regardless of the differences among the five bloggers and the posters on their blogs, however, there is no question that all five have strongly contributed to mobilizing the Egyptian public and enhancing the Egyptian youth's level of civic engagement by increasing their awareness about what was taking place on the political scene in Egypt. The type of cyberactivism that was practiced by these five, as well as other popular bloggers, and that culminated in the toppling of the Mubarak regime had been in the works for years before the January 25 revolution. "Collective consciousness in Egypt was building up in the period before the revolution to a great extent as a result of collective discontents. The events that unfolded in Tahrir Square pointed towards many festering economic, social and political issues that go back over twenty years in time" (Stroud & Ibrahim, 2011, p. 11). As was explained in chapter 3, the Egyptian bloggers, like the five whose blogs we analyzed, started shedding light on the political ills, human rights violations, and corruption in Egyptian society as early as the mid-2000s. "Starting as early as 2004 Egyptian bloggers began carving out spaces for communication, expression, and sharing of information.... [Today] blogs continue to be important centers for the spread of information, analysis and exchange of ideas.... Individual bloggers develop a particular reputation that enables them to act as alternatives to mainstream journalists or analysts and ultimately as opinion leaders regardless of their economic or social standing" (Stroud & Ibrahim, 2011, pp. 28–29).

In this context, Hassan Abu-Taleb, deputy director at Al-Ahram Center for Political and Strategic Studies, told the authors in 2009: "Blogs have encouraged the creation of new civil society activities or organizations with new functions. For example, we have seen new associations that provide help to females about how to avoid sexual harassment. These kinds of associations were created thanks to the blogs' role in increasing public awareness in this matter."

Mohammed Sharkawy, a prominent human rights activist, argued that the Egyptian blogs "negotiated new public spaces" that led to a "paradigmatic shift" from the print media to a more expressive online platform. According to Sharkway, "Blogging created a new opposition, a new literary movement that started discussing the problems that Egyptians face on a daily basis, problems that were silenced. It created a virtual reality, new virtual streets to demonstrate upon. This is what... [came to be] called new writing. Language there doesn't matter; all that matters is the act of expression itself" (Stroud & Ibrahim, 2011, p. 8).

Echoing the above comments, Noha Atef, a prominent Egyptian blogger whose blog titled *Torture in Egypt* has helped shed light on human rights violations, told the authors in 2009: "I think people were looking for alternative media such as the blogs because they used to get news in the same format and the same tone from the traditional media that were not that serious in tackling and presenting the problems facing Egyptians. With blogs, it is more interactive; people can speak up and express their views. People are not satisfied with the news they are getting through the mainstream media, and so they are resorting to the blogs to find an outlet to express themselves." Atef believed that her blog has strongly contributed to a more engaged and more politically responsive public inside and outside Egypt. "At least it makes people aware of the fact that torture exists in Egypt. Also, a number of NGOs are interested in making sure that these torture cases are posted on my blog so that people can become aware of it. My blog is also inspiring to many other bloggers and victims of torture. For example, my blog has encouraged some torture victims to start blogging about their experiences. I can say that my blog even inspired a blogger in Uganda to start a similar blog in her country called 'Torture in Uganda.' I met her and she told me that she was inspired by my blog."

Addressing blogs' role in Egyptian civil society, Ehab El-Zalaky, an Egyptian journalist who covered blogs since their introduction in Egypt, told the authors in 2009: "I think blogs have enriched the Egyptian civil society. They are considered a new platform for information, opinion, and for expressing various experiences. I think their biggest and most prominent role was in shedding light on the torture inside the Egyptian prisons. Blogs have been able to reach the average person despite the technical obstacles."

The role of blogging in invigorating Egyptian civil society and enhancing civic engagement, particularly among youth, was exemplified by the five blogs under study in this book. The analysis in chapters 4 and 5 indicated that all five bloggers were shown to utilize several of the civil society functions that were envisioned by Larry Diamond (1999). It was important to look into a theoretical, abstract concept like civil society and apply it to the analysis of these five blogs to obtain some empirical results, particularly because "conclusions about the impact of the Internet on civic engagement have been hampered by . . . a shortage of varied and multiple indicators of attitudes and behaviors regarding engagement" (Jennings & Zeitner, 2003, p. 311).

However, two highly critical issues have to be addressed in the context of our assessment of the Egyptian bloggers' effectiveness in energizing civic engagement: The normative nature of the concept of civil society and the role of the offline environment in the prognosis of the political future of postrevolutionary Egypt.

With regard to the first issue, the normative supposition "that civil society is per se a positive development leading to democratic governance, or to the strengthening of democratic rule where it already exists," has been subject to question on the basis that this normative assumption "represents an obstacle to a more genuine and hopefully more neutral, understanding of the dynamics of civil society in the Arab world.... Civil society in liberal thinking has always had positive normative connotations because it is intimately associated with the most positive of political values: democracy" (Cavatorta & Durac, 2011, pp. 9, 11). However, the critics of the normative-based civil society are opposed to associating the concept with the Western-based liberal democratic theory that does not account for the different nature of the non-Western societies. "The argument is that civil society does not... [on its own] have any normative liberal-democratic nature and does not necessarily promote liberal values. This means that what matters are the groups that make up civil society and, more importantly, the values to which they subscribe" (Cavatorta & Durac, 2011, p. 23). Proponents of the neutral, nonnormative approach to the study of civil society have argued that this approach can pave the way "for an examination of civil society without ideological or political prejudice" (Cavatorta & Durac, 2011, p. 141).

The authors of this study chose a middle ground between the "normative" and the "neutral" approaches to the study of civil society. The normative values serve as a foundation that provides guidance to the assessment of civil society in any given situation. However, these normative values should not be expected to automatically introduce or initiate change without the enthusiasm and readiness of the civic groups to democratize their societies. We used Diamond's normative civil society functions to assess the level of civic engagement on the five blogs under study, but we believe that these functions were empiricized and operationalized thanks to the efforts of the Egyptian youth groups on the ground. Our analysis in the two analytical chapters showed that the five bloggers under study provided a platform for leadership training, political participation, interest group representation, and conflict mediation. These normative values were the impetus for change, and they were translated in the collective action of protestors who led the January 25 revolution while carrying banners calling for freedom and social justice.

In this context, Fahmy Howeidy, a prominent Egyptian journalist and political writer, argued that while it is important to consider the causal relationship between a healthy civil society and democracy, one needs to consider the differences among institutions and political structures that affect how civil society is perceived. In a personal interview with the authors in 2009, Howeidy said:

> I think civil society is a new term that was introduced recently to the Egyptian context. Based on my understanding, a civil society is based on foundations or institutions and are not run by one particular person. Even the definition of institutions is relative. In other words, the way institutions are defined in a democracy are different from the way they are defined in non-democratic societies. For example, political parties can be considered independent institutions, but in our Egyptian context, political parties are mostly a representation of the government. So, overall, one cannot have a particular definition of institutions in civil society without knowing the type of political system that is available. The civil society is one of the consequences of democracy. In the Arab experience, the democratic structure was separated from the function of democracy, and this is a very non-healthy phenomenon. The functions of democracy are threefold: political participation, questioning the government, and power rotation. So, if there is a civil society without these three factors, we would have a structure or skeleton for democracy, without a function for democracy.

The second of the two highly critical issues that we referred to above has to do with the role of the offline environment in the political dynamics of postrevolutionary Egypt. In our assessment of the virtual world, particularly blogs' role in civil society, we should not neglect the circumstances in the real world, which did play a similarly important, if not a more important role in the success of the January 25 revolution in Egypt. "The exclusion of many groups—especially youth—from [the Egyptian] public space had contributed to the formation of...collective consciousness and marked one of the definitive features of the period leading to the Revolution" (Stroud & Ibrahim, 2011, p. 13). Despite the fact that the Mubarak regime cut off the Internet for close to a week during the 18-day revolution, protestors' numbers continued to increase on the Egyptian streets. Addressing the role of the offline activists in the revolution, Wael Khalil, an Egyptian blogger who participated in the revolution, told the authors in February 2011, a few days after the toppling of the regime:

> I saw millions of people on the streets who have never been online. Those people might have been instigated by what they watched on TV or what they heard from their friends. There is no revolution that is initiated by one single social class. In this revolution, there were people from all walks of life and all socio-economic backgrounds. So, the bottom-line here is that the Internet played a role, but the main source of success for this revolution were the people who were determined not to leave the streets until the regime was ousted. Under Mubarak, the online space was freer than the offline space, but now moving on, both spaces will be freer than before.

This book's lead author was at Tahrir Square on February 11, 2011—the day Mubarak was forced to step down—and he interviewed several protestors who were out celebrating. Several of them said they were not using social media. One protestor, a 25-year-old male medical doctor who was camping out on the Square for two weeks to treat the injured, told him: "We have been very organized here. For example, some people were assigned the task of cleaning the streets; moreover, several committees were formed by the protestors, such as a doctors' committee and a committee to handle the media interviews. Delegating responsibilities was done in a very efficient manner. We even had a corner on the Square for posting poetry and another corner for posting pictures and slogans commemorating the revolution."

A female protestor in her forties told the lead author: "This revolution is about principles. It is not about social media, but it is about the people who believed in some principles and who were persistent in their calls for change. Today, we have regained our dignity. I am here with my family at Tahrir Square to congratulate all the Egyptians who participated in this revolution and to tell the whole world that we are proud of being Egyptians."

The above discussion compels us to take another middle position, this time that of "cyberrealism," which lies between the two bipolar extremes of "cyberoptismism" and "cyberpessimism," as outlined by Muhlberger (2004), who explains that

> the cyberoptimist view holds that [information technology (IT)] will appreciably reduce digital inequality, ignorance, and apathy....The cyberpessimist view suggests IT will further increase the influence and knowledge of the advantaged, exclude the disadvantaged, and introduce new possibilities of social control and manipulation by the powerful.....Finally, a cyberrealist view [argues]...that the new capacities

> created by the Internet represent a potential that can be tapped under the right circumstance and that do empower more peripheral groups. (p. 226)

Of all the above views, which attempt to evaluate the role of the Internet and its potential implications on political life, we find the "cyberrealist" view to be the most relevant to our analysis of the role of political blogs in Egypt and their impact on the Egyptian political and communication landscapes. In light of this view, "By reducing the marginal cost of political information, communication, and organizing, at least the potential exists for IT to substantially mobilize political action. Structural factors resulting in a lack of political motivation [can] prevent mobilization . . . , but if an event of sufficient concern occurs, the Internet greatly increases the possibility of mobilization" (Muhlberger, 2004, p. 226).

Indeed, it could be said that the Egyptian revolution was an excellent example of this kind of event, since it was worthy of "sufficient concern," and the Internet played a crucial role in it in terms of mobilizing people to take action. However, while acknowledging these facts, we are also fully aware of some of the constraints that can limit the effectiveness of the Internet's role, especially in developing countries like Egypt, such as the high level of illiteracy, poor infrastructure, limited accessibility, and the suppressive measures adopted by the regimes in power, which can include their own manipulation of online means of communication to circumvent the activities of the political activists, thus turning the Internet into a double-edged sword and a battlefield for "cyberwars" (Khamis et al., 2012). This is in line with Shane's (2004) remark that

> technological potential is hardly the soul or even primary predictor of the likely impacts of electronic networks on democracy. First of all, [information communication technologies (ICTs)] are as inherently adaptable to programs of control as they are to programs of empowerment. The networks that facilitate information sharing and discourse also, and to an unprecedented degree, facilitate filtering, surveillance, and the evasion of democratically adopted norms. The capacities of new ICTs could thus be deployed as much to suppress democracy as to enhance it. (p. xii)

The measures taken by the toppled Egyptian regime during the revolution to block the activists' online communication efforts, which included shutting down the Internet for an entire week, provided clear evidence supporting the existence of these "push" and "pull" mechanisms and tensions between the regimes in power and the activists who are fighting against them, with both sides engaging in cyberwars (Khamis et al., 2012) to achieve their goals. This highlights the importance of adopting "'cyberrealist' thought about the prospects for electronic democracy" which "embrace[s] neither the hyperoptimistic technological determinism of the early 1990s nor the doomsday anxieties of the pessimistic backlash" (Shane, 2004, p. xii). This requires adopting a balanced and even-handed approach in thinking about "what ICT-enabled democratic revitalization would require of new technologies in principle and what those technologies are likely to offer in practice" (Shane, 2004, p. xii). This is the kind of approach that we adopted throughout this book in assessing the roles and functions of the studied political blogs and analyzing their multiple implications.

Adopting such a balanced and realistic approach in assessing the multiple roles of political blogs, with all their possible strengths and potential limitations, while staying away from the bipolar opposites of "technological determinism" or "sociological determinism," requires acknowledging that "digital space and digitization are not exclusive conditions that stand outside the nondigital. Digital space is embedded in the larger societal, cultural, subjective, economic, and imaginary structurations of lived experience and the systems within which we exist and operate" (Sassen, 2004, p. 299).

This "embedded media perspective," which we adopted throughout this book, "is a powerful analytical framework for describing the way in which new media are deeply set in our social and personal lives," because it helps us to see that "media that fit well with existing social habits become deeply entrenched, difficult for us to give up, and fixed mediators of our social interaction. Moreover, we seem quick to give up communication technologies that are ill fitting and not easily embedded in our daily lives" (Howard, 2004, p. 24). Additionally, "in terms of *status*, embedded media situate us as both producers and consumers of political, economic, and cultural information... [they] can help us form (or hinder us from forming) our own political opinions... in terms of *link*, these technologies connect different spheres of our lives more efficiently and effectively than do traditional media" (Howard, 2004, p. 24).

Most importantly, as the findings of this study clearly reveal, this "embedded media perspective" enables us to see that "communication tools provide both capacities and constraints for human action and that individual users are responsible for taking advantage of capacities and overcoming constraints in daily use" and that "there is mutual structuration; technological use patterns conform to relations in a personal network, but the habits of personal networking adjust to the communication tools available" (Howard, 2004, p. 25). Therefore, we agree with Howard (2004) that "these new technologies have been deeply embedded in multiple spheres of life—cultural, political, and economic—such that the global and personal contexts of our lives are fitted together and tightly linked" (p. 26).

Of special relevance to this study is the realization that "the embedded role of the Internet in everyday life is perhaps most prevalent for youth" and that "civic engagement... is one of the areas of activity that has made the transition to the online realm, with varied forms of implementation and varying degrees of success" (Raynes-Goldie & Walker, 2008, p. 161). However, it is equally important to realize that these forms of online communication should be best seen as "supplements" to offline efforts in the real world, rather than "substitutes" for such efforts, since "social software should empower rather than replace traditional forms of interaction... [and therefore] the role of online civic engagement tools [is] enhancing and empowering real-world action," and furthermore, "efforts in the online civic engagement space are often more strongly suited for enhancing or more deeply engaging young people who are *already* civically minded" (Raynes-Goldie & Walker, 2008, p. 161). This last point is certainly applicable to the young Egyptian bloggers studied here, most of whom had been active in the realm of political opposition before starting their own blogs, as well as many of their posters, who were equally engaged and actively involved in political life offline. This proves that "interactive Web sites and online communities aimed at promoting civic engagement, activism, or community involvement among youth are generally facilitators of the civic engagement that occurs in the offline world, but not necessarily the places where this engagement occurs... [, and] this role of online civic engagement tools is a valuable precursor to engaging young people in their physical communities" (Raynes-Goldie & Walker, 2008, p. 162).

In explaining how online civic engagement sites are primarily "facilitators of action," rather than "places of action," Raynes-Goldie and Walker (2008) provide the following example, which is of utmost relevance to the findings of this book:

> While actions such as writing to an official or signing a petition are positive actions that do occur online, the majority of civic engagement activities resulting from online engagement actually happens in the offline world. Online engagement sites are facilitators of these offline

> activities, providing access to three keys of change: information, people, and tools to organize. These sites enable youth to access information about issues, other relevant organizations, and how to take action effectively. They can connect with their peers to get feedback and support, and organize around issues important to them. Armed with the support of like-minded individuals, tools to organize, and the right information, youth are empowered by these Web sites to step out into the offline world to volunteer, raise awareness, educate others, and start their own organizations. (p. 162)

There is certainly ample evidence in this book that the political blogs under study have been performing all of these functions for the participating youth, thus facilitating their online and offline civic engagement efforts, through being "embedded" in their daily lives and social patterns. This is especially true since today "the core tools that young people use so readily [are] blogs, discussion boards, podcasts, and instant messaging—combined with collaborative action-planning tools, background information on...social issues, and connections to relevant organizations, groups, and their peers" (Raynes-Goldie & Walker, 2008, pp. 162–163). Therefore, what makes venues such as political blogs particularly attractive to youth and effective in boosting their political activism is the fact that "providing civic engagement opportunities online—where youth already spend their time—has great potential. It is accessible, familiar, and does not ask youth to change their habits or step outside their comfort zones to get involved" (Raynes-Goldie & Walker, 2008, p. 162). This helps us understand why and how the political blogs under study acted as important "facilitators" for young people's political activism that paved the way for the eruption of the Egyptian revolution.

At the time of writing this book, almost two years after the revolution took place, the Egyptian political scene is going through political turbulence, ideological ruptures, and serious divisions that may affect the future of political blogging and redraw the parameters of its impact on civil society. During the revolution, which did not have one specific leader, there was one youth coalition whose members were united around one objective: toppling the Mubarak regime. However, in the weeks and months following the revolution, the one coalition turned into more than 140 coalitions, with different agendas and conflicting demands with regard to the process of writing the new constitution, selecting parliamentary members, and voting for the president. This is posing an ongoing challenge to civic engagement and collective consciousness in Egyptian civil society. "When the message was simple and negative—'The people want to bring down the regime'—unity among the opposition groups was simple. When the message becomes complex and positive, it becomes harder to sustain both unity and participation. This is not to blame the idealistic groups that helped usher in political change. The absence of political discourse in Egypt for decades, the vacuous politics of Egypt's opposition parties, and the ways in which bureaucratic repression paved over any sort of charismatic or ideological leadership has taken its toll" (Alterman, 2011, pp. 113–114). Adding to the complex scene, there is a feeling among the revolutionaries that other than toppling Mubarak, their demands for social justice, an end to corruption and "institutional[izing] youth engagement at all levels of civic affairs" have not been met (Stroud & Ibrahim, 2011, p. 42).

In addition to the complexity of the Egyptian civil society structure, which has resulted in a more confusing political message, there is the problem of dogmatism and lack of political tolerance that has been dominating the political environment in Egypt. Addressing this problem, Nabil Abdel Fattah, former director of Al-Ahram Center for Political and Strategic Studies, told the authors in a personal interview in the summer of 2010:

> Generally, we have a big problem with the culture of dialogue in Egypt. This dialogue culture has been very weak and fragile. Very few cases and issues are subject to objective and critical thinking. Educational levels are very weak, and there is religious dogmatism. All these factors have led to an inclination to fight rather than engage in a civilized dialogue. Such an environment does not lead to rational critical debates. And what we are seeing in the virtual world in this context is nothing but an extension of what we are seeing in the real world. For example, if you read through the readers' comments on the articles posted on newspaper websites and the discussion forums, you will realize that profanities and accusations are used right and left and that people don't know how to disagree. The people are frustrated and they explode when they find a venue to express their views.

This sense of dogmatism that stands in the way of a rational-critical debate has increased after the January 25 revolution, fueled by serious divisions. There is the "digital divide" resulting from the huge gap between the technology haves and have-nots. As we mentioned in chapter 3, Internet penetration in Egypt was only 15 percent in 2009. Furthermore, there is the "democratic divide" resulting from the chasm "between those who do and do not use the multiple political resources available on the Internet for civic engagement" (Norris, 2001, p. 12).

In addition to the divisions mentioned above, more serious types of divisions and polarizations that are hampering any efforts toward collective civic engagement in the transition to democracy in post-revolutionary Egypt are the ideological, sectarian, and religious divisions. These divisions revolve around Islamism versus secularism, and they have become more critical since the election of Mohamed Morsi of the Muslim Brotherhood as the fifth Egyptian president in June 2012. Although Morsi announced his resignation from the Brotherhood's Freedom and Justice Party, he is still ideologically associated with the group. His victory has galvanized, rather than alleviated, the tensed polarization. This is especially true since "the secular politicians accused the Brotherhood of 'hijacking' the revolution, called the group a threat to the 'civil' character of the state, and charged that the Brotherhood would impose religious rule" (Kirkpatrick, 2012).

Proponents of the secularist trend in Egypt accuse political Islamism of being contradictory to democracy. However, there is a counterargument to this accusation:

> Indeed, it can be argued that Islamist movements can be a potential force for democratic change in light of four variables: First of all, their political discourse is often couched in the language of democratic procedures.... Second, the internal structure of the majority of these movements is surprisingly reliant on democratic procedures with a considerable role played by ordinary members.... Third, these movements have an indirect beneficial effect by generalizing activism in society because they have a polarizing ideology, which generates opposition from social groups that feel threatened by it. Finally, such associations... are increasingly tolerant of groups and associations that do not necessarily share their societal outlook. (Cavatorta & Durac, 2011, p. 27–28)

In our selection of the five blogs under study, we made sure to include an Islamist blogger—Abdel Monem Mahmoud—who told the authors in February 2011: "I left the Brotherhood, but did not give up my belief in the ideological school of the group. In my blog, I criticize the organizational structure of the Brotherhood, but I do not criticize the ideological bases or foundation of the Brotherhood as a moderate Islamist school." On April 4, 2011, Mahmoud announced through his blog *I am a Brotherhood* that he decided to stop blogging, and he wrote a farewell note to his followers, mentioning that his blog had already achieved its purpose of humanizing the group in a way that nobody had done before, while providing a constructive criticism of the group when needed. He ended his note by saying that he may start a new blog soon, but that he would always consider the Brotherhood to be his "Big House," where he was "taught the principles of moderate Islam."

Among the five analyzed blogs, we also included a secularist—Mahmoud Salem (akaSandmonkey)—who told the authors in June 2010: "I am a libertarian and I adopt this ideology through my blog. I am anti-Islamist, but I am not anti–human rights in Islamism. I call for the separation of church and state."

So, both trends—Islamism and secularism—were included in the five blogs we selected, and it was interesting to see that they both contributed to enhancing civic engagement in Egypt, albeit through utilizing different techniques.

Beside these two polarizing trends, we were also keen to include a blogger such as Maikel Nabil, who expressed more extreme, and unconventional, views through his blog, such as his outright support for Israel and his declared agnostic identity. In this context, it maybe useful to mention that the two remaining bloggers under study—Wael Abbas and Nawara Negm—refused to declare a specific ideological orientation through their blogs. They simply referred to themselves as political activists who are using blogging to induce sociopolitical reform in their country.

The question remains: What do bloggers need to do to help the Egyptian civil society end this division between Islamism and secularism and overcome these sensitive circumstances that may dictate the country's future? Bloggers can engage in "bridge-building" activities (Cavatorta & Durac, 2011, p. 157). An excellent example of the bloggers' bridge-building was the campaign they launched to free Abdel Monem Mahmoud, who was arrested in 2007 as part of the Mubarak regime's crackdown on the Muslim Brotherhood. In his own words, Mahmoud described this campaign by saying:

> Other bloggers launched a support campaign calling for my release. The good thing was that bloggers from various backgrounds and with various ideologies—socialists, liberals and Islamists—participated in this campaign. I believe that this campaign did play a critical role in my release. They put pressure on the prosecutors to release me. They posted messages online and collaborated with human rights organizations and disseminated the message through their blogs, YouTube, and international media venues about my case. As a result of this pressure and the bloggers' collaborative effort, I was released earlier than expected. Today, this campaign is still used as a model for how to pressure the government to release a blogger from prison.

The cross-ideological unity that characterized the campaign to release Mahmoud in 2007 is highly needed in today's political environment in Egypt. The bloggers set the example in the virtual world, and it paid off in the real, offline world.

Another strategy that can be adopted by the bloggers is to focus specifically on promoting human rights issues, boosting personal freedoms, and fighting governmental corruption, rather than focusing on democratic reforms on the broader institutional level, such as constitutional reform and parliamentary elections. Focusing on human rights cases can lead to more concrete outcomes that can serve civil society. This would be particularly constructive in bridging the gap and decreasing the divisiveness between different ideological trends, such as Islamists and secularists, because "Islamist groups rhetorically support individual rights, such as freedom of speech and association. In addition, they are also typically forthright to the issue of torture, because they are the primary victims of abuse. As a result, focusing on such individual human rights would not constitute as divisive an issue within the opposition as macro-institutional reforms might. The policy implications of this would mean sponsoring those secular and liberal associations that do not deny the commonality of interests they have with some Islamist groups on certain issues" (Cavatorta & Durac, 2011, p. 157).

The previous discussion reminds us that the differences between the analyzed blogs did not just encompass the aspect of cyberactivism that each of them chose to focus on, whether it was mobilization, documentation, or deliberation; the centrality of the blogger's role; the role played by the posters and their degree of interactivity on each blog; as well as the demographic characteristics of the posters, which had to do with whether the blog was in English or Arabic. Rather, they also included the uniqueness and individuality of the analyzed blogs in terms of the diverse ideological positions adopted by the bloggers (and the posters) vis-à-vis various political and religious issues.

The similarities and differences that manifested themselves through the various political blogs under study remind us of what Norris (2004) describes as the "bridging" and "bonding" roles of online communities "that function to bring together disparate members of the community . . . and . . . reinforce close-knit networks among people sharing similar backgrounds and beliefs" (p. 31). This classification "assumes that pure bonding groups are most likely to occur online where social homogeneity and ideological homogeneity overlap, deepening networks among people sharing similar backgrounds and beliefs. In contrast, where the internet draws together those from diverse social backgrounds and beliefs and thereby widens contacts, the typology suggests that this generates pure bridging groups" (Norris, 2004, p. 34).

In elaborating on this classification, Norris (2004) explains that, on the one hand "the result of participating in online communities could be expected to reinforce like-minded beliefs, similar interests, and *ideological* homogeneity among members. So many interest groups, organizations, and associations are available on the internet that it is exceptionally easy to find the niche Web site or specific discussion group that reflects one's particular beliefs and interests, avoiding exposure to alterative points of view" (p. 33). Yet, on the other hand "certain features of the internet could be expected to bridge traditional social divides. Textual communication via the internet strips away the standard visual and aural cues of social identity—including those of gender, race, age, and socioeconomic status—plausibly promoting heterogeneity" (Norris, 2004, p. 33).

In understanding this classification, however, it is important to bear in mind that "this conceptual distinction should be seen as a continuum rather than a dichotomy because in practice many groups serve both bridging and bonding functions, but networks can be classified as falling closer to one end of this spectrum or the other" (Norris, 2004, p. 32). Indeed, it could be said that we found enough evidence supporting the existence of both the "bridging" and "bonding" ends of this spectrum on the analyzed political blogs in this book. However, it is safe to conclude that the dominant function performed by most of these blogs fell closer to the "bonding" end, due to the prevailing similarities that mostly manifested themselves between the bloggers and the posters within each blog, especially in terms of ideological homogeneity. This finding "suggests that online contact does bring together like-minded souls who share particular beliefs, hobbies, or interests, probably due to the hyperpluralism and ideological diversity widely evident on the internet as well as widening social diversity" (Norris, 2004, p. 37).

The similarities and differences witnessed on the analyzed blogs are also closely linked to what Jones (1995b) described as "the tensions caused by differentiation and homogenization in the (re)production of space. In the case of CMC, what allows for the reproduction of space is the malleability with which identity can be created and negotiated.... Consequently, one must question the potential of CMC for production of social space. Could it perhaps *re*produce 'real' social relations in a 'virtual' medium?" (p. 14). In answering this question,

Jones (1995b) contended that online forms of communication have the potential to create new social formations and to form a new matrix of social relations, mainly because "identity as mediated in cyberspace carries no essential meanings. Alliances based on 'sameness' may form and dissolve . . . [and] . . . CMC users may use similar resources to develop and structure meaning" (p. 31). In thinking about these new online communities and their nature, however, it is important to bear in mind that they are closely linked to the particular nature of the computer itself, as Jones (1995b) argued, "Because these machines are seen as 'linking' machines (they link information, data, communication, sound, and image . . .), they inherently affect the ways we think of linking up to each other, and thus they fit squarely into our concerns about community" (p. 32).

The fact that new online communities formulated in cyberspace, as in the case of political blogs, not only combine the bipolar extremes of "bridging" and "bonding" or "differentiation" and "homogenization," but that in doing so they also restructure the social formations of the notions of "identity" and "community," compels us to pay attention to a number of important issues:

> First, understanding the place of these new technologies from a sociological perspective requires avoiding a purely technological interpretation and recognizing the embeddedness and variable outcomes of these technologies for different social orders. These technologies can indeed be constitutive of new social dynamics, but they can also be derivative or merely reproduce older conditions. Second, such an effort in turn calls for categories that capture what are now often conceived of as contradictory, or mutually exclusive, attributes. (Sassen, 2004, p. 303)

The recognition of the points mentioned above necessitates focusing on three important issues, which are of special relevance to the findings of this book, namely, "the embeddedness of the new technologies, the destabilizing of older hierarchies of scale when these technologies come into play, and the mediating cultures that organize the relation between these technologies and users" (Sassen, 2004, p. 303).

As previously mentioned, there is sufficient evidence in this book that these new forms of online communication are deeply embedded in the daily lives of the Egyptian political bloggers and the posters on their blogs. There is equally strong evidence that these forms of communication have restructured the participants' identities and their sense of community, both online and offline. Most importantly, there is a clear indication that these forms of communication played a crucial role in destabilizing the older hierarchies of power in society, as evidenced in their contribution to shaking the Mubarak regime and paving the way for sociopolitical reform.

The bigger question that still awaits an answer, however, is: Will the Egyptian bloggers be able to play as an effective a role in building civil society in the "New Egypt" as they did in toppling a corrupt regime? Addressing this question, Hassan Nafaa, a former general coordinator for the National Association for Change (a.k.a. the Kefaya ["enough"] movement) and a political science professor at Cairo University, told the authors in 2010: "In a country like Egypt where more than 40 percent of the population is between 15 and 40 years of age, the youth plays a vital and critical role by definition. And so, the youth is bound to continue to play an increasingly important role. Our youth is highly enthusiastic, politically aware and has the ability to adjust and create. And so I am hopeful that the youth will be able to initiate change in the Egyptian political scene. The Internet has provided this youth with the venue through which they can express their hopes and frustrations in an unprecedented way."

Echoing Nafaa's optimism with regard to the future of political blogging in Egypt, Ahmed Badawy, a blogger and political activist, told the authors in February, 2011, two days after Mubarak stepped down:

> Blogs will continue to flourish because people's political awareness has increased thanks to this revolution. I expect that the long-time bloggers in Egypt will start heading to the traditional forms of print journalism. And we have to remember that corruption will not go away totally in Egypt, and as long as there is corruption, we will continue to need the social media to uncover it. We also have to remember that the traditional forms of media do not have as many reporters on the ground to cover all what is going on. However, with blogging and citizen journalism, the ordinary people can take some photos, shoot a video and upload it online. Also, now the average Egyptians who used to make fun of the social media impact have come to realize that these social media can play a more powerful role in the political scene. If we have a full-fledged democracy in Egypt, it will enhance the online discourse and contribute to its flourishing.

Another prominent blogger and civil society activist, Hussam El-Hamalawy, was cautiously optimistic regarding the future of political blogs. In his interview with the authors in 2009, he said: "What I see is an expanding sphere of blogs, microblogs, and Internet activism in Egypt, and I can see more and more people getting online, which means that I can see more influence. But our role as bloggers will continue to be mainly disseminating information. Some bloggers believe that if they call for a general strike through their blogs, people will follow. But things don't work that way. We have to always have one foot in cyberspace and one foot on the ground. We should not be totally immersed in virtual reality."

El-Hamalawy's last sentence was right on the mark. One must always remember that blogs could never, on their own, enhance civic engagement without a vibrant civil society to complement their role in the offline world. This is especially true since blogs are "an ideal tool for connecting loose networks of association, bringing together otherwise disparate groups and individuals to support a common cause" (Wilkinson, 2011, p. 7).

All five bloggers included in this book were well aware of the role of political blogs in complementing offline civic engagement, since they all started out as political activists on the ground before turning to online activism. It is our hope that the current and future generations of Egyptian bloggers will draw upon sufficient resources in the offline world and facilitate their transfer to the domain of civic engagement, both online and offline, in an effort to supplement the ongoing challenges of sociopolitical reform in Egypt. In doing so, we also hope that they will be able to reduce some of the political divisions and ideological tensions that set the Egyptian people apart from one another and, thus, contribute to their integration into a more active and effective community, both in the virtual and real worlds, for the sake of a better Egypt.

References

Abdel-Dayem, M. (2009). *Middle East bloggers: The street leads online.* Committee to Protect Journalists. Retrieved from http://www.cpj.org/reports/2009/10/middle-east-bloggers-the-street-leads-online.php

Abdel Rahman, A. (1985). *Studies in the contemporary Egyptian press.* Cairo: Dar Al Fikr Al-Arabi (in Arabic).

———. (2002). *Issues of the Arab press in the twenty-first century.* Cairo: Al-Arabi lilnashr Wal Tawzi' (in Arabic).

Abdulla, R. A. (2006). An overview of media developments in Egypt: Does the Internet make a difference? *Global Media Journal (GMJ)* (Mediterranean edition), *1*, 88–100.

———. (2007). *The Internet in the Arab world: Egypt and beyond.* New York: Peter Lang Publishing.

Acosta-Alzuru, C., & Kreshel, P. J. (2002). "I'm an American girl . . . whatever *that* means": Girls consuming Pleasant Company's American Girl identity. *Journal of Communication*, *52*(1), 139–161.

Agati, M. (2007). Undermining standards of good governance: Egypt's NGO law and its impact on the transparency and accountability of CSOs. *International Journal of Not-for-Profit Law, 9*(2), 56–83.

Agre, P. E. (2004). Growing a democratic culture: John Commons on the wiring of civil society. In H. Jenkins & D. Thorburn (Eds.), *Democracy and new media* (pp. 61–67). Cambridge, MA: The MIT Press.

Ajemian, P. (2008). The Islamist opposition online in Egypt and Jordan. *Arab Media & Society.* Retrieved from http://www.arabmediasociety.com/topics/index.php?t_article=183

Al-Anani, K. (2007). Brotherhood bloggers: A new generation voices dissent. *Arab Insight.* Retrieved from http://www.arabinsight.org/aishowarticle.cfm?id=186

Allan, S., Sonwalkar, P., & Carter, C. (2007). Bearing witness: Citizen journalism and human rights issues. *Globalization, Societies and Education*, *5*(3), 373–389.

Al Malky, R. (2008). Blogging for Reform: The Case of Egypt. *Arab Media & Society.* Retrieved July 15, 2012 from: http://www.arabmediasociety.com/?article=12

Al-Saggaf, Y. (2006). The online public sphere in the Arab world: The war in Iraq on Al-Arabiya website. *Journal of Computer-Mediated Communication*, *12*, 311–334.

Alterman, J. (2011, Fall). The revolution will not be tweeted. *The Washington Quarterly, 34*(4), 103–116.

Atia, T. (2006, July). Paradox of the free press in Egypt. USEF Expert Panel Discussion, Washington D.C.

Bainbridge, W. S. (2004). The future of the Internet: Cultural and individual conceptions. In P. N. Howard & S. Jones (Eds.), *Society online: The Internet in context* (pp. 307–324). California: Sage Publications.

Barlow, A. J. (2007). *Blogging America: The New public sphere.* New York: Praeger.

Baym, N. K. (1995). The emergence of community in computer-mediated communication. In S. G. Jones (Ed.), *Cybersociety: Computer-mediated communication and community* (pp. 138–163). California: Sage Publications.

Beckerman, G. (2007). The new Arab conversation. *Columbia Journalism Review, 45*(5), 17–23.

Beierle, T. C. (2004). Digital deliberation: Engaging the public through online policy dialogues. In P. Shane (Ed.). *Democracy online: The prospects for political renewal through the Internet.* (pp 155–166). New York: Routledge.

Bennett, W. L. (2008). Changing citizenship in the digital age. In W. L. Bennett (Ed.), *Civic life online: Learning how digital media can engage youth* (pp. 1–24). Cambridge, MA: The MIT Press.

Berenger, R. D. (2006). Introduction: War in cyberspace. *Journal of Computer-Mediated Communication, 12*(1), article 9. Retrieved July 20, 2012 from: http://jcmc.indiana.edu/vol12/issue1/berenger.html

Bers, M. U. (2008). Civic identities, online technologies: From designing civics curriculum to supporting civic experiences. In W. L. Bennett (Ed.), *Civic life online: Learning how digital media can engage youth* (pp. 139–159). Cambridge, MA: The MIT Press.

Bohman, J. (2004). Expanding dialogue: The Internet, the public sphere and prospects for transnational democracy. In N. Crossley & J. Roberts (Eds.), *After Habermas: New perspectives on the public sphere* (pp. 131–155). Oxford: Blackwell Publishing.

Booth, J. A., & Richard, P. B. (1998, August). Civil society, political capital, and democratization in Central America. *The Journal of Politics, 60*(3), 780–800.

Boulianne, S. (2009). "Does Internet use affect engagement? A meta–analysis of research," *Political Communication 26*(2), 193–211.

Boyd, D. (1999). *Broadcasting in the Arab world: A survey of the electronic media in the Middle East* (3rd ed.) Ames: Iowa State University Press.

Bratton, M. (1994). Civil society and political transition in Africa. *Institute for Development Research Reports, 11*(6), 1–21.

Brauer, M. (2008). Citizen action groups and online communication. In Carpentier, et al. (Eds.), *Democracy, journalism and technology: New developments in an enlarged Europe* (pp. 229–240). Estonia: Tartu University Press.

Browers, M. L. (2006). *Democracy and civil society in Arab political thought: Transcultural possibilities.* New York: Syracuse University Press.

Brown, F. (2005). "Citizen" journalism is not professional journalism. *Quill Magazine, 93*(42), 42.

Bunbongkarn, S. (2004). The role of civil society in democratic consolidation in Asia. In Y. Sato (Ed.), *Growth and governance in Asia* (pp. 137–144). Honolulu, HI: Asia-Pacific Center for Security Studies.

Calhoun, C. (2004). Information technology and the international public sphere. In D. Schuler & P. Day (Eds.), *Shaping the network society: The new role of civil society in cyberspace* (pp. 229–251). Cambridge, MA: The MIT Press.

Cammaerts, B. (2008). Critiques on the participatory potentials of Web 2.0. *Communication, Culture & Critique 1* (4), 358–377.

Carr, S. (2010, March 5). Egypt's cyber battles: An ambivalent relationship with the Internet. *Daily News Egypt.* Retrieved from http://www.thedailynewsegypt.com/article.aspx?ArticleID=28251

Cavatorta, F., & Durac, V. (2011). *Civil society and democratization in the Arab world: The dynamics of activism.* London: Routledge.

Cesario, M. (2009). Arab civil society? It is already in the future (and waiting for politics). *ResetDoc.* Retrieved from http//www.resetdoc.org/EN/Arab-civil-society.php#

Christians, C. G. (1999). The common good as first principle. In T. Glasser (Ed.), *The idea of public journalism* (pp. 67–84). New York: The Guilford Press.

Chung, D., Trammell, K. D., & Porter, L. V. (2007, Autumn). Uses and perceptions of blogs: A report on professional journalists and journalism educators. *Journalism & Mass Communication Educator, 62*(3), 305–322.

Civil society index report for the Arab Republic of Egypt. (2005). Cairo, Egypt: Center for Development Services. Retrieved from www.civicus.org/new/media/Egypt%20Executive%20summary.pdf

Coleman, S. (2005). Blogs and the new politics of listening. *The Political Quarterly, 76*(2), 272–280.

———. (2008). Doing it for themselves: Management versus autonomy in youth e-citizenship. In Bennett, W. L. (Ed.), *Civic Life Online: Learning how Digital Media can Engage Youth* (p.p. 189–206). Massachusetts: MIT Press.

Committee to Protect Journalists. (2009). *Ten worst countries to be a blogger.* Retrieved from http://www.cpj.org/reports/2009/04/10-worst-countries-to-be-a-blogger.php

Cooper, S. (2006). *Watching the Watchdog: Bloggers as the Fifth Estate.* Wisconsin: Marquette Books.

Crack, A. (2007, September). Transcending borders? Reassessing public spheres in a networked world. *Globalizations, 4*(3), 341–354.

Crocker, D. C. (2009). *Ethics of global development: Agency, capability, and deliberative democracy.* Cambridge, UK: Cambridge University Press.

Dahlberg, P. (2001). The Internet and democratic discourse: Exploring the prospects of online deliberative forums extending the public sphere. *Information, Communication & Society, 4*(4), 615–633.

Dahlberg, L. (2007). The Internet, deliberative democracy, and power: Radicalizing the public sphere. *International Journal of Media and Cultural Politics, 3*(1), 47–64.

———. (2007). Rethinking the Fragmentation of the Cyberpublic: From Consensus to Contestation. *New Media & Society 9*(5), 827–847.

Dahlgren, P. (2001). The public sphere and the net: Structure, space, and communication. In W. L. Bennett & R. M. Entman (Eds.), *Mediated politics: Communication in the future of democracy* (pp. 33–55). Cambridge, UK: Cambridge University Press.

———. (2009). *Media and political engagement: Citizens, communication, and democracy.* Cambridge, UK: Cambridge University Press.

Davies, C. (2011). Ten must-read blogs from the Middle East. *CNN.* Retrieved June 12, 2012 from: http://www.cnn.com/2011/WORLD/meast/04/14/bloggers.middle.east/index.html

Day, P., & Schuler, D. (2004). Prospects for a new public sphere. In D. Schuler & P. Day (Eds.), *Shaping the network society: The new role of civil society in cyberspace* (pp. 353–375). Cambridge, MA: The MIT Press.

Dennis, K. (2007). Technologies of civil society: Communication, participation and mobilization. *Innovation, 20*(1), 19–34.

Deuze, M. (2003). The Web and its journalisms: Considering the consequences of different types of newsmedia online. *New Media & Society, 5*(2), 203–230.

Diamond, L. (1997a, June). *Civil society and the development of democracy.* Working paper presented at the Center for Advanced Study in the Social Sciences of the Juan March Institute, Madrid, Spain.

———. (1997b, March). *Prospects for democratic development in Africa.* Paper presented to the University of Zimbabwe, Department of Political and Administrative Studies, Democratic Governance Project, Harare, Zimbabwe.

———. (1999). *Developing democracy: Toward consolidation.* Baltimore: The Johns Hopkins University Press.

———. (2001, June). *What civil society can do to reform, deepen, and improve democracy.* Paper presented to the Workshop on Civil Society, Social Capital, and Civic Engagement in Japan and the United States. Sponsored by the Japan Foundation Center for Global Partnership, The Asia Foundation, and the program on U.S. Japan Relations at Harvard University, Tokyo, Japan.

Domingo, D., & Heinonen, A. (2008). Weblogs and journalism: A typology to explore the blurring boundaries. *Nordicom Review, 29*(1), 3–15.

Drezner, D. W., & Farrell, H. (2004). *The power and politics of blogs.* Paper presented at the American Political Science Association Annual Meeting, Washington, D.C. Retrieved from http://www.cs.duke.edu/courses/spring05.cps182s/readings/blogpowerpolitics.pdf

Earl, J., & Schussman, A. (2008). Contesting cultural control: Youth culture and online petitioning. In W. L. Bennett (Ed.), *Civic life online: Learning how digital media can engage youth* (pp. 71–95). Cambridge, MA: The MIT Press.

Edwards, M. (2004). *Civil society.* Cambridge, MA: Polity.

Elbayar, K. (2005). NGO laws in selected Arab states. *International Journal of Not-for-Profit Law, 7*(4), 3–27.

El-Gundy, Z. (2011, July 20). Egyptian police officer El-Batran was killed by a single shot rifle: Alleged official forensic report. *Ahramonline.* Retrieved from http://english.ahram.org.eg/NewsContent/1/64/16890/Egypt/Politics-/Egyptian-police-officer-ElBatran-was-killed-by-a-s.aspx

El-Mahdy, R., & Marfleet, P. (2009a). Introduction. In R. El-Mahdy & P. Marfleet (Eds.), *Egypt: The moment of change* (pp. 1–13). London: Zed Books.

———. (2009b). Notes. In R. El-Mahdy & P. Marfleet (Eds.), *Egypt: The moment of change* (pp. 155–163). London: Zed Books.

El-Masry, S. (2006). *Civil society in Egypt.* Unpublished master thesis. Sweden: Jonkoping International Business School.

El-Mikawy, N., & Mohsen, R. (2005, January). *Civil society participation in the law making process in Egypt.* Paper presented at the Center for Academic Research, University of Bonn, Germany.

El-Naggar, A. (2009). Economic policy: From state control to decay and corruption. In R. El-Mahdy & P. Marfleet (Eds.), *Egypt: The moment of change* (pp. 34–50). London: Zed Books.

el-Nawawy, M., & Khamis, S. (2009). *Islam dot com: Contemporary Islamic discourses in cyberspace.* New York: Palgrave Macmillan.

Eltahawy, M. (2008). The Middle East's generation Facebook. *World Policy Journal.* Retrieved from http://www.mitpressjournals.org/doi/abs/10.1162/wopj.2008.25.3.69

Encarnacion, O. G. (2000). Tocqueville's missionaries: Civil society advocacy and the promotion of democracy. *World Policy Journal, 17*(1), 9–18.

Etling, B., Kelly, J., Faris, R., & Palfrey, J. G. (2009). *Mapping the Arabic blogosphere: Politics, culture, and dissent.* Internet and Democracy Project, Research Publication No. 2009–06, The Berkman Center for Internet & Society at Harvard University, Cambridge.

Eveland, W. P., & Dylko, I. (2007). Reading political blogs during the 2004 election campaign: Correlates and political consequences. In M. Tremayne (Ed.), *Blogging, citizenship, and the future of media* (pp. 105–126). New York: Taylor & Francis Group.

Fairclough, N. (2003). *Analyzing discourse: Textual analysis for social research.* London: Routledge.

Fanselow, J. (2008). Community blogging: The new wave of citizen journalism. *Wiley InterScience, 97*(4), 24–29.

Faris, D. (2008). Revolutions without revolutionaries? Network theory, Facebook, and the Egyptian blogosphere. *Arab Media & Society.* Retrieved from http://www.arabmediasociety.com/topics/index.php?t_article=232

Fioramonti, L., & Fiori, A. (2010). The changing roles of civil society in democratization: Evidence from South Africa (1990–2009) and South Korea (1987–2009). *African and Asian Studies, 9*, 83–104.

Ford, T. V., & Gil, G. (2001). Radical Internet use. In J. Downing et al. (Eds.), *Radical media: Rebellious communication and social movements* (pp. 201–234). London: Sage Publications.

Fox, J. (2000). *Civil society and political accountability: Propositions for discussion.* Paper presented at the Helen Kellogg Institute for Institutional Studies, University of Notre Dame, Indiana.

Franklin, S. (2008, July). The hunger. *Columbia Journalism Review, 47*(2), 37–40.

Freeland, C. (2011). The Middle East and the Groupon effect. *AFP.* Retrieved from http://blogs.reuters.com/chrystia-freeland/2011/02/18/the-middle-east-and-the-groupon-effect/

Froomkin, A. M. (2004). Technologies for democracy. In P. Shane (Ed.), *Democracy online: The prospects for political renewal through the Internet* (pp. 3–20). London: Routledge.

Fuchs, C. (2006, June). *E-participation research: A case study on political online debate in Austria.* Salzburg, Austria: Information and Communication Technologies & Society Center, University of Salzburg.

Gelvin, J. L. (2012). *The Arab uprising: What everyone needs to know.* London: Oxford University Press.

Ghannam, J. (2011). *Social media in the Arab world: Leading up to the uprisings of 2011.* A Report to the Center for International Media Assistance. Retrieved from http://cima.ned.org/publications/social-media-arab-world-leading-uprisings-2011–0

Gharbeia, A. (2007, July). Lost in process. *Index on Censorship, 36*(3), 51–55.

Gill, K. E. (2004). *How can we measure the influence of the blogosphere?* Paper presented at the American Political Science Association Annual Meeting, Washington, D.C. Retrieved from http://faculty.washington.edu/kegill/pub/www2004_blogosphere_gill.pdf

Goode, L. (2005). *Jürgen Habermas: Democracy and the public sphere.* London: Pluto Press.

———. (2009). Social news, citizen journalism and democracy. *New Media & Society, 11*(8), 1287–1305.

Haas, T. (2004, March). The public sphere as a sphere of publics. *Journal of Communication, 54*(1), 178–184.

———. (2005). From "public journalism" to the "public's journalism"? Rhetoric and reality in the discourse on Weblogs. *Journalism Studies, 6*(3), 387–396.

———. (2007). *The pursuit of public journalism: Theory, practice, and criticism.* New York: Taylor & Francis.

Habermas, J. (1989). *The structural transformation of the public sphere: An inquiry into a category of bourgeois society.* Cambridge, MA: MIT Press.

Hall, S. (1975). Introduction. In A. C. H. Smith (Ed.), *Paper voices: The popular press and social change, 1935–1965* (pp. 11–24). London: Chatto and Windus.

Hall, R. S. (2006). *The blog ahead: How citizen-generated media is radically tilting the communications balance.* New York: Morgan James Publishing.

Hamdy, N. (2009). Arab citizen journalism in action: Challenging mainstream media, authorities and media laws. *Westminister Papers in Communication and Culture*, *6*(1), 92–112.

Hamelink, C. J. (2004). Human rights in the global billboard society. In D. Schuler & P. Day (Eds.). *Shaping the network society: The new role of civil society in cyberspace* (pp. 67–81). Cambridge, MA: The MIT Press.

Hardaker, D. (2008, December). *Putting the genie back in the bottle: Ruling regimes and the new media in the Arab world*. A Report by Lowy Institute for International Policy, Sydney, Australia.

Hassan, H. (2010, December). State versus society in Egypt: Consolidating democracy or upgrading autocracy. *African Journal of Political Science and International Relations*, *4*(9), 319–329.

Haugbolle, S. (2008). From A-lists to webtifadas: Developments in the Lebanese blogosphere 2005–2006. *Arab Media &Society*. Retrieved from http://www.arabmediasociety.com/topics/index.php?t_article=91

Herring, S. C., Scheidt, L. A., Kouper, I., & Wright, E. (2007). Longitudinal content analysis of weblogs: 2003–2004. In M. Tremayne (Ed.), *Blogging, Citizenship, and the Future of Media* (pp 3–20). London: Routledge.

Hindman, M. (2008). *The Myth of Digital Democracy*. New Jersey: Princeton University Press.

Hofheinz, A. (2005). The Internet in the Arab World: Playground for political liberalization. Retrieved from http://library.fes.de/pdf-files/id/ipg/02941.pdf

Howard, P. N. (2004). Embedded media: Who we know, what we know, and society online. In P. N. Howard & S. Jones (Eds.), *Society online: The Internet in context* (pp. 1–27). California: Sage Publications.

———. (2011). *The digital origins of dictatorship and democracy: Information technology and political Islam*. Oxford: Oxford University Press.

Hunt, W. (2008). Baghdad burning: The blogosphere, literature and the art of war. *Arab Media & Society*. Retrieved from http://www.arabmediasociety.com/topics/index.php?t_article=189

Ibrahim, B. (October–November, 2005). *Strengthening philanthropy and civic engagement in the Arab world: A mission for the John D. Gerhart Center*. Paper presented at the American University in Cairo.

Idle, N., & Nunns, A. (2011). *Tweets from Tahrir: Egypt's revolution as it unfolded, in the words of the people who made it*. New York: OR Books.

Internet filtering in Egypt (2009, August). OpenNet Initiative. Retrieved from http://opennet.net/research/profiles/egypt

Isherwood, T. (2008). A new direction of more of the same? *Arab Media & Society*. Retrieved from http://www.arabmediasociety.com/?article=693

Jamieson, K. & Waldman, P. (2004). *The Press Effect: Politicians, Journalists, and the Stories that Shape the Political World*. UK: Oxford University Press.

Janack, J. (2006, June). Mediated citizenship and digital discipline: A rhetoric of control in a campaign blog. *Social Semiotics*, *16*(2), 283–301.

Java, A., Finin, T., Song, X., & Tseng, B. (2009). Why we Twitter: Understanding microblogging usage and communities. *Advances in Web Mining and Web*

Usage Analysis. Retrieved from http://www.scribd.com/doc/230982/Why-We-Twitter-Understanding-Microblogging-Usage-and-Communities

Jennings, M. K., & Zeitner, V. (2003). Internet use and civic engagement: A longitudinal analysis. *Public Opinion Quarterly, 67,* 311–334.

Johnson, T. J., & Kaye, B. K. (2004). Wag the blog: How reliance on traditional media and the Internet influence credibility perceptions of weblogs among blog users. *Journalism & Mass Communication Quarterly, 81,* 622–642.

Jones, J. (2007). *Negotiating change: The new politics of the Middle East.* London: I. B. Tauris.

Jones, S. G. (1995a). Introduction: From where to who knows? In S. G. Jones (Ed.), *Cybersociety: Computer-mediated communication and community* (pp. 1–9). California: Sage Publications.

———. (1995b). Understanding community in the information age. In S. G. Jones (Ed.), *Cybersociety: Computer-mediated communication and community* (pp. 10–35). California: Sage Publications.

Kaid, L. L., & Postelnicu, M. (2007). Credibility of political messages on the Internet: A comparison of blog sources. In M. Tremayne (Ed.), *Blogging, citizenship, and the future of media* (pp. 149–164). New York: Taylor & Francis Group.

Kalaycioglu, E. (2004). State and civil society in Turkey: Democracy, development and protest. In A. Sajoo (Ed.), *Civil society in the Muslim world: Contemporary perspectives* (pp. 247–272). London: I. B. Tauris Publishers.

Katz, J. E., & Rice, R. E. (2002). *Social consequences of Internet use: Access, involvement, and interaction.* Cambridge, MA: The MIT Press.

Kent, M. (2008). Critical analysis of blogging in public relations. *Public Relations Review 34* (1), 32–40.

Keren, M. (2006). *Blogosphere: The new political arena.* Lanham, MD: Lexington Books.

Khalid, M. (2007). Politics, power and the new Arab media. In *Information warfare monitor.* Retrieved from http://www.infowar-monitor.net / modules.php?op=modload&name=News&file=article&sid=1380&mode=thread&order=0&thold=0

Khamis, S. (2007). The role of new Arab satellite channels in fostering intercultural dialogue: Can Al-Jazeera English bridge the gap? In P. Seib (Ed.), *New media and the new Middle East* (pp. 39–52). New York: Palgrave Macmillan.

———. (2008). Modern Egyptian media: Transformations, paradoxes, debates and comparative perspectives. *Journal of Arab and Muslim Media Research, 1*(3), 259–277.

Khamis, S., Gold, P., & Vaughn, K. (2012). Beyond Egypt's "Facebook revolution" and Syria's "YouTube uprising": Comparing political contexts, actors and communication strategies. *Arab Media & Society.* Retrieved from http://www.arabmediasociety.com/index.php?article=791&p=0

Khamis, S., & Sisler, V. (2010). The new Arab "cyberscape": Redefining boundaries and reconstructing public spheres. *Communication Yearbook, 34,* 277–316.

Khazen, J. (1999). Censorship and state control of the press in the Arab world. *The Harvard International Journal of Press/Politics*, *4*(3), 87.

Kirkpatrick, D. (2012, June 24). Named Egypt's winner, Islamist makes history. *The New York Times.* Retrieved from http://www.nytimes.com/2012/06/25/world/middleeast/mohamed-morsi-of-muslim-brotherhood-declared-as-egypts-president.html?pagewanted=all

Kittilson, M. C., & Dalton, R. J. (2008). *The Internet and virtual civil society: The new frontier of social capital.* Center for the Study of Democracy, Irvine, California. Retrieved from http://repositories.cdlib.org/cgi/viewcontent.cgi?article=1155&context=csd

Kline, D. & Burstein, D. (2005). *Blog! How the newest media revolution is changing politics, business, and culture.* New York: CDS Books.

Kraidy, M. (2007). *Public media in the Arab world: Exploring the gap between reality and ideals.* Center for Social Media. Retrieved from http://www.centerfor socialmedia.org / files/ pdf/ arab_public_media.pdf

Kranich, N. (2004). Libraries: The information commons of civil society. In D. Schuler & P. Day (Eds.), *Shaping the network society: The new role of civil society in cyberspace* (pp. 279–299). Cambridge, MA: The MIT Press.

Kreutz, C. (2009). Exploring the potentials of blogging for development. *Participatory Learning and Action*, *59*(1), 28–33.

Lehning, P. (1998). Towards a multicultural civil society: The role of social capital and democratic citizenship. *Government and Opposition*, *33*(2), 221–242.

Lemert, J. (1981). *Does mass communication change public opinion after all?* Chicago: Nelson-Hall.

Leonard, T. C. (1999). Making readers into citizens—The-old fashioned way. In T. Glasser (Ed.), *The idea of public journalism* (pp. 85–96). New York: The Guilford Press.

Lerner, R. M., Alberts, Amy E., & Bobek, Deborah L. (2007). *Thriving youth, flourishing civil society: How positive youth development strengthens democracy and social justice.* A Report for the Carl Berterlsmann-Prize, Institute for Applied Research in Youth Development, Tufts University, MA.

Lunat, Z. (2008). The Internet and the public sphere: Evidence from civil society in developing countries. *The Electronic Journal of Information Systems in Developing Countries*, *35*(3), 1–12. Retrieved from http://www.ejisdc.org/ojs2/index.php/ejisdc/article/viewFile/501/253

Lynch, M. (2003). Beyond the Arab street: Iraq and the Arab public sphere. *Politics & Society*, *31*(3), 55–91.

———. (2007). Blogging the new Arab public. *Arab Media & Society.* Retrieved from http://www.arabmediasociety.com/?article=10

Maher, K. (2011). Interview with Frog Design (Video). Retrieved from http://www.youtube.com/watch?v=zulsoFZ-Kqs&feature=player_embedded

Makumbe, J. (1998). Is there a civil society in Africa? *International Affairs*, *74*(2), 305–317.

McCullagh, K. (2008). Blogging: self presentation and privacy, *Information & Communications Technology Law*, *17*(1), 1–23.

McKee, A. (2005). *The public sphere: An introduction.* London: Cambridge University Press.

———. (2006). *Textual analysis: A beginner's guide.* London: Sage Publications.

McLaughlin, M. L., Osborne, K. K., & Smith, C. B. (1995). Standards of conduct on usenet. In S. G. Jones (Ed.), *Cybersociety: Computer-mediated communication and community* (pp. 90–111). California: Sage Publications.

Mehanna, O. (2008). *Internet and the Egyptian public sphere.* Paper presented at The twelfth general assembly governing the African public sphere, Yaoundé, Cameroon. Retrieved from http://www.scribd.com/doc/20964344/Internet-and-the-Egyptian-Public-Sphere

Mellor, N. (2007). *Modern Arab journalism: Problems and prospects.* Edinburgh: Edinburgh University Press.

Mesch, G. & Talmud, I. (2010). *Wired Youth: The Social World of Adolescence in the Information Age.* London: Routledge.

Meyer, P. (1995, September). *Public journalism and the problem of objectivity.* Paper presented at the Investigative Reporters and Editors Convention. Cleveland, Ohio.

Mildner, J., & Tate, N. (2004). The league of women voters' DemocracyNet (DNet): An exercise in online civic engagement. In P. Shane (Ed.), *Democracy online: The prospects for political renewal through the Internet* (pp. 195–206). New York: Routledge.

Miller, R. (2005). Journalism returns to its (grass)roots. *EContent Magazine.* Retrieved from http://www.econtentmag.com/Articles/Editorial/Feature/Journalism-Returns-to-its-%28Grass%29-Roots-8065.htm

Monteiro, B. G. (2008, August). Blogs and female expression in the Middle East. *Media Development,* 55(3), 47–53.

Montgomery, K. C. (2008). Youth and digital democracy: Intersections of practice, policy, and the marketplace. In W. L. Bennett (Ed.), *Civic life online: Learning how digital media can engage youth* (pp. 25–49). Cambridge, MA: The MIT Press.

Muhlberger, P. (2004). Access, skill, and motivation in online political discussion: Testing cyberrealism. In P. Shane (Ed.), *Democracy online: The prospects for political renewal through the Internet* (pp. 225–237). New York: Routledge.

Muhtaseb, A., & Frey, L. R. (2008). Arab Americans' motives for using the Internet as a functional media alternative and their perceptions of U.S. public opinion. Journal of Computer-Mediated Communication, 13(3), 618–657.

Mustafa, H. (2006). *A policy for promoting liberal democracy in Egypt.* White Paper Series: Voices from the Middle East on Democratization and Reform. Foundation for Defense of Democracies, Washington, D.C.

Nakamura, L. (2004). Interrogating the digital divide: The political economy of race and commerce in new media. In P. N. Howard & S. Jones (Eds.), *Society online: The Internet in context* (pp. 71–83). California: Sage Publications.

Nelson, A. (2008). Arab media: The Web 2.0 revolution. *Carnegie Reporter.* Retrieved from http://carnegie.org/publications/carnegie-reporter/single/view/article/item/70/

Nichols, S. L., Friedland, Lewis A., Rojas, Hernando, Cho, Jaeho, & Shah, Dhavan V. (2006, Spring). Examining the effects of public journalism on civil society from 1994 to 2002: Organizational factors, project features, story frames, and citizen engagement. *Journalism & Mass Communication Quarterly, 83*(1), 77–100.

Nip, J. Y. M. (2006). Exploring the second phase of public journalism. *Journalism Studies, 7*(2), 212–236.

Norris, P. (2001). *Digital divide: Civic engagement, information poverty, and the Internet worldwide.* Cambridge, UK: Cambridge University Press.

———. (2004). The bridging and bonding role of online communities. In P. N. Howard & S. Jones (Eds.), *Society online: The Internet in context* (pp. 31–41). California: Sage Publications.

Papacharissi, Z. (2007). Audiences as media producers: Content analysis of 260 blogs. In M. Tremayne (Ed.), *Blogging, citizenship, and the future of media* (pp. 21–38). New York: Taylor & Francis Group.

Paulussen, S. (2008). User generated content in the newsroom: Professional and organizational constraints on participatory journalism. *Westminister Papers in Communication and Culture* 5(2), 24–41.

Perez, O. (2004). Global governance and electronic democracy: E-Politics as a multidimensional experience. In P. Shane (Ed.), *Democracy online: The prospects for political renewal through the Internet* (pp. 83–94). London: Routledge.

Poor, N. (2005). Mechanisms of an online public sphere: The website slashdot. *Journal of Computer-Mediated Communication 10*(2), article 4. Retrieved from http://jcmc.indiana.edu/vol10/issue2/poor.html

Posner, R. (2005). "Bad News." *The New York Times.* Retrieved August 15, 2011 from: http://www.nytimes.com/2005/07/31/books/review/31POSNER.html?pagewanted=all&_r=0.

Putnam, R. (1993). *Making Democracy Work: Civic Traditions in Modern Italy.* New Jersey: Princeton University Press.

Putnam, R. D. (2000). *Bowling alone: The collapse and revival of American community.* New York: Simon & Schuster Paperbacks.

Radsch, C. (2007a). Blogging in Egypt. *Reset Magazine.* Retrieved from http://www.resetdoc.org/EN/Radsch-blogging.php

———. (2007b). Speaking truth to power: The changing role of journalism in Egypt. International Studies Association Conference, Chicago. Retrieved from http://www.allacademic.com//meta/p_mla_apa_research_citation/1/8/0/2/8/pages180287/p180287-1.php

———. (2008). Core to commonplace: The evolution of Egypt's blogosphere. *Arab Media & Society.* Retrieved from http://www.arabmediasociety.com/?article=692

———. (2011). Assessing the economic impact of the Egyptian uprising. *Arab Media & Society.* Retrieved from http://www.arabmediasociety.com/?article=778

Rainie, L. (2005). *The State of Blogging.* Pew Internet and American Life Project. Washington, D.C.

Rasmussen, T. (2007). *Two faces of the public sphere: The significance of Internet communication in public deliberations.* Paper presented at the Schuman Center for Advanced Studies, Florence, Italy. Retrieved from www.regione.toscana.it/regione/.../RT/.../1211883113188_rasmussen.pdf

Raynes-Goldie, K., & Walker, L. (2008). Our space: Online civic engagement tools for youth. In W. L. Bennett (Ed.), *Civic life Online: Learning how digital media can engage youth* (pp. 161–188). Cambridge, MA: The MIT Press.

Reich, Z. (2008). How citizens create news stories: The "news access" problem reversed. *Journalism Studies 9*(5), 739–758.

Rheingold, H. (2000). *The virtual community: Homesteading on the electronic frontier.* Cambridge, MA: The MIT Press.

———. (2004). What do we need to know about the future we're creating? Technobiographical reflections. In D. Schuler & P. Day (Eds.), *Shaping the network society: The new role of civil society in cyberspace* (pp. 254–277). Cambridge, MA: The MIT Press.

———. (2008). Using participatory media and public voice to encourage civic engagement. In W. L. Bennett (Ed.), *Civic life online: Learning how digital media can engage youth* (pp. 97–118). Cambridge, MA: The MIT Press.

Rifaat, Y. (2008). Blogging the body: The case of Egypt. *Surfacing: An Interdisciplinary Journal for Gender in the Global South 1*(1), 52–72.

Rinnawi, K. (2011). The Internet: Schizophrenic trilogy. In N. Mellor, M. Ayish, N. Dajani, K. & Rinnawi (Eds.), *Arab media: Globalization and emerging media industries* (pp. 123–148). London: Polity.

Rosen, J. (1994). *Public journalism: Theory and practice.* Dayton, OH: Kettering Foundation.

———. (1999). *What are journalists for?* Binghamton, NY: Vail-Ballou Press.

Rugh, W. (2004). *Arab mass media: Newspapers, radio, and television in Arab politics.* Westport, CT: Praeger.

Rutigliano, L. (2007). Emergent communication networks as civic journalism. In M. Tremayne (Ed.), *Blogging, citizenship, and the future of media* (pp. 225–237). New York: Taylor & Francis Group.

Salama, V. (2007). Arab and Iranian bloggers: Emerging threat to official line. *PoynterOnline.* Retrieved from http://www.poynter.org/content/content_print.asp?id=118010

Salmon, C. T., Fernandez, L., & Post, L. A. (2010). Mobilizing public will across borders: Roles and functions of communication processes and technologies. *Journal of Borderlands Studies, 25*(3&4), 159–170.

Salter, L. (2004). Structure and forms of use: A contribution to understanding the "effects" of the Internet on deliberative democracy. *Information, Communication & Society, 7*(2), 185–206.

Sassen, S. (2004). Sited materialities with global span. In P. N. Howard & S. Jones (Eds.), *Society online: The Internet in context* (pp. 295–306). California: Sage Publications.

Schneider, S. M., & Foot, K. A. (2004). Crisis communication and new media: The Web after September 11. In P. N. Howard & S. Jones (Eds.),

Society online: The Internet in context (pp. 137–153). California: Sage Publications.

Schuler, D., & Day, P. (2004). Shaping the network society: Opportunities and challenges. In D. Schuler & P. Day (Eds.), *Shaping the network society: The new role of civil society in cyberspace* (pp. 1–16). Cambridge, MA: The MIT Press.

Seib, P. (2004–2005, Winter). The news media and the clash of civilizations. *Parameters: US Army War College, 34*(4), 71–85.

———. (2007). New media and prospects for democratization. In P. Seib (Ed.), *New media and the new Middle East* (pp. 1–18). New York: Palgrave Macmillan.

Seif El-Dawla, A. S. (2009). Torture: A state policy. In R. El-Mahdy & P. Marfleet (Eds.), *Egypt: The moment of change* (pp. 120–135). London: Zed Books.

Sen, A. (2000). *Development as freedom.* Delhi: Oxford University Press.

Seymour, R. (2008). Middle East bloggers set cat among the pigeons. *The Middle East* 388, 62–63.

Shah, D. V., Cho, J., Eveland, W. P. Jr., & Kwak, N. (2005). Information and expression in a digital age: Modeling Internet effects on civic participation. *Communication Research, 32* (5), 531–565.

Shane, P. M. (2004). Introduction. In P. Shane (Ed.), *Democracy online: The prospects for political renewal through the Internet* (pp. xi–xx). New York: Routledge.

Shapiro, S. (2009, January). Revolution, Facebook style. *The New York Times.* Retrieved from http://www.nytimes.com/2009/01/25/magazine/25bloggers-t.html

Siapera, E. (2008). The political subject of blogs. *Information Polity, 13*, 51–63.

Silver, D., & Garland, P. (2004). "sHoP onLINE!" Advertising female teen cyberculture. In P. N. Howard & S. Jones (Eds.), *Society online: The Internet in context* (pp. 157–171). California: Sage Publications.

Simone, M. (2006). Codepink alert: Mediated citizenship in the public sphere. *Social Semiotics, 16*(2) 345–364.

Skelly, J. (2008). Fostering engagement: The role of international education in the development of global civil society. In R. Lewin (Ed.), *The handbook of practice and research in study abroad: Higher education and the quest for global citizenship* (pp. 135–152). London: Routledge.

Smeltzer, S. (2008). Blogging in Malaysia: Hope for a new democratic technology? *Journal of International Communication 14* (1), 28–45.

Sparks, C. (1998). Is there a global public sphere? In D. Thussu (Ed.), *Electronic empires: Global media and local resistance* (pp. 108–124). London: Arnold.

Stroud, S., & Ibrahim, B. (2011). *Youth activism and public space in Egypt.* A report presented at the John D. Gerhart Center for Philanthropy and Civic Engagement, Cairo, Egypt.

Su, N. M., Wang, Y., and Mark, G. (2005). *Politics as usual in the blogosphere.* Proceedings of the 4th International Workshop on Social

Intelligence Design, Irvine, California. Retrieved from http://www.ics.uci.edu/~yangwang/papers/SID05.pdf

Sullivan, A. (2002, October 13). An honest blogger will never make a quick buck. *Sunday Times*, p. A4.

Talat, M. (2011). Jailing Maikel Nabil betrays the Egyptian people's revolution. *The Guardian*. Retrieved April 20, 2012 from: http://www.guardian.co.uk/commentisfree/2011/apr/24/egypt-blogger-maikel-nabil-jailed

The Economist. (2007, April 12). Bloggers may be the real opposition. p. 54.

Trammell, K., Williams, A., Postelnicu, M., & Landreville, K. (2006). Evolution of online campaigning: Increasing interactivity in candidate Web sites and blogs through text and technical features. *Mass Communication & Society*, *9*(1), 21–44.

Tremayne, M. (2007). *Blogging, citizenship and the future of media*. London: Routledge.

Tsekeris, C. (2009). Blogging as revolutionary politics. *Research Journal of Social Sciences*, *4*, 51–54.

Tusalem, R. (2007). A boon or a bane? The role of civil society in third- and fourth-wave democracies. *International Political Science Review*, *28*(3), 361–386.

Vatrapu, R., Robertson, S., & Dissanayake, W. (2008). Are political Weblogs public spheres or partisan spheres? *International Reports on Socio-Informatics*, 5(1), 7–26. Retrieved from http://www.itu.dk/people/rkva/docs/2008-IRSI-Political-Blogs-Public-Spheres.pdf

Wallsten, K. (2005). *Political blogs and the bloggers who blog them: Is the political blogosphere an echo chamber?* Paper presented at the American Political Science Association Annual Meeting, Washington, D.C. Retrieved from http://www.journalism.wisc.edu/blog-club/Site/Wallsten.pdf

Walters, T., & Barwind, J. (2004, January). Media and modernity in the United Arab Emirates: Searching for the beat of a different drummer. *Free Speech Yearbook*, *41*, 151–163.

Ward, I. & Cahill, J. (2007) Old and new media: Blogs in the third age of political communication. *Australian Journal of Communication*, *34* 3: 1–21.

Ward, W. (2007). Uneasy bedfellows: Bloggers and mainstream media report the Lebanon conflict. *Arab Media & Society*. Retrieved from http://www.arabmediasociety.com/ topics/index.php?t_article=54

Warnick, B. (2007). *Rhetoric Online: Persuasion and Politics on the World Wide Web*. New York: Peter Lang.

Weyman, G. (2007). Western journalists report on Egyptian bloggers. *Nieman Reports*, 61(2). Retrieved July 15, 2011 from http://www.nieman.harvard.edu/reportsitem.aspx?id=10021

Whitaker, J., & Varghese, A. (2009). *Online discourse in the Arab world: Dispelling the myths*. A briefing by the United States Institute of Peace, Washington, D.C.

Wild, L. (2006). *Strengthening global civil society*. Institute for Public Policy Research, London. Retrieved from http://www.globalpolicy.org/ngos/intro/general/2006/04strengthening.pdf

Wilkinson, A. (2011, April). *Driving civic participation through social media.* A paper presented at the European Workshop on Perspectives of Web 2.0 for Citizenship Education in Europe. Brno, Czech Republic.

Witschge, T. (2004). Online deliberation: Possibilities of the Internet for deliberative democracy. In P. Shane (Ed.), *Democracy online: The prospects for political renewal through the Internet* (pp. 109–122). London: Routledge.

Witt, L. (2004). Is public journalism morphing into public's journalism? *National Civic Review, 93*(3), 49–57.

Woo-Young, C. (2005). Online civic participation, and political empowerment: Online media and public opinion formation in Korea. *Media, Culture & Society, 27*(6), 925–935.

Xenos, M., & Foot, K. (2008). Not your father's Internet: The generation gap in online politics. In W. L. Bennett (Ed.), *Civic life online: Learning how digital media can engage youth* (pp. 51–70). Cambridge, MA: The MIT Press.

York, J. (Winter/Spring 2012). The Arab digital vanguard: How a decade of blogging contributed to a year of revolution. *Georgetown Journal of International Affairs, 13*(1), 33–42.

Zayani, M. (2011, Summer). Social media and the reconfiguration of political action in revolutionary Tunisia. *Democracy & Society, 8*(2), 2–4.

Zelaky, E., Eid, G., Sami, S., & Ziada, D. (2006). *Implacable adversaries: Arab governments and the Internet.* Cairo: The Arabic Network for Human Rights Information.

Index

Printed in the United States of America